SUNDAY TALKS

SUNDAY TALKS
At Coombe Springs

JG Bennett

Ken W.F. Pledge, Editor

BENNETT BOOKS
Santa Fe, New Mexico

First Edition 2004

Bennett Books
PO Box 1553
Santa Fe, New Mexico 87504
office@bennettbooks.org · www.bennettbooks.org

cover design: Elizabeth Brown
book design: AM Services
cover photo: Coombe Springs Manor House, photographer unknown.

Library of Congress Cataloging-in-Publication Data
Bennett, John G. (John Godolphin), 1897-1974
    Sunday talks at Coombe Springs / J.G. Bennett.-- 1st ed.
    p. cm.
    ISBN 1-881408-14-0 (alk. paper)
    1. Spiritual life. I. Title.

BP610. B46164 2002
299'.93--dc21   2002028390

LIST OF ILLUSTRATIONS & PHOTOGRAPHS

Part 1

CONTENTS

Part 2

CONTENTS

John Godolphin Bennett, 1960

FOREWORD

SUNDAY TALKS AT COOMBE SPRING is a unique collection of some of JG Bennett's most creative thinking, and they cover an astonishing range of subjects from "true freedom" to the deceptively simple question of "why we have a body." They were presented as a starting point for practical study, but they also provided—and continue to provide—inspiration for work and reflection.

Each talk starts with a clear proposition that Bennett expands to a profound discourse and then, usually, brings back to a simple practical task, which his audience—and today's reader—could use to help verify the validity of what he was saying.

The talks were given at a particularly creative period of Bennett's life, when he returned to the practice of techniques he had derived from Gurdjieff but was still strongly influenced by his experience of Subud* in the preceding half-dozen years. In characteristic fashion, Bennett had plunged wholeheartedly into the practice and dissemination of Subud, and the rapid worldwide spread of Subud in the late 1950s owed a great deal to his commitment and energy. Bennett's autobiography, *Witness,*** describes the effect that the Subud experience had on his spiritual life, and people who knew him before and after this phase of his life can attest to the fact that Subud brought about a profound change in him. To put it simply, it helped him to dis-

* *Concerning Subud.* London: Hodder and Stoughton, 1958.
** *Witness: The Story of a Search.* Santa Fe: Bennett Books, 1997.

cover his "heart." This is apparent from these talks, which have an unmistakable compassion, even when they are presenting ideas that are unpalatable for people to face.

Although the talks cover a very diverse range of subjects, there are common themes. One of the most powerful of these is what Bennett has to say about "help." He makes it clear that "work on oneself" is not possible without help—for which one might substitute the word "grace"—but he emphasizes in a number of talks that the source of this help is intimately close. It is not some source "out there" at an unattainable distance, but something with which we can learn to have an intimate connection, and can call on repeatedly, and with confidence.

Two talks can serve to illustrate the diverse ways in which Bennett spoke of help. The first is entitled "Inner Help and Inner Freedom." Here Bennett is concerned with the idea that help is always available and always close, but he points out the usually neglected fact that we are not accustomed to ask for help. Moreover, we rarely allow ourselves to be helped, either from pride or from the mistaken impression that transformation is something we can—or should—achieve through our efforts alone. Asking for help, he says, is something we need to practice, and the talk ends with the simple suggestion that people work at asking for help in small things, in order to have developed the ability to seek for help when faced with more intractable problems: "What we do a hundred or a thousand times in small moments we shall find ourselves able to do when a big moment comes."

This emphasis on help forms an important counterbalance to the idea that human transformation depends largely on our own efforts. It is possible to caricature the message of Gurdjieff, particularly as presented by Ouspensky, as an unremitting struggle that has to come entirely from one's own work. Various of Bennett's talks here remind us that while we must make continual efforts to "work on ourselves," ultimately we depend on help to make any progress.

The second example of this theme is the talk given on the feast of Pentecost in 1964. Here, as Ken Pledge once pointed out, Bennett went to church early in the morning, pondered the significance of the feast day, and then, later in the morning, produced an extraordinary and moving exposition not only on the significance of the Holy Spirit as a source of help that "abides within us," but also of the true role of the power of "representation," which we can learn to develop. This power of representation is the key to some of the most significant techniques that Bennett developed and taught in the courses he ran at Sherborne, Gloucestershire, at the end of his life, and which have proved very effective to those who have worked with them. Elsewhere, in his book, *The Way to be Free*,* he describes the power of representation as being intimately connected with will, and careful study, inner work, and outer practice can verify that this is so.

Herein lies the power of these Sunday Talks. They are not theoretical expositions, but the result of years of study and practical experiment, delivered with an understanding and authority that is unmistakable. The talks were given to be used in an immediate and practical way by the participants in the "Work Sundays" at Coombe Springs, and each talk is accompanied by questions and answers based on participants' work during the day. Though these answers were in direct response to individual questions and observations they, and the talks themselves, retain a striking freshness and relevance forty years on, a testament to the unusually creative power with which they were given.

The individual reader, or group, would be well advised to read an individual talk, try for themselves any suggested practical task that accompanies it, and only then move on to the questions and answers. Many of Bennett's former students have found that, used in this way, the talks remain a very profitable guide to inner and outer work, and can provide an astonishing variety of inspiration.

—George Bennett
Royalston, Massachusetts
August 2004

---

* *The Way to Be Free*. York Beach, Maine: Red Wheel/Weiser. All current editions are out-of-print. A Bennett Books edition is scheduled for November 2005.

"If a new world is to come,
we must first create it in ourselves."*
—JG Bennett

* from *Is There "Life" on Earth?* This and all the following facing-page quotes are from JG Bennett.

EDITOR'S INTRODUCTION

THE TALKS BROUGHT TOGETHER HERE (for the first time in one definitive volume) were given during Sunday Work-Days at Coombe Springs—the research community near London that Bennett led between 1946 and 1966—and were inspiration for reflection and practical study. In one of the later talks Bennett refers to them as "conversations," and that does convey some of their informal flavor. Nevertheless, an overriding impression remains of his certainty and authority in domains ordinarily supposed impenetrable. Some talks emphasize the converse: how little is really known. Some are experimental essays at communicating principles and methods of work involved in human transformation; others are near perfect five-finger exercises in creative thinking upon some well chosen theme. The arguments are clear, their reasoning cogent.

Often it is obvious that Bennett is speaking directly from his own hard-earned experience: he knows the pitfalls nearly everyone inevitably encounters and how to avoid or survive them and, eventually, transcend them. Thus his workmanlike psychology is both objective and practical (one is reminded of Pascal's remark: "That a religion may be true, it must have knowledge of our nature.") Sometimes, his replies in the after-lunch discussion sessions have a fine taste of compassion; yet others are terrifying, at first reading, by their sternly realistic attitude towards life and death. And one talk reads like a fine piece by William James. Yet here and there a happily chosen image, allusion or analogy is peculiarly Bennett's own. Surely, only he would think of supposing that Noah must have worked part-time on building the Ark because, even in the face of impending flood, the ordinary duties of everyday life must not be neglected.

Individual Sunday Talks were first published by Coombe Springs Press as a series of slim eighteen-page booklets, nearly always containing two talks. Their thin blue card covers bore on the front an autumnal sketch of a rustic bridge over a stream at Coombe Springs. The path crossing it led to the Djamichunatra,* a large nine-sided wooden building looming in outline in the background.

Coombe Springs was an estate of about seven acres near Kingston-upon-Thames, not far from London. Bennett acquired Coombe Springs for work with his groups in 1946, shortly after the Second World War. Years of devoted care had since been lavished on the lawns, trees, flower gardens, pools, paths and artificial stream. In 1965 a community of sixty was living there, that included Bennett and his family.

In order to attend a Work Sunday at Coombe Springs one had to book beforehand so that appropriate catering and other arrangements could be made. A typical Sunday would begin with an assembly at 10:30 AM, in the Djamichunatra, for a talk by Bennett. This finished at about eleven o'clock, often with a recommended inner task to be practiced during the remainder of the morning. Everyone was then allotted a practical work task in the house, in the grounds, in the kitchen, child-minding, and so on, until lunchtime, at one o'clock, in the dining room of the main house. After lunch (usually a silent meal) Bennett would ask for questions and observations—preferably arising from whatever practice he had suggested at the end of his morning talk—and give replies and explanations.

Work then resumed as before until about 4 o'clock—when all would meet for tea—followed by a movements class in the huge Djamichunatra. Both morning talk and after-lunch questions and answers were recorded and later transcribed, most often by Olga de Nottbeck** who, until her death, was a close associate and dedicated assistant. If eventually the talk was chosen for publication in a Sunday Talks format, Bennett would edit it at lightning speed for final retyping and duplicating in the Coombe Springs press.

The Coombe Springs period lasted from purchase in October 1946 until 1966. The property was owned by The Institute for the Comparative Study of History, Philosophy and the Sciences, an organization incorporated on 2 May 1946: "(a) To promote research and other scientific work in connection with the factors which influence development and retrogression in man and their operation in individuals and

---

* Spelled *"djameechoonatra"* in GI Gurdjieff's book, *Beelzebub's Tales to His Grandson*. A *djameechoonatra* is a terrestrial monasterial refectory, in which second being-food is collectively taken.
** "'Notty,' the human recorder." See page P1, photo insert section.

communities; to investigate the origin and elaboration of scientific hypotheses and secular and religious philosophies and their bearing on general theories of Man and his place in the universe; and to study comparative methodology in history, philosophy and natural science. (b) To promote and prosecute theoretical and experimental researches in the physical and biological sciences particularly in the field of psychokinetics."

In 1946 Bennett first contracted to publish his masterwork The Dramatic Universe, which appeared in four volumes between 1956 and 1967. From 1948 to 1949—the Institute was devoted to work with Gurdjieff in Paris until his death. In 1953 and 1955 Bennett visited the Middle East, seeking guidance "in the field of psychokinetics," and also making detailed measurements of the dimensions of dervish meeting halls or tekkes. On his return he soon initiated the design and building of the Djamichunatra, which was completed as a hall in October 1958 (its gallery was finally finished only in January 1965). In 1957 he met with Subud and devoted the Institute's resources to spreading Subud worldwide, writing, in only a few weeks, Concerning Subud,* which ran into a second 1958 edition and, of all his books, sold the most copies. For years Bennett gave weekly talks on Subud to members and applicants; they appeared in booklets as late as 1963. Three collections of them were published.

The Spring of 1961 marks the transition from the 1957-61 period, when the Institute was wholly concerned with Subud and its affairs, to the return of disciplined group work, in which context these Sunday Talks eventually emerged. Thus March 1961 dates Bennett's original preface to Witness,** his autobiography, which culminated with an account of his intense experiences with Subud since 1957. Bennett's notion that Subud's "working from within" was insufficient to provide balanced development and that Gurdjieff's methods of "working from without" provided the requisite balancing factor, was catalyzed into conviction by a first meeting that Easter, 2 April 1961, in Nepal with the Shivapuri Baba, a Hindu sage of extraordinary spiritual attainment.[†]

On his return from Nepal, Bennett formed a group of twenty people with whom he resumed the disciplined kind of work that had been followed up to 1957. This reached its own culmination in August 1962

---

* Concerning Subud. London: Hodder and Stoughton, 1958.
** Witness: The Story of a Search. Santa Fe: Bennett Books, 1997.
† cf. JG Bennett. The Long Pilgrimage. The Shivapuri Baba died in 1963 at age 137. JG Bennett's "Conversations with the Shivapuri Baba" (tape) and Long Pilgrimage [book] detail the life and teaching of the Shivapuri Baba, and are available from Bennett Books. The book and tape compliment each other with very little information overlap.

when Bennett gave two successive Summer Schools at Coombe Springs. Their proceedings were, as usual, tape-recorded, and a remarkable account, blending both into one, was produced from them by Isabel Turnadge. It became one of Bennett's best loved books: *A Spiritual Psychology*, a wonderful tour de force bringing together Subud experiencing and Gurdjieff understanding, each throwing light on the other.*

There is even an admixture of Aquinas present in this book, for Bennett had become a Roman Catholic in October 1961 and eagerly absorbed Aquinas' *Summa Theologica*. It displays the buoyancy of a man who is at last finding his own voice and has much of significance to say. Three months after the Summer Schools, we find the first surviving Sunday Talk of 2 December 1962, published in the Spring of 1965.

The work of the Institute "in the field of psychokinetics" began again in earnest with groups, movements classes, Work Sundays on the first and third Sundays of most months, a variety of seminars on the weekends between, the "French Week," and Summer Schools. Young research fellows in Education and Science were appointed, took up residence, and began their work. An Institute quarterly "Systematics" was launched with a first issue in June 1963 and a house style intentionally reminiscent of the journal, "Philosophy".

A Spiritual Psychology finally appeared in 1964, the same year as Idries Shah's book, *The Sufis*, which all Bennett's groups were, in due course, directed to study for its content of "second-level teaching." And, with its author, we enter the final phase of Coombe Springs and its connection with the Institute.

Bennett had first heard of Shah in June 1962 while preparing for the Summer School. "At first," he reports in *Witness*, "I was wary. I had just decided to go forward on my own and now another teacher had appeared." Nevertheless his first meeting with Shah convinced him that Shah had come to England to fulfill a vital mission and that he had access to special resources; but only after many meetings did Shah disclose his own pressing need for somewhere to work. Bennett had meanwhile pressed on with development of Coombe Springs, and provisional town planning approval was obtained from the local authorities in January 1965 for building a new refectory and common room. But Shah's needs were urgent and his arguments compelling, and so Bennett, later in 1965 after much heart searching, finally

* *A Spiritual Psychology*. Santa Fe: Bennett Books, 1999.

offered to give Coombe Springs to Shah for his work.

We can now see why Part 1 of this collection, *Sunday Talks at Coombe Springs,* covers only the two-and-a-half year period from December 1962 to July 1965. After Coombe Springs re-opened on 15 April 1962 Bennett conducted exploratory "research in the field of psychokinetics." It must have been the success of the Spiritual Psychology Summer School in August 1962 that decided him at last to go forward again on his own—not merely as he had before meeting Subud, but very greatly changed and invigorated by his Subud experiences. And, as we shall see from these Sunday Talks, he was proceeding from strength to strength. And yet, three Summer Schools later—two months after the Summer School in August 1965—the hammer fell. At an Extraordinary General Meeting of the Institute convened in October 1965 the members voted to transfer Coombe Springs to Shah's S.U.F.I. society. One final movements' demonstration in the Djamichunatra was given, and a feast celebrated Gurdjieff's birthday on 13 January 1966. In April 1966 Shah moved in and, within a year, sold Coombe Springs to a developer. In 1956-8 Bennett's groups had painstakingly built the Djamichunatra with its main axis directed towards Gurdjieff's grave in Paris. Now the massive concrete foundation with its underground cloakroom, changing-room and passageway was bulldozed to rubble in a few days; the nine-sided wooden hall and gallery, copper-clad roof and stained glass windows broken up for scrap.

At first Bennett found relinquishing Coombe Springs—where he had hoped to end his days—hard to bear; but Shah, like a classical Sufi teacher in one of his own stories, forced him to be free and break completely with the past. Bennett, in characteristic fashion, rapidly learned much from this necessary suffering. We can see it transmuted into his further evolved understanding two years later, from his profound treatment of struggle, sacrifice and help in his book, *Transformation,** and later still, in his account of the essential role of Judas Iscariot (a talk Gurdjieff foretold he would give) in his book, *The Masters of Wisdom.*** But those books, along with his Sherborne experiment,† were still to be realized in Bennett's own future. Meanwhile, as a venue for Work Sundays and Sunday Talks, the role of Coombe Springs was over.

—Ken W.F. Pledge
London, July 2004

---

* *Transformation.* Santa Fe: Bennett Books, 2003.
** *The Masters of Wisdom.* Santa Fe: Bennett Books, 1999, chapter 4.
† *see,* Allen Roth. *Sherborne: An Experiment in Transformation.* Santa Fe: Bennett Books, 1998.

"I wonder whether I should be pleased or sorry that God has made me so that I prefer to learn rather than to teach? All my life when someone has set out to teach me, I have set myself to learn. Perhaps it is laziness or perhaps it is lack of faith, but I think it is rather the realization that unless a person wishes to learn one wastes one's breath in trying to explain anything. These observations are prompted by nearly four hours of talk with Emin Bey. I honestly tried to show him some of the limitations of his way of understanding, but I could see that it never once crossed his mind that there is something he might learn from me. This complete assurance of superior wisdom that people have in speaking to others never fails to surprise me. I always see what I can learn from them, even if it is only how to make Turkish coffee."

—from *Journeys in Islamic Countries*

1.
TRUE FREEDOM

15 November 1964

ALL OUR HOPES rest in the possibility of being free from the influences that bind us to this present state of existence. Our present condition does not correspond to the true destiny of man and yet there is little we can do about it because we have been conditioned to see everything "not as it is in reality." This conditioning is not wholly our own fault and it is not wholly in our power to overcome it. We must be prepared for a wholesale deconditioning if we are to become free beings. Today I want to draw your attention specially to the kind of deconditioning that we need to bring about voluntarily in ourselves. Conditioning goes easily enough, but deconditioning is something different, and the kind of deconditioning we require will not come by itself, if only because we are constantly exposed to the very same conditioning influences that we are trying to free ourselves from. I refer to the conditioning that makes us take as reality only what we can see and touch, in other words, the material objects with which we have to deal. This conditioning makes us look for, and take an interest in, the supposed security that is given by material possessions. We take all this as being in contact with the "real world." From all that, we become accustomed to thinking in terms of everything as if it were like this material world with which we have to deal all the time. When we begin to see the limitations of this material world and to look for something beyond it, we do so partly in our thoughts, by picturing to ourselves that there is another, an invisible world or a spiritual world, and partly with our feelings. There may also be some memory and perhaps even sometimes an immediate present experience of something quite different, so that, although we see the same thing, it is altogether different because we are different. And this we describe as becoming aware of a spiritual reality within a material reality.

All this is very good, but it does not stay with us, so that we are not able to live our lives with full acceptance of a reality that is beyond the senses, and of all that that acceptance implies. The constantly acting influences of the material things in themselves, and also of the worlds attitude towards them, causes us to be conditioned to belief in the visible and skeptical about the invisible, without our being aware of what is happening to us.

Our language is permeated through and through with forms that are taken from the material world. Those who have taken part in some of our seminars, and particularly the seminar about time that we completed yesterday, know how difficult it is. Special mental exercises are required to liberate oneself from the conditioning of material views of time and space before one can even begin to think freely about them. At the same time, you also know that it is really possible, if one sets oneself to do it, to see things differently at least for a long enough time to realize that the ordinary way of seeing things is no more than conditioned habit. What seems to us to be the reality proves, on closer examination, to be nothing else but our own habitual way of looking at our own experience. We have come to a peculiar situation where our minds and even our souls seem to be governed by the same laws as govern tables and chairs.

Then comes a time when we begin to search and look for another reality. At that point, another kind of mistake can creep in: of thinking of it as far away. We know the honest-to-God criticism of the notion of God as a "huge man" and of heaven as a "place in the sky." This kind of foolishness is not really the fault of the religious teaching, it is the fault of the habitual language which cannot express itself in any other way.

Many of you have no doubt noticed that when you come to our Work—to the search for a reality in yourself through the transformation of your own nature—you carry this conditioning to it and think of this change as remote, as something very far away, something that has no meaning for us such as we are now. The idea that this is near, that this is immediately present, that this is part of the reality that we are now experiencing, is what is hard to come to. We either think of one world or of two worlds, but when we think of one world we do so as if this were the only real world. What we cannot think of is a world where the invisible and the visible are really one and the same: not apart like earth and sky, not apart like everyday experience and the ecstasy of the mystics, but intimately all the time woven into one another.

If we try to bring home to ourselves that the invisible world is really near to us we may ask: "Well, if it is so, why do I not experience it? Why do I not find it? Why am I not aware of it?" You cannot see it because it is invisible. That is accepted. And you cannot be aware of it because it is not your ordinary awareness that brings you to it. But everyone knows that we do have experiences of wonder and astonishment, when the whole world looks different—not another world, but this very world looks totally different to us. This must convince us that the failure to see is not in distance or in strangeness, but in our own inability to open ourselves to a different kind of experience.

I said at the beginning that I would speak about deconditioning. I believe that it is possible, by steadily pegging away at it, to change our mode of thinking about these things. For example: by constantly reminding ourselves that the spiritual reality is here and not in another place, that my own spiritual reality—that is, my real "I"—is here and now and not in some other world. And if I use even the phrase "other world," that "other world" is not far away, it does not belong to the end of time, as people have been accustomed to think of it. It does not require that we should die and go somewhere else to find it. Because we are accustomed to think that the other world has to be "reached" by some kind of journey in space and time, we have to dissaccustom ourselves. That will come about only if we frequently remind ourselves of it in the ways we think, in the ways we look, in our attitude to ourselves, to people, to things, to events, to everything. There is here, in intimate contact with what we are at this moment, an invisible world that we have had glimpses of, and these glimpses have shown us how very close it is.

This does not mean of course that the highest levels of being for man are easily attained, and that the transformation is simply a matter of changing our attitude. The transformation of man to make him such a being that he is really free in relation to the invisible worlds, is a very great thing. This is not because the reality is different; it is because a tremendous reconstruction of our nature is required. This reconstruction has to begin with accepting that it is possible.

We must really accept—not merely dream "wouldn't it be nice if one could be different"—that this transformation is something that is possible for me, for you, for everyone. It is possible because it is nothing but a reconstruction, a reformation of what has been wrongly assembled. As things are, we have become assembled in such a way that our apparatus for knowing the outside material world has been put together without means of communication with another apparatus that is there for knowing the spiritual world. We can bring about this reconstruction by the act of reminding ourselves of the immediate presence of what we are looking for. If I think of it as distant, I do something to keep the breach open, to keep this barrier closed inside me: but, when I remind myself that this reality for which I am looking is here, intimately present in me, already this gap narrows, the barrier grows less impenetrable. By doing this constantly, we come to be able to accept that the change of everything in our life, everything that we see in the material world and the other, is indescribable for the very reason that the whole glory of reality is in the union of the material and the spiritual, not in their being isolated from one another. One should not allow oneself the kind of thoughts that imagine the invisible world as something remote and the possibilities of our own transformation as some kind of dream we do not really believe in. Nor should we treat our memory of the glory of this contact of the spiritual and the material as a strange experience but as the natural state for man that we ought to be in the whole time.

As I said earlier, we are under the influence of the attitudes and behavior of other people, all of which point in the opposite direction: of taking the material as here and now and treating the spiritual as far away. To become free from this attitude is not a battle to be won in a single encounter. Constant renewal, constant return to this inner work that brings an awareness of the immediacy of a spiritual reality, is needed to decondition us from our old habits of thought.

The nearness of the invisible world is vividly expressed in the well-known poem, "The Kingdom of God," by Francis Thompson, *which was* first shown to me by the headmaster of my school when I was a boy. It was one of the turning points in my life when he said: "You read this, learn it by heart; you will keep it with you all your life." He was right, it is extraordinary in its truthfulness, and that truthfulness has become a greater and greater reality to me as the years have gone by.

"O world invisible we view thee,
O world intangible we touch thee,
O world unknowable we know thee,

Inapprehensible we clutch thee!
Does the fish soar to find the ocean,
The eagle plunge to find the air—
That we ask of the stars in motion
If they have rumour of thee there?
Not where the wheeling systems darken
And our benumbed conceiving soars!—
The drift of pinions, would we hearken,
Beats at our own clay-shuttered doors.
The angels keep their ancient places;—
Turn but a stone, and start a wing!
Tis ye, tis your estranged faces,
That miss the many-splendoured thing."

The wonder of the penetration of the invisible into the visible and the transformation of the invisible through its entry into the visible, all this is what we can experience ourselves, if only we will practice this deconditioning. It is important because this will give us the courage and determination to submit to the action that is required to bring about the radical reformation of our own nature, which is a hard and painful business. We must and can see what it will bring us to.

You can begin to work this way this very morning. Whenever you remember yourselves, remind yourselves that there is an invisible reality here and now, and all about and within us.

After-Lunch Discussion

Questioner. The exercise, as far as I was concerned, was extraordinary. I was in a rather confused state and I sat quietly. It was not that I did anything, but something entered, something changed, and it lasted right through to lunchtime.

JG Bennett. Yes, confusion is an important notion that you have incidentally referred to here. It is confusion that separates us from this direct awareness. Confusion is in our minds, or at least it starts in our minds and afterwards penetrates into our bodies, until everything becomes confused and we can no longer bring anything into focus in ourselves, not even in the external world. What I called deconditioning can also be called "removal of the state of confusion," because we are conditioned to confusion. When we work in this way then the opposite of confusion begins to come, that is, clarity.

Q. It seems to me that this conditioning starts very early in our culture. Even from the Bible we get the idea that heaven is in some other place and that we shall only get there after death.

JGB. It is very true that, for a very long time, men have been in the habit of dividing the world in that way. It should not be so but it is, and I agree that this is taken to be a cultural matter. It implies that some people have the secret and others have not, and that those who have the secret are somehow privileged, and that the "other people" cannot expect anything unless they get into this privileged circle. The privileged people know the reality of things. They are cultured and the others are uncultured. And so it becomes totally absurd. For instance, the difference between seeing and non-seeing is then taken to be much the same as between literate and illiterate. Whereas, in reality, it is very often the literate people who cannot see. In the end, it becomes quite inverted: what started by being something which is straightforward for everyone and is always presented as such, begins to be a private possession of a few. But, that it is very difficult to get oneself reconstructed and adjusted so that one can do something about it that is not a privilege, that is something which requires very hard work and readiness to pay a very great price. Certainly those who do their hard work and will pay the price are in a different situation.

Q. I find that confusion is brought about in me by an intensity of energy which the inner self cannot control.

JGB. This happens through ignorance. There needs to be an intensity of energy, but we must be prepared for it. If light is suddenly turned on in the darkness, people are blinded by it. If there is a great intensification of the energy of our inner state and we are not organized to deal with it, then it does increase the state of confusion. That is why it is necessary to go about this patiently, by constantly repeated small acts. I know this from my own experience and that is why I recommend this exercise. Little by little, it strengthens our ability to see things more often as they really are, without being confused and distressed, or overexcited by it.

Q. What is one to do when one is struggling to keep a central peace, and the periphery is chaotic? For instance, just before lunch started I noticed that my hair was untidy and quickly went to brush it. These two minutes of doing the outer action and at the same time inwardly trying to become recollected did the trick. Very often I find the outer settles the inner, which is rather the opposite way round to what you were saying?

JGB. That is simply one form of it. What I was saying is also done in

6

the outer. Our thoughts are, after all, still the outer; and if we put our thoughts in order we are doing something very much like brushing our hair. But it is still only the instruments that we are putting right. With the help of that we come to an inner clarity and so eventually to peace and faith. They are all indications of the same thing. But it is true that this technique is one that can be learned and can be profitably used. We can see that it is very often possible to deal with an inner confusion—which we cannot get at—by putting right some outer confusion, which we can get at. Even the simplest things such as merely arranging better some external things that are in a muddle. This external act of putting things in order reflects back on to an inner part that we cannot reach. So, it is not really right to say that the outside does not matter so long as the inner is right. Muddled thinking interferes with our power of perceiving directly how things are; and, therefore, getting one's thinking clear is a means of getting what we cannot reach, that is, this inner state of our will. One of Ouspensky's favorite sayings was that "it is a myth to think that the good professor loses his umbrella."

Q. This seems to fit in with what came to me this morning. I remembered something written in Idries Shah's book, *The Sufis,* that the rightness of our actions reflects on our inner state. This struck me very much and stayed with me the whole day.

JGB. It is so. The material world remains the foundation. There is no soundness in the idea that we should put aside or abandon, or lose interest in the material world. It is the foundation, it is the primary scene of action, but it is a mistake to expect from it what it is not able to give. One can make this sort of distinction: that what we need is in one place and what we are longing for is in another. What we long for is an imperishable perfection and some state of realization where everything can be reconciled, where all contradictions can be seen to make sense, where the purposes of things are revealed as well as the means of fulfilling these purposes. We long to know our place in the scheme of things and how to fill it.

We must remember, however, that we need to *exist.* First of all, as material objects and, secondly, as living organisms dependent upon environment to renew our existence. We make a mistake, when we begin to transfer our longings into the world of needs, or to transfer our needs into the world of longings. We can exist without this fulfillment. There is no need for this realization, which is a goal attainable for those who long for it enough. When there is some kind of balance between recognizing our needs and understanding also the significance of our longings, and the conditions for fulfilling them, then the world begins to make sense. Out of this world of needs, we begin to build up this other world of our longings, of our aspirations. And it is true that in the right performance of our actions there is something that can affect our whole character, but it is not immediately obvious why doing outer tasks in the right way is so important for us.

Q. I can see that something has changed in my life. The idea of wanting to put the whole world right has now become wanting to manage my own life better, such as managing my household chores, my clothes and so on. And then it seems to come even nearer, right into your mind and your movements, and the relationship you have with other people, and because of that there is less of a feeling of confusion.

JGB. What you say is quite right, and even hopeful! Confusion is closely mixed up with rejection: and by this I mean not being willing to accept things as they are. They are so involved in one another that, between them, they close the door to this little place in ourselves where it is possible, at any moment, to make the connection between the two sides: the side where the meanings are and the side where the facts are. As long as they are separated, nothing can make sense, because then the meanings are in our imagination and the facts are there for us to stumble against. This block prevents us from connecting the two. This block partly comes from our not accepting but making demands, expecting things to be shown to us, proved to us, or that they should be according to our preconceptions of what they ought to be—all of that closes the door.

The other obstacle is the bad habit that has come from the whole of our culture, as K. R. remarked, of not using language in the right way, which, on the face of it, does not seem a very serious matter. But it really is a very serious matter, because what should be understood literally, we understand figuratively, what should be understood figuratively, we understand literally. We are doing that all the time and therefore we never come to grips, nothing really comes into focus for us. When you begin to see this in yourself then something begins to become clear, with often quite extraordinary results. As L. H. was saying, one short moment of clarity can make many other things change and alter our state even for hours.

Q. The other day I had to wait for a bus for about twenty minutes on a cold and wet evening and it was all I could do not to allow myself to be pervaded by a feeling of physical misery and annoyance and even a kind of peevish and stupid resentment. I was aware though that this discomfort was only temporary and that there are many people who are permanently, or at least for long periods, subjected to that kind of thing; and I felt ashamed to see how very fragile and weak my inner detachment is. Can you say something about this?

JGB. Yes. There are two things here. First of all, the human organism and also with it the human psychic functions are enormously adaptable; they are able to adapt themselves to a range of external conditions far wider than any other living thing. As far as heat and cold are concerned, human beings can adapt themselves to live in climates varying from the hottest and driest or wettest parts of the world to the Arctic Circle. I remember the extreme conditions of physical discomfort many others and I had to endure during the trench warfare of the First World War. In a very short time one got accustomed to sleeping on boards, in mud, in freezing temperatures, for long periods on end.

The two points to note in this question are therefore, firstly that the human organism and the human psyche adapt themselves to a very great range of external conditions and secondly, that what we notice are changes, even comparatively small changes, in the conditions.

It is a very awkward thing to be conditioned to one very stable set of circumstances because this diminishes our power of response. People who want to keep themselves alive inwardly must be ready to subject themselves to changes of conditioning. The kind of experience you describe can in fact be used for a deconditioning purpose. To remain comfortable in a certain narrow set of conditions is not really conducive to a state of freedom; however, if one subjects oneself to changes in one's way of living, a certain deconditioning takes place and with that a certain freedom comes. So if one really understands one's own true profit, one will not mind being subjected to discomforts, especially to changes of this sort.

2.
WISHES ARE CONTROLLABLE

20 December 1964

WHERE IS THE POINT at which we are all free, at which we have power to do what we choose? This depends on what we really wish for. This power of wishing is ours and it is never taken away from us. We can wish what we decide to wish. But that decision must be taken by ourselves, we cannot push it off on to anyone else.

We must be sure that we know the difference between wishing and wanting, desiring, or even needing. The way I shall use the word "wish" in talking to you now refers to the inward decision that every one of us has to take as to what really matters to us. But it does not mean that because we wish for something, we also have the power to achieve it. Nor have we even the power to want, because our wants are divided: one part of us wants one thing and another, another; one part desires one thing, another hates it. We cannot get away from this conflict of desires in ourselves or in the changing of our wants: we now want this, then forget all about it and want something quite different. This is how we are, but none of this touches a true wish, because wish is where will is anchored. Wish is really the simplest thing because wish can either be to belong where we do belong and to fill the place that is destined for us, or it can be a wish to occupy the place that we want, that we desire. In another and a still simpler way of putting it, we either can wish to serve God or we can wish for the satisfaction of our own egoism. It is said that there is no place for two in the soul: it must be either God or I, not both. I say it is at this point that we have full power to wish for what we choose. That is why the place of supreme responsibility is where we have to decide what it is that we wish. None of us need be confused about this question. It does not require any learning; it does not require any particular articles of faith nor belief in this or that creed. It is before and beyond and more intimate than all of that.

So long as this is not faced, life is troublesome. We approve of this or of that, we are affected by things, by people, by their behavior, by success and failure, by pleasure and pain, but none of these can touch us when we know what we wish. If you see a person who is affected by what others think, by how they stand in other people's eyes, you must know that they have no stable unchanging wish, and if you find that you yourself are such a person, you must know that your wish is not clear. If you wish for God, for Reality, for Truth, for what is right, none of these things will matter. They cannot, because they all belong to the wish that you have rejected; that is, the wish for your own egoistic satisfaction.

Until you have cleared up this question of wish, you will be afraid, because you will not know how to face the future. If you are clear about this, fear disappears, because you will know that whatever happens and whatever may come, your wish will remain unchanged. When people have a strong wish they are strong in their lives. We must not forget that the power of wish also applies to people whose wishes are founded on their own egoism. They wish for success, they wish for dominance, they wish to stand well in the eyes of people, and they go all out to get it, ruthlessly. And because of this, they have not got these kinds of subservience to what people think, or to pleasure or pain. They will face being affronted, having to suffer overwork; they will deny themselves, because they know what they wish for.

You know the parable of the unjust steward [Luke 16]. When he saw that he was going to lose his job he took every precaution to see that he would be all right, and to everyone's surprise he is commended. Even Christ says that the children of this world are wiser in their generation than the children of light. Why? Because it is necessary to know what one wishes for and who does not know what he wishes for is nothing at all, because this is the center of everything for us. There are many people who can be called children of light, who are sincerely drawn towards truth and reality, and yet they are all the time looking over their shoulders to see what is going on behind them, or looking at other people to see whether they are approved or disapproved of, or waiting to be commended. They are the kind of people of whom it is said: "The children of this world are wiser than they." When one is really clever, how can any of these things matter?

It may be that we cannot make the image of what we wish for clear to ourselves, but we can, without any question, make the direction clear. By that I mean that a person may say "I wish to serve God, I wish for the realization of truth, I wish for the love of God, for impersonal objective love" without being able to fully comprehend what these things mean. But everyone can be clear about whether the wish is for his own self or for what is right. We must all of us see without any doubt that about this there can be no self-deception. When this wish is clear, then all the other things will come, and that again is expressed by the saying of Christ: "Seek ye first the Kingdom of God and His righteousness." Even if you do not really know what it means, this is the direction to which you can turn and then the rest will become clear by itself. There has to be an implacable, uncompromising demand of oneself that one will not deceive oneself, because with self-deception we fall into every kind of misery. We become afraid. We depend upon people. We have no kind of confidence.

When I say we must be clear about what we wish, I do not mean that this solves all our problems. Far from it. We will still want the wrong things. We shall still forget all about it. We will still be drawn towards stupidities. This is how things are. We have very little power over all that. But once we are clear about our wish, and return to it again and again to be quite certain that it remains unchanged in us, and once we really know that we do not want our own egoism to be fed, pampered, by anything whatsoever—then we shall have that extraordinary assurance that enables us to face anything. But as soon as we are again caught by this egoism of ours, every misery enters again. This must be clear.

After-Lunch Discussion

Questioner. Suppose we find that what we really wish for is the fulfillment of our destiny, how can we put this wish to the test?

JG Bennett. If I can say to myself, "Does it touch me if I am praised or blamed?" and I find that it does touch me, I can then ask myself why, and I will find that there is something in me that minds. But what does it mind? It minds that I should be touched, that I should be praised or blamed. If I cared for nothing whatever except to do my duty or to serve, I would be indifferent to praise or blame. That does not mean that I would not be pleased if I was praised or sad if I was blamed, but I would not be touched. I would know that it would not affect me in any way. If one has this certainty, that one is not affected that there is no inner disturbance when one is praised or blamed, then this is a good indication that the wish to fulfill our destiny and not to please our self is clear and stable. Again, if I do something well and I succeed in what I am doing and I see that this matters to me; or I fail and I am downcast and this matters to me, this shows that I am not free. Because, if I do my duty, it should not matter to me whether I succeed or fail. What matters of course is that I should do what is required of me in order to fulfill my destiny with all my heart. I should know that I can work with the same strength and energy because it is right, as I would do if I should be praised for it, or get some reward for it. Another very interesting observation is to see whether one acts just in the same way if nobody knows what one is doing as one would do if people were watching. You see that these kinds of tests are not difficult to apply.

Q. Supposing that one knows one is obsessed with egoistic fears and so on, does that quite clearly mean that one has not got a true wish?

JGB. No, to have a real wish does not of itself free one from egoism. If the wish is really to be free, it is not enough only to wish. If you have to go to the dentist to have a tooth pulled out, you know that this is necessary for you, but it does not make it any more pleasant. Either we shirk the dentist or we do not. Egoism is worse than a tooth, and it does not want to be pulled out. In the same way we can shirk or not shirk what is needed to extirpate our egoism. If you know and face this, I believe that to attain a clarity of one's own, looking at the situation, is the decisive thing. If I ask myself whether there is any point in serving my own egoism, I see quite clearly that there is no point in it; it cannot possibly do me any good. And then this ceases to be a question of moral "ought" or "ought not": I simply see that my egoism cannot possibly be satisfied, it cannot possibly have peace, and it cannot possibly arrive at anything. And therefore my attitude towards it does not mean that my egoism will quietly vanish away. Certainly it does not, but something in me is now clear and settled. I see what is right for me and once this is done, other things begin to move. But to come to this clarity is hard. It seems a very small step to become clear about something when one cannot do anything about it yet, when one is still obsessed, as you say; but once that step is made, you cannot deceive yourself any more into thinking that feeding your egoism can have any sense.

Of course egoism is very deceptive. We think it is right that people should be encouraged if they are doing well. We say "isn't praise a good thing, isn't it desirable that people should be comforted and encouraged?" Yes, all these things are perfectly true, all those things are desirable, but we must know that this is only something that can help us temporarily until we are strong enough to be able to do without them.

I think that if man were intended to do right for any other reason than just that it is right, this would be shown to him. We would see the rewards of virtue, if virtue were something that depended upon reward. We do not see the rewards of virtue and this means that fundamentally we have to do right without looking to rewards.

Q. How can one stabilize the experience of clarity?

JGB. By renewal. The experience is quite out of the ordinary because people in general have no wish to be clear. We are ready for anything but the simple truth. The truth turns everything upside down because the whole world lives by motives that are either open or disguised egoism. Even when people do good, they do it because they want to be pleased with themselves, they want others to admire them, they want some sort of personal satisfaction from it. When they do harm, they justify it to themselves rather than admit that they are like they are: some good reason is found. So the whole world lives by a vitiated, upside-down motivation. To get ourselves the right way up we have to become accustomed to living the right way up and this, as I say, is done only by renewal.

Suppose people can be hypnotized and persuaded that the right thing to do is to stand on your head, and they all stand on their heads and get accustomed to hobble about as best they can in this way. And then some are de-hypnotized for a moment and stand on their feet. First of all, everyone will think them crazy; and, secondly, this habit of standing on their heads is so strong that half an hour after being de-hypnotized and having seen how absurd it is, over they go again on their heads and feel comfortable again. What does "standing on your head" mean? It means putting "I" first. This habit of standing on one's head takes time to get rid of, even if one has seen the absurdity of it.

Q. But are we not right in thinking that everyone who is born on this Earth has to acquire a complete ego in order to give it away? So that when we are "standing on our heads," is it not that we just do not grow up into the casting off of our ego? Is it not absolutely necessary for each of us to acquire an ego, whatever we may do with it afterwards? Think how pleased we are when our children become individuals, and does not individuality necessitate a streak of egoism?

JGB. Egoism and Individuality are not the same thing. Individuality one must have. By egoism I mean worshipping oneself, putting oneself first. I do not mean being a real person, because this is not egoism. Each person should be wholly themselves, not lost in the masses. The more one is oneself, the more right it is to be so, and the more one is able to fulfill one's own destiny. But it is the spoiling of this very thing that I am talking about. We do just this to our children. You say we are pleased when we see them begin to be independent. This is true, but it is very hard to avoid suggesting to them also that they are important, or better, or more clever than others are. If they are made to feel unimportant and suffer from it, this is by contrast with people who are full of egoism, so they get exposed to it either way, for egoism can be either self-assertive and bold, or plaintive, timid and self-effacing. There is no difference because in both cases one's tenderness is for one's own person.

With our children, our great aim should be to create conditions in which they can acquire the first stage of Individuality; that is, their own "I," without the taint of egoism. This is far more important than all the learning and skill in the world. It is even more important than acquiring discipline and the capacity for work, though Heaven knows these are necessary enough for modern man!

Q. I would like to be really friendly with people, to be connected with them, but it seems as if there always is a separation between people. Can one do something about being integrated?

JGB. Yes, there is very much we can do about this. Just bring back to your mind an occasion when you have done some really hard bit of work with someone so that both of you have put everything you could into it. Do you ever forget the connection you had with such a person? The connection does not come from wishing to be connected, but from doing. You ask about how one can be integrated? Integration between people depends on how they live. If we, all of us, could understand that we exist to serve one purpose, and if we could really be decided that what matters is that we should serve that purpose, we should soon be integrated.

Q. When people have been hospitable to me, I often saw that they were wearing two faces all the time, and I did not feel at home.

JGB. Being integrated has little to do with being nice or nasty, behaving in a kindly, friendly way to people or in an unfriendly way. It depends on a bond being formed between you: on what you do together. Consider, for example, the act of giving and taking. You talk

15

about being "hospitable." In hospitality it looks as if one person gives and the other receives. This, by itself, can separate people: there can be resentment, the host can feel that he was not appreciated or the guest can feel that he was not properly understood or well-treated or something like this; or there can be some kind of awkwardness due to imagination. Obviously, no sort of connection is made in such situations. You should see for yourself that the act of hospitality—of receiving a guest and being received as a guest—is something that belongs to the reality of things. That it is something to be shared and enjoyed. That both—the one who gives and the one who receives—are partaking in something that concerns not just their personalities but something more than that. When you come to that feeling—that you are really doing something that is to be enjoyed, is to be done as well as possible and so on—then hospitality becomes something quite different, and people really can become integrated through it. The actions that integrate are not superficial; they have to go to a certain depth before something happens. Otherwise, if they remain on the surface, they do not connect and may even separate.

3.
OTHER PEOPLE

17 November 1963

THIS MORNING I want to direct your attention TO some of the ways in which other people affect our own inner development. What happens inside us, the transformation that we hope and believe is going on within each one of us, we can think of as private and connected with other people only through our outward relations with them.

The idea that our inner development is first of all a private matter and only in a second degree connected with our being in a life with others is very strongly held by some people. One great philosopher (Whitehead I think) said, "Religion is what man does with his solitude," and there is obviously a great truth in this. We have to be totally alone, totally turned towards the innermost experience possible for us, in order to come nearer and nearer towards the reality we are looking for. It is also quite true that insofar as we have something inside us it must manifest for the benefit of others, and therefore this manifestation and benefit is an inevitable result of what we have gained inwardly.

But this is only one side of the picture. It is also true that our connection with other people is an essential, a primary part of our own spiritual life. It is not just a consequence of what happens or fails to happen in us. It is a part of the whole of what is happening to us. In many obvious ways we can help one another; we learn from those who know; we transmit to those who can learn from us; we help others by our example and we are very greatly helped by the example of those who have very evidently made progress in spiritual development. But this is still outward, still really secondary. If we can learn from those who know, some inner change has had to happen to them: they must really know something in order to teach. Similarly, if we are to teach, we must really have acquired something inside ourselves which we understand and can live by, otherwise we cannot teach it in any genuine way. The example of others and the example we can be, depends upon what there is inside us and inside them. So, if this connection with other people is to have a primary place, it must be something more and different from that.

When I am in front of you I am in front of a person. I am a person and you are a person, and a person means a being who has an inner life. As long as we depend just upon the outward show to recognize other people, this is definitely a secondary thing. But if we can contrive to meet them directly as people, then it is a primary thing: it is no longer going out from our solitude to meet somebody else coming from their solitude; it is a meeting in a company where we are not alone. We are only alone when as a person we are unable to meet other people as persons. Of course this is a very difficult thing, and we recognize only too well that even with those who are nearest to us—parents with children, loving husbands with loving wives—there is still some gap between person and person, perhaps only to be bridged in moments. This is partly because we do not give enough importance to this truer kind of relationship in our lives and we expect or imagine that we can be people with people without having done anything special about it. And yet experience shows us that something quite special has to happen so that this meeting of person with person can be a reality.

Now it is possible for us all to strengthen that kind of relationship. And one way is to remember when we are in front of people that each one is an individual person with an inner life of his own. This act of recognition is something that is in our own power, whereas it is not within our power to break through this barrier by thought or by feeling. This does not mean that the kind of exchange that comes through the outside—through our senses, through seeing and hearing and touching—is not important; or that all the things that are comprised in friendship—in giving and taking, in setting and receiving examples—are not important. But none of them by themselves do that particular thing which is to take our inner life out of its solitude.

It is to be taken very seriously that in our conversation with people, in our exchanges of every kind, we should try to add to the outer, visible, exchange also an inward movement, an inward awareness that we are in front of a person and that this person is the same as we are in this fundamental thing. That he has an inner life, an inner experience that is in the process of transformation. With some people this transformation may go very weakly, with some perhaps even not rightly; perhaps it may be a transformation that is a disintegration. With others it may be a transformation that is certainly a creative integration. But whatever it is, with everyone—whoever they may be—there is that unseen inner life. Maybe all of us here accept and do not question the reality and importance of the inner life in other people, but we forget it. And a great many of our actions, behavior, thoughts, feelings—hidden or visible—would be different if we remembered always that when we are dealing with "people," we are dealing with *people*! We forget this obvious thing, and therefore we expect from them something that cannot be—a degree of perfection, a degree of integration which we ourselves do not possess.

By remembering that "people" are *people* we become free. When we forget it we fall into a slavery of fears and cruelties. We know perfectly well that there is something within us that is quite different from what other people are seeing and hearing when they talk to us, and this is what we should remember about them.

How can we remember this? Experience shows that the mind is a bad rememberer. The good rememberer is the body. When the body is trained to remember, it will do so even when the attention of the mind is quite distracted. If I were to ask you to remember what I have been saying when you are in front of people, even though you may wish to do so, you will not be able to if your mind is occupied with something else. Perhaps a minute or two afterwards you will remember and feel sorry. This sorrow may serve to remind you that can also happen, but the simplest thing is to evoke the memory power of the body. Suppose we do it in this way: that we connect our own selves with our right hand and other people with our left hand, and through remembering the presence of our hands we remember the connection between people. For example, take the well-known commandment in which it is said "One hand must wash the other," and remember that this means that between people there must always be a giving and taking, and that what we are looking for is this deep giving and taking between us as persons, as one person to another person. It does not matter at all whether we achieve this or whether we do not, for that depends upon factors we are not yet able to control. What we want to do is simply to have this wish.

Before we stop I want you now—just sitting where you are—to bring your attention to your two hands very intently, so that you are not only thinking about them but really have sensation in them and so are aware that your hands are alive. Now connect the life of your right hand with yourself, and the life of your left hand with the people whom you will meet and speak with during the day.

When I ask my two hands to remind me of this, I find that as I do so I am saying the words "I" and "thou," which had not occurred to me before. You can say I am asking my right hand to remember "I" and my left hand to remember "thou." This is something formed in a movement of my own memory and intention, not just something to be expressed in outward actions. (The outward actions are another matter.) Now I shall speak. What I shall do to people, that I shall do in my usual way. But this memory and intention I wish to keep separate: the memory that the person in front of me is a person with a life and an understanding of his or her own; and the intention to accept him or her as such. My left hand is not yet really accepting all this—I have to tell it to behave. Now it is better, now it will remember.

If you will try this experiment this morning, while you are occupied with various activities, we can talk about it after lunch.

After-Lunch Discussion

Questioner. Is it possible that our behavior is altered by a bodily memory even if our thinking is not present?

JG Bennett. Yes, of course it is. What matters in this is our intention or decision, our commitment. This makes a kind of inner orientation, almost as if we were magnetizing ourselves. When you do that through your physical body, it remains with you. It can touch your thinking, it can touch your feelings, it can touch your actions. Sometimes you are aware of it; sometimes you are not aware of it until later and you may notice that you have behaved differently. What is important is to learn how to take a commitment in such a way that it will really stick, so that it is not just on the outside. You do not produce this condition in yourself just by thinking "Wouldn't it be nice?" or something like that. One has got to know how to transfer it into one's organism so that it becomes an organic reminder, and then it works.

Q. Has it something to do with the quality of the energy in the thinking?

JGB. No, the thinking here is only a kind of pipe through which something flows; it does not do anything else except transfer an idea into the place where we can make a decision. We cannot take a decision by thought. There is no power of decision in our thinking because thinking is essentially fluid, mobile. It has to be by its nature. You cannot use it as a fixed point on which to turn something. The body is the fixed point on which you can do that, because it is always there. That does not mean that the thinking has no part. Something other than thought itself is transferred through the thinking, but there has to be a particular quality of thinking or it will not be transferred.

Q. Sometimes I take a decision and I know perfectly well that I am just not going to do it!

JGB. Yes, it is very good when you know in advance the difference between having committed yourself and not having done so. The power to make real commitments has to be built up little by little until we know when our word is our bond. When we know that, then this word to ourselves will be kept and cannot be put aside.

Q. How is this "bond" made? It seems to me as though there has to be a certain intensity in one's thinking first, to make this recollection possible.

JGB. That is true. At that moment there must not be any confusion in our thinking. At that moment we must really know what we are doing and what it means to be deciding something. Then it reaches us. It may be that at that very moment we have the awareness that we are not going to decide it, we are not ready to take this commitment. As you say, one can know in advance that one is not going to do it; and one can also know in advance that one is going to do it, because when they reach our will, our decisions cannot be taken in obscurity. The role of the thinking at that moment is to see that the situation is brought out into the open in order that I should really know what it is I am setting in front of myself. Then, when faced with seeing the situation objectively, either I will decide or I will not. Of course it is not easy to come to that, so your remark that it requires a certain intensity of thinking is quite true. There must not be any woolliness at that moment, because if there is all sorts of excuses will follow. We always wriggle like anything to get out of our own decisions. But if we have really decided clearly, then that wriggling does not avail: we have to do it.

Q. Do you think words help? I find that for me words like "I" and "thou" mean a tremendous amount.

JGB. Yes, but the words in themselves are no use unless they actually evoke in you something quite clear. It is the something they evoke that matters. Words can equally well hinder. You may wrongly imagine that you understand something if you blindly trust the words and do not get at the reality. Words can be big deceivers.

Q. Is it possible to reinforce the decision taken?

JGB. Up to a point it is possible, by a kind of self-reasoning that brings me to see that if I cannot commit myself to this which it is in my power to do, what about all the other things? "At this moment this is the opportunity which is in front of me and if I do not take it, what will happen to me?" With that kind of self-reasoning one can bring just that additional clarity which enables one to say "I must."

Q. About loneliness ... I feel that we are not really alone, or does one become aware of loneliness only after a certain amount of work?

JGB. We have the possibility of not being alone; but in order to make that possibility into something real for ourselves, we have to be able to meet people, and to meet people one has to be strong. People are weak in themselves, they cannot bear to meet other people and therefore they hide. Of course we are not really alone, we are all connected with one another. But that reality has got to be made into something.

Question: At first the exercise used to help a great deal. Now it no longer helps.

JG Bennett: Quite so. You must understand that this is a principle. No technique in this kind of work can be always the same in its result. Sometimes, even to continue a technique beyond the point where it no longer serves its purpose is dangerous. This is why we need groups, and the experience of other people who have gone through other and different experiences; and people trained in the understanding of how to apply techniques. More than once I have known people to go away when they've found they got positive results from some technique; then after they've gone away things have not gone well with them. In reality, everything needs to be adapted to circumstances. There is nothing—no technique—that gives the same results at all stages of development. There is a saying: "You don't give strong meat to babes!" People need different strengths of food at different stages of development. If we use powerful techniques before we have entered into ourselves, they can split us apart. To do that is to use techniques without what Gurdjieff calls Science. You must understand as a principle that everything—every exercise you are shown—should not be continued unaltered for more than six months. If someone goes abroad, for example, the necessary modifications can be sent to them by letter. Sometimes it is not harmful to continue a technique, because it may just peter out. But sometimes to continue it produces the wrong kind of result.

—Coombe Springs Group "S" Notes, 1964.

4.
UNDERSTANDING

1 December 1963

WHILE I WAS SITTING HERE waiting, I was thinking how difficult it is to say something that will not be misunderstood. One reason for this is that we are so different that a clear and easy idea for one person to understand is often quite incomprehensible to another, and that kind of situation may easily lead to great confusion. When that happens, we should not take it as an indication that either we ourselves have failed or that what is told us is necessarily confusing or wrong. It may not be confusing at all for someone else and the fact that we cannot understand need not be a weakness in ourselves: it may just be that the particular correspondence which enables us to see it is lacking.

But this is not all. It happens also that at one minute we can see clearly and understand just what is meant by something that is said and perhaps a few minutes later, when we try to return to it, it no longer makes sense to us. You know how it can happen, in listening to a talk like this one, that what was said seems quite clear, but a little later in the day, when we try to remember it, we either cannot recall anything at all or it is quite confused. It is not only that one person is different from another but also that all of us are subject to such fluctuations in our inner states that what we understand at one moment seems meaningless at another.

This is not at all a disaster. The fact that different people understand in different ways is the very condition that allows understanding to progress. Imagine what would happen if everyone understood and agreed about everything. We should just come to a standstill. But there is an infinite world to be understood—not only because it is so large but also because it is so deep, and each one of us can catch glimpses of it which are unnoticed by others. And it is also true that our own changes of states are something to be thankful for.

Supposing that the state of understanding of any one of us were twenty degrees—because of the strength of our own nature, let us say—and that it always remained at that level. This would immediately set a limit to what could happen to us: nothing that was beyond twenty degrees would make any sense to us at all. But supposing that it fluctuates, that sometimes our understanding is at ten degrees and sometimes at forty or fifty degrees; then we could penetrate into realms that our average understanding could not possibly touch; but because our average is only twenty, we inevitably lose it all again. This does not really matter, because in the moment of seeing more deeply something has changed in us, and when it is necessary we shall be able to return to it. Therefore these fluctuations of our state are really the condition of our progress.

We have to learn to use fluctuations in our understanding in such a way that they will really help us. If we are always waiting to touch some higher level—say forty degrees, when our average is only twenty—and think we cannot do anything except when we are in this special state of clear understanding, clear vision, we shall miss nine tenths of the opportunities in our lives. A great deal has to be done when our understanding is even below our own average, in moments when we are obliged to go on in what seems like darkness and confusion to us. In those moments of darkness and confusion we are inclined to think that it is not worth doing anything, and perhaps it will not even occur to us to think, because we feel so wretched and so hopeless, and we just wait for something to happen. The truth is that there is a great deal to be done in those moments if we understand that the amount of what we do is not so important, but that the quality of what we do is what matters. The quality of a very feeble effort made in a state of confusion and weakness can have more value—be, in fact, of much greater value objectively—than an apparently much greater effort made in a state of clarity.

At the same time, it has to be accepted that for most of the time we are somewhere near our own average, or below it, and this is really not enough for us to understand and face what has to be done; which brings us to realize the necessity for other people. But just as there can be a combination of understanding, so there can also be a mutual disruption of understanding. Two or three people together can very easily drop below the average for the worst of all of them. They can talk real nonsense, for example, or act foolishly and wonder afterwards why they did so, or find themselves coming out of meetings in a depressed and weakened state. But when there is real union and building up of understanding, then it raises all of them to a much higher level than is possible for one alone; although usually we do not see how this happens because the understanding in which we share is above our own level. One of the principles of understanding is that one can only understand as far as one can reach oneself. When one person has only twenty degrees of understanding available at a given moment, then something which belongs to the twenty-fifth degree seems just nonsense or is totally unperceived, unseen. The words are just words. If we wish to understand something beyond the degree we are in at a given moment, then we have either to change our own degree—which is possible—or we have to share in something with others. And then it happens in a mysterious way that we find ourselves understanding things which are normally beyond us and afterwards may even wonder whether we really did or not.

Something has to happen between people for this positive working of understanding to occur. There has to be a positive instead of a negative correlation between their states and their understanding; that is, there has to be an acceptance instead of a rejection. For example, if I look at someone and put my attention on his inability to understand, this will bring things down. If, on the contrary, I look at someone and put my attention upon what he is able to understand, then there is a pool of understanding between us on which we both draw. Something happens. Strangely enough, for this to happen it is not even necessary for us to communicate in the ordinary way; that is, it is not necessary for people to talk together and discuss things in order to share in understanding. This sounds very absurd, for we have got in the way of believing that it is only by talking that anything can happen. It is not like that; it comes through acceptance.

It is possible for us to practice this acceptance of other peoples understanding; and this is what I want to propose to you today as a useful exercise when we are all together. When you look at other people or when you see them going by or are in some way aware of them, remind yourself that that person whom you are looking at has his or her own understanding, which is sure to be different from yours. At that moment you can accept; which means acknowledge to yourself that there is a person who has some experience not like your own, and out of that experience something has been distilled; that is, their understanding. Do not try to assess their degree of understanding by saying to yourself, for example, "this is only a five degree person" or something similar. That is not the point.

I have found that just through this act of looking at a person and accepting that here is an experience of life with some degree of understanding, your own state changes; you find that you are connected, not only with that person, but in a way that liberates you from this shutinness which comes over us whenever we separate or isolate our own understanding from other people, and especially when we deny the understanding of other people. When we say to somebody, or think: "You don't understand," it seems as if we are saying or thinking something rather harmless and perhaps even true. In reality, it is not a permissible thing to say, for he or she does understand, but it is their own understanding. If I say to somebody "You don't understand," I really mean "You don't prove to me that your understanding is the same as mine, which is of course the true one."

If we could train or develop in ourselves the tendency, when looking at people, of seeing that each one is a repository of a certain positive degree of understanding, and refrain from saying—either inwardly or outwardly, "You don't understand," many good things would result.

This exercise I am proposing to you today requires a certain focusing of attention. If you bring a person into focus and you look and see that person as someone who has his or her own experience, you also realize that this person has understood in his or her own way.

All degrees are low, what of it? In suggesting twenty degrees, it may be twenty out of a thousand, who knows? It does not matter. What is valuable for us to have, is a positive attitude towards the understanding of others.

I have not said anything about what understanding is, but it does not matter. Do not let yourself be worried by this problem at this stage by saying: "What on earth is understanding?" Understanding is not really something to be described or defined. So just tell yourself that there is something we call understanding which enables us to build upon our experience. It is very good in this sort of experiment to refrain from letting oneself be drawn away by the desire for definitions or explanations. The word "understanding" evokes something for each of us. That is sufficient at the moment.

After-Lunch Discussion

Questioner. Why do we feel quite justified in complaining that other people do not understand the needs of a situation, whereas we are ready to take a more tolerant view of ourselves?

JG Bennett. That is the whole tragedy of the situation. When we look at ourselves, what we see is the reflection of our own imagination as to what we are; and when we look at other people we see the reflection of our imagination of what they are. So we neither see ourselves nor other people objectively: we see ourselves on the rosy side of the mirror and other people on the jaundiced side. The exercise I was advising you to try today is really a help to break through this; not to have this sort of cloud between us and other people that makes us see them differently from the way we see ourselves. When I first began to see this in myself it seemed such an absurdity that I could not believe it to be true that I really had two completely different standards of valuation according to whether they were applied to myself or to other people. Not only was I tending mostly to think myself wonderful and other people bad, but I also sometimes thought myself bad—but in quite a false sort of way, and other people good—in quite an illusory and imaginary way. For example, I took for granted that everyone else could remember themselves, and that I was the only person who could not. This is all connected with the kind of cloud that is between people—an unnecessary cloud that we should really set ourselves to dissipate.

Q. I am never sure what really makes me behave in a certain way and this is very confusing.

JGB. It is no use indulging in self-analysis or self-questioning. One must just get on and act. Doing the task will show up your motives. You must not first ask yourself if you are doing it just to feel good about yourself or to look good in other people's eyes, or for any other sort of mixed motive. Do not let that sort of thing happen in you, just go on and do what has to be done. In the course of doing it you may have painful moments when you see that your motives were not what you thought they were. It is of course a very unpleasant thing to become aware that one is doing something in order to impress someone and not just because it is right. As far as possible we should not deceive ourselves, but if we waited to have pure motives for doing things we would not do anything at all.

Q. I never trust my own understanding; I always think it is better to rely on what other people think.

JGB. When you do something not from your own understanding you are not a man, you are just being pushed around.

The first thing is to distinguish between a state where you are only a machine being pushed around by events or by people and a state where you have some control over what is happening to you and what you are doing. Either a state in which there is no one present and everything happens, or a state where at least something is present and you are acting from yourself. Once we have the taste of this distinction, there is no longer any doubt in us about which is the better state. If you have not had the bitter taste in yourself of realizing that you were just carried along by a stream of events over which you had no control, you cannot understand what I am talking about; but if you have had this taste, you know. And if you have had the taste of inward freedom in realizing that you were not being carried along by the stream of events, then you took some decisions by yourself, then also you have no doubt. Nobody can tell you anything about that because it is *your* taste. Little by little this becomes clear to you and you see what makes you a slave and what make you free. As you begin to see this your understanding goes up a degree or two. You then only have to summon back this feeling, which will always give you strength to increase this inner freedom. It is only when you forget the taste you had that you allow yourself to fall into a state of fear and weakness.

Q. But surely there are moments when we have to accept what other people decide. Is that a sign of weakness and helplessness?

JGB. Certainly not! To accept a situation is not helplessness. I was only speaking of the very first crudest distinction in our experience that tells us what is the taste of reality: which means discrimination between one way of living and another. A life that counts does also include this quality of acceptance, from which freedom can come. If we have not got the first taste clear for ourselves, then we can deceive ourselves about the finer things. For example, until we have understood this distinction, we can confuse laziness and weakness for with acceptance, but if we know the inward taste of freedom and the inward taste of slavery—the taste of life and the taste of death—then we will know when what we were calling acceptance was really not life but death. At another moment we would know by the taste that, this time, acceptance is life. Also, if I do not know this taste, I will confuse activity with life. Sometimes we can be desperately active, very busy, but really dead. Many people take refuge in activity and think that activity is life, because they do not know the taste. If they have the taste, they know that there are some kinds of activity which are really nothing at all, which, as the saying goes, are running round and round like a squirrel in a cage, pretending to be free. We have to know when activity is life, when it is death; when acceptance is life, when it is death. When we know the difference, then our understanding has grown and we can now use it for quite a number of different situations.

Q. Someone I know always assumed he was right and the other person wrong, so he told his son to remember that the other person was sometimes right. It is very difficult to stand up to the thought that other people may understand as much as we do or perhaps more ... how can we know?

JGB. The question is not whether they understand as much, or more, or less, but simply to realize that this person has his own understanding. Whether it is better or worse does not matter, it is the acceptance of the reality of that person which matters. There is always this tendency to either overrate ourselves or belittle ourselves and therefore to be different towards oneself than towards other people. By this experiment I suggested to you this morning, by reminding oneself that every person has got some experience and some understanding, something happens to us. It is like an inner shock that takes us out of ourselves, out of this condition of being enclosed.

After having spoken to you this morning, it occurred to me—as it may have to you—that the seriousness of the denial of understanding in others may be one way of interpreting the enigmatic phrase in the Sermon on the Mount: "Whosoever sayeth to his brother 'Thou Fool,' is in danger of hell fire."* A rooted denial of understanding in others undoubtedly engenders various things such as self-love, self-pity and isolation.

* Matthew 5,22.

5.
FINER SUBSTANCES

16 June 1963

WE SHOULD BE ABLE to connect—in a way that is certain and verifiable for us—our beliefs in man's destiny and the everyday experience of our own life. That is, we need to have some way of being confident of a connection between the visible and the invisible worlds. Otherwise, we may think of the invisible worlds as something only connected with quality—something that just turns on how well things are done—instead of having a substantial reality of their own.

To start you thinking about this, studying it, and also to remind those of you who have studied it in the past, I will speak of the notion of "finer substances," which indicates this connection most strongly and helps us to verify it for ourselves.

There are finer substances within the ordinary coarse substance of what we can see and touch—what we ordinarily call matter—and within those finer substances there are others still finer that are beyond our experience, which we can only become aware of in rare and special states of consciousness. There are, of course, other things to be said about finer substances. Those of you who have been following my talks about energies* will recognize that when I speak of finer substances I am talking of the different energies on which our different ways of experiencing depend.

There is something that carries the material energy; there is something finer than this that carries the energy of consciousness and, finer still, is the substance that carries the creative energy. Finest of all is the

* cf. JG Bennett. *How We Do Things*. Coombe Springs Press.

energy of Cosmic Love, which is the highest that can enter any human experience.

If we speak about these as energies, we put our attention on what they are able to do, because the word "energy" really means capacity for doing, for producing results, and for any given kind of result an appropriate kind of energy is required. Therefore, whenever we are concerned in knowing what will be obtained from an action, we need to know what quality of energy is going into that action.

When we talk about substances, we put our attention on a somewhat different aspect of this same quality, and that is the aspect of "building." Out of substances, things and beings are made; with energies, actions are performed and things are done. In reality, there is no such sharp division; that is, there are no substances lacking the special energy associated with them, and there is no energy without a certain substance to support it. But now I want to speak to you especially about substances as materials of construction.

This physical body of ours is made out of one kind of substance. Another, finer, body is made out of a finer kind of substance and a still finer one out of yet another substance. The necessary substance has to be supplied in order to make these bodies and to allow them to grow.

That is how it concerns each one of us personally. If my total being is to achieve the completeness of which it is capable, then I have to obtain a supply of all the different substances required. In some ways they can be looked upon as food; in other ways these substances can be looked upon as actual constructional materials out of which a certain structure is formed.

When it is formed, it has a degree of stability and permanence which depends upon the way it is put together. The stability and permanence of our physical body is very limited because it is dependent upon the material world. The stability and permanence of the second body is very much greater because the forces of the material world much less influence it. But we require substances not only for our own private purposes—that is, for our completion—but also for greater purposes beyond our private interests. Substances are required for the general ordering of human life on the earth. If the substances of the right kind are not available, then some part of human life is starved. Or if required substances are in some way spoiled, or poisoned, or adulterated, then they produce diseased conditions in the whole of the body of human life on the earth. Therefore the way in which mankind is able to build itself into a structure, or a body, or a society depends upon the supply and purity of these substances, and towards this everyone has some responsibility.

That, broadly, is the situation as regards substances, about which at other times I will give you more explanations. But today I want to say one more thing about the production and storage of substances.

The basic substances for man's spiritual development are produced by his own experiencing and by his attitude towards his own experiencing. That is, if he allows himself to enter into any kinds of experiences without discrimination, then the substance produced is the same as that of an animal; which also allows itself to enter indiscriminately into any experiences of which its kind of animal species is capable. But if man brings to his experiencing a certain discrimination, that is, if he begins to select, to accept some and reject others, then, by so doing, he concentrates substances of a finer quality. One part of our destiny, of the purpose of human life on earth, is just precisely to separate and make available these substances of a finer quality, and if we neglect this duty we fail in one of our basic obligations. Some people even say it is the obligation of man as far as this life on earth is concerned. So the condition for the production of the finer substance—the truly human substance we can call it, to which Gurdjieff gives the name of *hanbledzoin*—is discrimination. If you understand and practice discrimination, then by that you will bring this finer substance into a place where it can be preserved and concentrated. Otherwise, it is dissipated and there is no separation and then our lives go in the same way as animals' lives do.

The next thing is the conservation or preservation of this substance. Here, man has to learn to be careful. He has to recognize that when these finer substances begin to concentrate in him, he becomes what is called a "sacred vessel." He now contains something that is precious, and he must learn to experience and accept the responsibility that accompanies this sacred state. This can be very easily understood by comparing it with a woman who has conceived a child. She has in her womb something of a different quality. With her conception she becomes herself a sacred vessel for a new life to be born on earth. As soon as she is aware that she has become a sacred vessel, she recognizes and feels her responsibility. She cannot permit herself things that will hurt the new life she is bearing.

It is the same with us, with man and woman alike, when we begin to enter into and to recognize this state of being a sacred vessel. When we begin to have within us a concentration of finer energy, it is only by

33

this recognition that we are able to concentrate this energy to the point at which it begins to transform our own nature. It clearly is useless—even worse than useless—to produce something that is very precious and then throw it away. The discrimination that enables us to set this finer substance free is not sufficient if there is not also with it a sense of the value, the special character, of what has been obtained in this way. There is, for man—according to all teachings—a responsibility that cannot be escaped, inherent in his very nature—which is, that he is a being of such a kind and so-made that he has the power to concentrate finer substances.

Since finer substances are produced by nature, even by certain plants, the nature of man that makes him special among the beings living on this earth, is not so much that these substances can be separated in him but that they can be preserved and made available for a higher purpose. And, as it always is in the economy of this Creation, whenever a service is performed, that service carries its own reward. If man performs this cosmic service. If he prepares in himself a vessel in which fine sacred substances can be preserved—then that vessel becomes his own property, and with that he is able to enter a totally different domain of being and to be transformed into a being of eternal significance: an immortal soul.

The immediate practical significance for us, if we understand this, is that we should see how important it is for us to learn to recognize these substances when they are present, and begin to practice in ourselves the acts whereby they are taken care of and preserved. The way to have this inner care cannot be described; it has to be found out for oneself. One important part of it is abstaining from doing harmful things, as is so strongly emphasized in the Indian teachings, where it is given basic importance. Harmful actions destroy or perhaps damage this vessel very badly. Not harming is a much wider thing than just not sticking knives into people; one has to learn what abstaining from harming means.

As that sense of care and of responsibility begins to grow, it is accompanied by suffering whenever we neglect, or make a mistake about it. As a woman will suffer if she has carelessly done some act that will put her unborn child in danger, so we have to come to the point where the presence in us of these substances is equally important for us.

It would be very misleading, though, if one thought that the only important action for liberating and concentrating these finer substances is discrimination. There is another action which serves this purpose, and that is intentional sacrifice; such as, for example, sacrificing the impulse to justify our actions in the name of "fairness" or "justice" when they really stem only from our self-love.

After-Lunch Discussion

Questioner. I would like to ask about "inner considering." It seems to affect people's behavior in so many different ways. Does it come from having the wrong kind of substance in us?

JG Bennett. There are various ways of human behaving that are due not to a wrong something being present in a man, so much as to his being empty at some point. He lacks something, some strength, and some capacity for feeling, for understanding. This lack determines a particular kind of behavior and is often associated with fear. This fear is strange; it is pictured in the *Masnawi* of Jellaleddin Rumi as the fear of the naked man that someone will steal his clothes. People do not want their real nakedness to be seen and this engenders a constant fear of being shown up. This shows itself in different ways. In some people, it is quite a mechanical and automatic behavior that has been adopted as a result of education or imitation. There are people whose behavior is dominated by the quite superficial habit of dependence on the opinion of others. They have no confidence in their own inner life and therefore they are all the time adapting themselves to the opinions of others and making the appearance they show to others conform with this pattern.

There is another kind of inner considering and this is also of a relatively superficial kind. It comes from the sensitivity and is much more difficult to deal with. This is commonly called "self-consciousness," and there is a much finer substance, or a stronger energy, associated with it. It actually influences the physiological systems and people can be sick from it.

The first is not like that. The first is so mechanical that nothing is really experienced, so that such people are not even emotionally disturbed, or anything of this sort. They live entirely by what the neighbors think but they do not even care what the neighbors think, and this is really very peculiar. The second kind of inner considering, where they really care, is where the reactional self is brought in, and then they suffer because it has no foundation, no strength of its own.

A third kind of inner considering is when a man or a woman projects on to the world his own image and expects everyone to agree with his own picture of himself and the world. He has got his own world-pattern, which is purely subjective, governed by nothing but his own nature, and he seeks to impose this as a reality. This kind of inner considering is chiefly manifesting in the form of demands—quite outrageous demands sometimes and yet very often successfully made—that the whole world should be what they wish it to be. That kind of considering comes also from the absence of a real "I" in the person; that is, the person is not free and therefore makes these demands to hide the fact that he is not free, that he has no "I" of his own. Therefore, instead of this real "I" he produces an extremely strong and coherent simulacrum of an "I." It is very different from the other kinds I have described, as this one can be strong and dominant. And very often such people really get away with it. They surround themselves with those who submit to their demands, as they will not tolerate near them those who do not.

In all these cases, as I said, it is the absence of a real "I" which determines peoples' behavior in such different ways. When there is no "I," a pseudo-I takes its place and this is always in danger of being taken away. If I have my own "I," I have no fear, because it is my own and cannot be taken away.

6.
SPECIAL PLACES

7 July 1963

THIS MORNING I wish to speak to you about finer substances in relation to places. The question is whether a place—such as we have here at Coombe Springs—has any special significance or whether it is just convenient for meeting. In one way, there is no place more significant than another, and everywhere man can find the same reality and he can always work. But there is something else connected with work, which is that it is a process of transformation and for this, particular substances are required. All life is such a transformation, and all experience is a different and finer transformation than is life just by itself. But there is another special transformation beyond that of material energies and life energies and sensation and feeling and thought—and that finer transformation is connected with doing. It begins to touch the will and it requires special conditions of both time and place. That means that for doing anything there is both a certain place where it can be done and also a certain time when it can be done. Any attempt to do something right in itself in an inappropriate place or at the wrong time will fail.

The importance of place is that there are certain concentrations of substances at some places which are not present in others, and from ancient times men have understood that in certain places things can happen because there is something special there. When once such a place is recognized, then a certain kind of experiencing will occur there so that its latent possibilities can take shape.

The fact that men have, for such a very long time, given special importance to certain places cannot be explained unless we accept that there have always been men on this earth who had quite different powers, different insights, from ordinary people, and that they have been able to see things other people could not see. Because of that, they were able to show people, who were willing to be shown, the real situation behind the visible appearances.

Some places, say like Delphi, are evidently powerful just by their natural surroundings. Not many other places have the same kind of striking nature as Delphi. But Delphi has something special, and men understood at one time that there was something in just that part of that valley, where a concentration of substances made it possible for people to have experiences which would guide the whole life of the Hellenic world. That is why Delphi was also called the "navel of the world," the center about which the world turned, because people felt that there was a movement round about this place which reached out. There have been other places, all over the world, which have been recognized as having special qualities and people came to them, sometimes in order to receive answers to their questions through what were called oracles, and sometimes to receive healing. Delphi and Epidaurus in Greece are examples of these two. There were also places of special spiritual and religious significance where certain religious events could take place—as Jerusalem, for example. Or very simple ones where it was felt that to be in that place brought peace, or a feeling of the reality of the spiritual world, and people were drawn towards such places. Other places again have more special tasks, and there the substances require a great deal of work in order to be made suitable for the performance of those tasks.

Further, there are certain places that are almost timeless, that for literally thousands of years have been found to be localities with a special power. They were at times lost and forgotten, then found again. Again and again men have been drawn back to such places because there was unmistakably something imperishable in terms of human time in those particular localities. Others had a special importance only for a limited time, for some event to take place in them, and when that event was completed, their character changed and they became, not places of preparation, but repositories, where the power of the event was kept for those who came later.

Now it does seem that this place here at Coombe Springs has a certain significance: how great or how small we cannot tell, but some. I never can forget the day—it was 8 April 1941 when I first came into these grounds, which were then completely desolate, covered from end to end with brambles and almost impassable once one got off the drive—and into the house, inhabited by a totally deaf old lady with her Italian maid, and smelling of innumerable cats and seven or eight very fierce chows. And yet, in spite of all this, I could not doubt that I was somehow going to live here and that there was a destiny to be fulfilled in this place. And since then, in the twenty-two years since that time, many happenings here have confirmed this sense of destiny I felt so strongly when I first came.

It has been a place where encounters, meetings, could take place; a place which could receive the impact of such an extraordinary action as that of Subud. No doubt its destiny is not yet completed. At the next stage, there is something that has to be understood about the substances here, and it is just about that that I wanted to say something this morning. Perhaps I will say more at other times.

There are certain substances associated with this place that can easily be affected one way or the other. They have a particular sensitiveness and they can, as we might put it, absorb influences of a very high order or they can also absorb influences that are quite negative and distasteful, and people have felt all these things here. Because of this, it is really a duty for those of us who have a feeling for the destiny of this place to be very careful about the quality of the experiencings that are brought here. I do not mean by that that it is possible to avoid every kind of painful, distressing or even negative experience. Strangely enough, those things are also necessary, so that the transformation of substances should take place. In other words, it is not just by "roses, roses" that the place acquires the right quality, but also by "thorns, thorns;" not only by pleasant experiences, but also by unpleasant ones. You may ask: "Why is there any need then to have special care?" The answer is that it is neither by means of the pleasant nor of the unpleasant experiences that the real transformation takes place, but by our attitude towards them; by certain qualities that we ourselves have to bring; that are independent of pleasure and pain and like and dislike.

This necessary inner attitude can be formed by a certain looking towards destiny and fulfillment. The simplest way in which this expresses itself is by a certain valuation, or respect. Through some people treating this place with respect, a transformation becomes possible. But also, there necessarily are and always will be people who feel what you could call disrespect. That attitude in other people should also always be accepted; that is to say, nobody who really wishes to understand how things truly are should ever be disturbed by any kind of negative manifestation. On the contrary, they should always be accepted as a necessary factor in any creative work or any realization.

God would not have taken such an extraordinary step as to create a being who could occupy the position of Satan, if it had not been a necessary step. In other words, we must never wish that there were no satanic forces. They are necessary for the creative work. Only, it is necessary that we should not ally ourselves with them and that we should learn to keep a very understanding attitude towards both satanic and angelic forces. We men are not destined to be either angels or devils, we are destined for something more difficult than the task of a devil—which is a very hard one—because we have to be the representatives of God, which is the hardest task of all.

It is through that attitude, that kind of understanding, that we can make possible this transformation of substances here, and proceed in such a way that this place can be prepared for what will come to it. And we know that knowledge of the future is reserved for others than we are, therefore we can prepare, but we have to prepare without knowing the times and seasons.

When this is translated into the simple minute-to-minute experiencing of our days, and especially when so many of you come here and we all work together, it takes the form of an inward collectedness that enables us not to be drawn towards either negative or positive, either pleasant or unpleasant experiences, but to keep an inward balance. It is not easy to find what is necessary, because this inward balance is not aloofness, not inactivity, it certainly does not cast aside the positive or the negative forces; rather it is an attentiveness that makes sure we have in us also the third force. We should be able to see in ourselves the impulses of affirmation and negation, of accepting and rejecting, the impulse to do and the impulse to withdraw from doing. All this we should be able to watch in ourselves at every moment, and yet, with that, keep separate this inward freedom that allows us to carry out what is necessary.

There is one simple very ancient secret connected with this, and that is not to let oneself be taken by unnecessary and useless activity. A very big secret, requiring very little from us, but a most difficult thing. Because there is in us a very great tendency to do what is unnecessary; that means, to occupy ourselves at all costs with something instead of taking the opportunity to be free when there is not something necessary to be done.

Everyone, I suppose, can agree that the elimination of unnecessary and useless activities is something desirable, and can see that it will give us freedom and strength and enable us to play our part as we should play it in this world. But how many people can really put this into practice? Inwardly to be free and attentive and outwardly to abstain from unnecessary things is a simple rule of life, but not easy. And because it is so hard, we need all sorts of other things to help us.

After-Lunch Discussion

Questioner. Could you explain what Gurdjieff means by the *Fulasnitamnian* Principle?

JG Bennett. This is an invented term, used by Gurdjieff in *Beelzebub's Tales* to stand for virtually the same thing as is meant by the word *Susila*: "Right living according to the Will of God." Gurdjieff emphasizes one particular side of this, and that is, that people are not able to live this way because they are already spoiled, and that this is something that cannot be imitated, nor can people do it just by wanting to. There are really two ways of living for man; one as an animal, and the other as a man. The way of living as an animal is by reactions to the changing stimulation of our outside world. The animal, with its own appetites and needs and instincts is constantly being stimulated by what is outside—sights and sounds, and especially smells—and that is what keeps him moving. Nothing of his own is brought into this except just what kind of animal he happens to be. Men can live in the same way, and that way is called by Gurdjieff the *Itoklanoz* way of living, which really means living under causal influences, living as things happen to come. If there is any kind of order in that kind of living, it is because patterns of reactions have already been formed in a person, which Gurdjieff compares to gramophone records. In the chapter "Hypnotism" in *Beelzebub*, he describes the formation of these mechanical patterns of reactions to life. The nature of these being material, they wear out, and as they wear out, capacity for reaction diminishes. People who live in that way little by little lose their power of living until finally they have nothing left to live with. He also says that each of the different centers—thinking, emotional, instinctive and so on—has its own record, and they can wear out differently. Sometimes people who still have something left to run out in their instinctive center or intellectual center may have exhausted all their capacity for response in the feeling center. Then such people cannot feel any more, they only live with their bodies and their thoughts, but without realizing it, they have lost the capacity for any sort of feeling. If people have lost the capacity for thought, it is more obvious because then you can see that they are no longer able to remember or connect things together, although the rest of their organism continues to operate, to live. This he called "dying by thirds."

The Fulasnitamnian Principle is totally different from this, because when a man is able to begin to live in accord with this then he is no longer dependent either upon his own records or on outside stimulation. He lives in accordance with his own true pattern, and when he becomes connected with this pattern his life acquires a creative value. Gurdjieff says that once somebody has come to this, he will not die on this earth until he has completed what is necessary for him to learn or to do on this earth; whereas anyone living under the Itoklanoz Principle may die without having completed it. In a simple kind of way one can say that the Itoklanoz Principle of living is living from the outside, controlled and determined by what is outside; the Fulasnitamnian Principle is living from the higher centers; that is, directed and governed by the higher wisdom and power that lies behind our ordinary consciousness. There is an assurance of fruitfulness in that second kind of life which is absent from the first, but this is a very difficult thing for people to realize, because they have formed very strong habits of depending upon external stimulation's and of being also dependent upon their own habitual reactions. And to get away from this is both difficult and painful; that is, really to begin to live one's own life is the most painful thing. So it is not true, really, to say that one has only to want to change over and one will.

Q. Do these two principles actually mesh together?

JGB. No. A man who allows himself to live by the Itoklanoz Principle comes under the laws of animal existence, which are different from those of human existence.

Q. What happens to the gramophone records if one begins to live by the second principle?

JGB. They can be used economically and then they will last the required time. Life is not really dependent upon them and when we know how to do without them, there is no fear that they will not last the necessary time. This is connected with what I was saying in the *Djami* this morning, about avoidance of unnecessary actions. This is the simplest way of beginning to bring oneself under the Fulasnitamnian Principle, and it has a very powerful effect upon one's aging. People grow old—and I am not referring to just the body—not by the necessary things they do but by the unnecessary ones. The Shivapuri Baba, for example, was a man 137 years old when I last saw him, as fresh as a daisy and as interested in everything as a child could be. Why was that? Because there had been no wearing out of his mechanisms of reaction; because he had, from early youth, followed his discipline of avoiding anything unnecessary. I have known other people, also of great age, who retained very great freshness for the same reason. But we are slaves to unnecessary things and to break that slavery is hard.

Q. Could he have lived as we live?

JGB. You mean in the Western world? Yes, he spent forty years of his life in the Western world. He traveled round the world, mostly on foot at that, and mixed with this Western society all the time, wherever he was, in England, in the United States. From the time he was fifty to the time he was ninety he lived in the thick of everything.

Q. You have suggested that the chapter on "Ashiata Shiemash" in Beelzebub has a special significance in our time. What is the significance of the destruction of the work of Ashiata Shiemash?

JGB. One thing about Beelzebub that Gurdjieff always insisted upon is that there are seven interpretations to everything he has written in it. If you can see two or three, you are already very perspicacious. One of them, he said, we should understand literally. There is another sense in which we should understand it psychologically. What he says about the subsequent destruction can quite clearly be taken psychologically as showing this tendency of ours to reject the idea of work and to consider it is somebody else's duty to provide what we need. The destructive actions of Lentrohamsanin illustrate the rejection of the notion that man is a responsible being. There are always people who are infected by the notion that work is not real, and that man has no real responsibility. That is the psychological interpretation of this chapter. There may also be an interpretation that applies to the future. When the present work of regeneration is completed, as it will be, mankind will live for quite a long period under very favorable conditions. Then again there will come a time when people will say that these conditions should be destroyed, and it will seem very plausible and right that they should be.

Q. Is that a secular inevitability?

JGB. Yes. It is inevitable that this doctrine of irresponsibility should be preached, but it is not really inevitable that mankind should fall for it. Men will probably continue to do so for a good long time to come, say one and a half million years. Then, after that, maybe thcy will begin to see that this has to change and then the whole world will be quite different. Maybe it will not take so long, but a long time it will take, I am sure, because people are nowhere near it yet. There is no sign in any of us of really taking our responsibilities as human beings seriously. We would be simply appalled, terrified, if we could see how man should behave on this earth and were to confront it with how he actually does behave. There is no "ought" without "can," but the immense disparity between what man could do and what he does do is so strange.

Q. Is it because conditions are so bad now that something could be made out of the present situation, which could not be made in any other way?

JGB. We cannot say that conditions now are especially bad. Things are not worse now than they were a thousand, two thousand, or five thousand years ago. Things simply change. Now we have this plus and that minus; before we had another plus and a different minus. But what is true—and this certainly is a very deep truth—is that there are periods of transition which are periods of much greater tension, and those periods, if they are rightly used, are very beneficial for individuals. It is really a very big challenge to be born in such times because at such times one has the possibility of getting very much, more quickly than is possible at other times. But one must know how to do it. One must have two things: one must have knowledge and one must have courage. It applies to us all, and not only to individuals but, even more so, to brotherhoods, to societies of people who come together and so have more continuity in time than individuals can have.

November 11th 1953: This morning I gave myself the task of pretending not to know a word of Turkish. It was interesting to see that the chief difficulty was not to laugh when one of my fellow passengers made a joke. It nearly proved awkward at the Turkish frontier where they made an efficient customs search. I showed all my purchases and they were in trouble about explaining that I could not take all that in without paying heavy duty and the suitcase containing all the purchases must go in transit to Istanbul. One explained this in very halting English and they were delighted when I at once agreed and repacked as they wanted. I heard them saying: 'There is a really cultured man: he makes no difficulty; even picks out the things himself. You can see from his face that he is an honest man. How different from those Americans who went through last week and made such a row!' I felt rather ashamed because my ready acquiescence was solely due to my understanding all that they were saying and realizing it was all perfectly in order and safe for my property. But I had to watch very carefully to avoid giving myself away. When we reached Iskenderun I managed to make the transformation in going from one garage to another: and resumed my role as a man who has lived many years in Turkey.

—from *Journeys in Islamic Countries*

7.
LIBERATION AND TRANSFORMATION

2 December 1962

THERE ARE TWO WAYS of describing the goal of our striving; one is
called liberation and the other transformation. We shall try to understand how these two expressions differ and what they have in common.

We all see that we are tied up in the attractions of the world and
held by the pull it has upon us through our senses. We can see also,
how we are tied up in our own feelings, in our likes and dislikes, fears
and hopes. We can see how we are tied up in our own character, in our
own nature; how we are not able to do the things we see are right to be
done, that we wish to do; just because we are such as we are. And seeing this, there arises in us the wish to be free from it all, the wish not to
be helplessly drawn in directions we do not want to go.

This helpless state is variously described as attachment, identification or slavery. In it we are not our own masters. As a result comes the
desire to be free, and from that arises a feeling that the great thing to
come to is liberation: freedom from every possible limitation. This can
be put forward as the whole aim of our existence in the Eastern religions and particularly Buddhism. In Buddhism, there is that repeated
promise "You can become free, here in this very life," and sometimes
we use that formula ourselves when we think of freedom. Maybe we do
not go as far as envisaging the "ultimate freedom," the state of Nirvana,
but we may hope to reach a state of relative freedom from our present
imprisonment: a condition of detachment from all earthly cares.

When one hears the word "detachment," one sometimes tends to ask the question: "Does detachment mean indifference, in which one loses the power of caring for things and people?" The answer is that, on the contrary, the man who is detached has an infinitely richer capacity for feeling than the man who is a slave to everything that comes his way, whose feelings are always narrowed down to the experience of the moment.

But although detachment is an indispensable quality for reaching completeness, we must now consider whether the ultimate goal is to achieve freedom from this nature of ours in the sense of "liberation" from existence itself; or whether it consists in "transforming" into another nature.

Do we really want to get away from it all or do we only want to get far enough away from it to enable us to be transformed? There is a real difference between the attitude towards the destiny of man which is depicted by saying "It is to become free, completely and finally free from everything, even from existence itself," and the view that existence is itself to be transformed and perfected. With this second view, some sacrifice of freedom is inevitable, because as long as this remains—not merely this body, not even this mind and these feelings only, but this "I," this self of mine—as long as this remains, it is somehow still involved. It has some responsibility, and if it is really opened towards reality, it will see the suffering of the world and will inevitably accept to participate, and in participating, it cannot but lose the freedom of complete liberation.

On the view therefore that the aim is to achieve transformation, freedom is not the whole story. The perfect man does not pass out of existence, but has the power to stand between freedom and involvement. He can, when it is necessary, and as much as it is necessary, enter into the freedom where nothing can touch him and also, when it is necessary and as much as it is necessary, go out altogether into this creative, conditioned world in order to participate, to accept, to share and to act. If what we really want is this transformation by which a man can become such that he is able to belong to two worlds (I mean by that, in a rough and ready way, the inner world where one can become free "from" and the outer world where one becomes involved "in"), then we must learn to find that middle place where we are able to choose.

If transformation is really our aim, then this must affect everything we do, because then all our actions are concerned with its process. On the other hand it is possible to say that in the search for freedom only those actions which are in the direction of renouncing, putting everything aside, are important and all the rest are a mere passing duty from which little by little we shall be able to withdraw. That is how it appears to be if one reads the Buddhist Scriptures. These and other "liberation" doctrines teach man that to be involved in the world, even for a good purpose, is a limitation. To withdraw, to renounce entirely, is seen as a step forward, for it leads to the path which is liberation. For those who hold that life and even existence itself is only evil and suffering, all external activity is unimportant, whereas the inner life is all-important. Of course, there is obviously the opposite way—to which we are only too accustomed in the world—which puts all the importance on the outside, which makes us look only at what we achieve and what we do, as the measure of what we are worth—to the exclusion of what we are inwardly.

Clearly there is a difference between those who see everything on the outside, those who see everything on the inside, and those who see the real goal as in the middle. The middle is the place of transformation. Here a very extraordinary work can be performed in the soul of man, by which that soul itself becomes a bridge between what is inside and what is outside, between what is visible and what is invisible, between what is temporal and what is eternal.

This, it seems to me, is the true meaning of human life, and shows us the really great work that we have to do. In that process, of course there also has to be a setting free, a liberation from our slavery, because as long as we are attached, stuck to and involved in all the outside things and in our own likes and dislikes and hopes and fears, and in our own character, the work in the center cannot be balanced. Therefore this "unsticking" liberation is a necessary thing and for that there has to be a stronger consciousness of the reality of the inner life, strong enough to dissolve these attachments: to see that these things are not what matters.

But of course, if what we seek for is to be the work in the center, if it is to be transformation of man so that we become a conscious willing bridge for the work of the spirit, then we cannot turn our backs upon the outer world any more than upon the inner. For the attainment of perfection, everything is going to count; everything we touch and see, everything we feel and think about and all that we are in ourselves—that is, our character—all this is going to count. We cannot turn our backs upon anything, except what is false to our great aim and to the Work that we wish to serve.

The truth is that man has to become such that he is complete on all sides and on all levels; according, of course, to the potentialities latent in his nature and the Task he is destined to perform. This notion that the center of man should be like a sphere—able to see in all directions, able to look down into the material world, able to look up towards the spiritual world, able to look to the right and to the left—gives us a picture of what is meant by transformation.

It may be that I have made too hard and fast a distinction. It is certainly true that people who do seek only to put their external lives right, can come to a balanced development. Those who search only for liberation and for complete purity, free of all that stains man's nature, can also come to balanced development. But when the conscious aim is too far removed from the true destiny, there is always a great risk of losing one's way. It is said that "All roads lead to Rome," but not all are equally direct or equally safe. This is why the assurance of reaching the goal is greatest for those who follow the way of understanding and wisdom, that accepts all ways. Our task is to be a bridge between what is on every side—above, below, right and left. If we remember that before and behind mean future and past, that bridge too can be built within us, for we should also be the means of transmitting from the past to the future. It is right, therefore, to look upon our task as a threefold one: to link the spiritual and the material worlds, to link together our fellow-men in this life, and also to be a channel by which the past can flow creatively into the future. This can only occur if this flowing involves a transformation; that is, the past should not disappear behind us dead, but live in us, so that it will be able to be transmitted to the next generation as a living heritage.

8.
THE SIN OF VAGUENESS

3 February 1963

ONE OF OUR great enemies is vagueness. Those of you who have read *The Dramatic Universe* will remember that I put vagueness among the six deadly sins, or six negative triads; that is, among the six kinds of illusory action which undermine the reality of our experience. This may surprise some people, as vagueness—in opposition to clarity, which may represent something rather hard and unfriendly—seems too harmless and cozy to be called a sin.*

Vagueness is failure to keep distinct things that are, and must be, distinct from one another. Because of failure to keep them separate from one another, we prevent them from playing their right roles. If you reflect on this, you then will begin to see in how many ways our lives are hurt by vagueness: how many promising and hopeful things come to nothing because of it. In our relationships with one another we must not be vague. We must "know our own minds," as it is said, "have the courage of our convictions" and all that is expressed in such clichés. We may laugh at them, but they refer to a real need not to confuse, not to allow the sharpness of our experience to be blurred. It does not mean that this is the whole story and that there is no other secret to right living than the preservation of distinctions. It is one factor among many, but nothing else will compensate for it if it is lost. One example of this need to be clear is in our inner and outer lives; their requirements are different, and our relationship to each of them is fundamen-

---

* *The Dramatic Universe, Vol. II.* Santa Fe: Bennett Books, 1999, Chp. 31. The six negative triads are: Imagination, or Negative Expansion; Narcissism, or Negative Concentration; Fear, or Negative Identity; Waste, or Negative Interaction; Vagueness, or Negative Order; and Identification, or Negative Freedom.

tally different. There is a different kind of responsibility and that distinction must be held on to.

One of the many contributions that Pak Subuh has made to the understanding of human problems is that he has so firmly emphasized the distinction between what man can do for himself and what he cannot do; between his responsibility for his outer life and his dependence with regard to his inner life. When people become vague about this, they begin to worry and concern themselves with parts of their own being which they cannot even reach, let alone take care of, and neglect those regions of their own being of which they can be aware, and can study and know clearly enough to take responsibility for their condition and development. That is an example of not holding fast to these distinctions.

Those of us who have been working together in the science group have agreed to use the word "complementarity" for indicating inescapably fundamental distinctions, and you will come, in time, to hear this word used quite a lot. It may seem to be a special philosophical word, coined by physicists to refer to particular properties of the physical world; but it stands for a characteristic element of our experience that is of universal importance. Every one of us can understand it quite well, if we see that the first way of overcoming vagueness is to be clear when things are different from one another and not to turn our backs or shut our eyes to differences. Let us take again the example of the inner and outer lives of man. They are complementary because neither would be anything at all without the other. Only a machine is totally "outside" and only a dream state is totally "inside." Most people most of the time are in a mixed condition in which they are neither fully in touch with the outside nor fully conscious of the inside. In terms of energies, we say that they are in a condition of confusion or vagueness in which "sensitive energy" and "conscious energy"* are not distinguished and their complementarity is lost. This results in ineffectualness and diminution of human being.

Complementarity and the awareness of distinctions does not mean that one element excludes the other, nor that we have got to make a choice between them. This is one of the mistakes which has constantly dogged man's footsteps in his search for reality. It has so often seemed to people that they were confronted by an either-or—"If this is right, then that must be wrong"—either this or that. The reality is not like

* For a detailed description of Bennett's scale of energies, see: JG Bennett. *Energies—Material, Vital, Cosmic.* Sherborne, England: Coombe Springs Press, 1964.

that. For example, what I said about our inner and outer life does not imply a choice between the inner and the outer. Everyone can see that the person who does reject one of the two and holds only to the other, will get lost. Either he will become psychopathic, incapable of living in this world, or he will become just a gross materialist incapable of looking for anything else except this world. It should be very evident to us, if we reflect upon it, that the truth of these complementarities is not that one has to choose the one and reject the other, but that one has to see how they differ and how they are needed to complete one another. We cannot have a sound inner life unless we have a sound outer life; we cannot have a sound outer life unless we have a sound inner life. We must simply accept the necessity for certain pairs of complementarities of this kind, such as the pair I have just been speaking about. There is certainly no one among us who would say that a choice has to be made in the sense of wholly accepting one and wholly rejecting the other. But even if we accept the need for this sort of complementarity in one situation, we nearly always reject it in some other situation in which we think we must go wholly over to one side and wholly reject the other, whereas a more mature reflection might show us that they are necessary for one another.

It does very often happen in personal relationships—sometimes just in a certain incident, sometimes in a whole lifetime—that this principle is lost and tragedy follows. One form of it is "I am right and you disagree with me: therefore you must be wrong." Instead of two people being able to see that their attitudes are different and have to be different, and that the value of their relationship lies in the difference of their attitudes, they make a demand upon one another: "You must see things my way. The way I see it is right and, therefore, the way you see it must be wrong." This truly is something that we constantly have before us, again and again. Perhaps every day of our lives situations arise where we can see whether we have really accepted or not the necessity for complementarity, its importance and value. Contradictions are not to be feared and shunned, rather they are the fruitful source from which life breaks forth.

What is more contradictory than a man and a woman? They really contradict one another in their natures, in the roles they have to play, and yet neither can exist without the other. How could there be human life if there were not this difference? And how tragic it is when this difference begins to be submerged and vagueness comes in as to what a woman is and what a man is.

Of course this is not something new, there have always been sages who have taught mankind to seek "The middle path, the middle way"—Buddha, Pythagoras, and many other wise men. It sometimes may appear to people that the middle way is the way of negation, of compromise. There is a false middle path, which is the path of vagueness and compromise; but there is also a true middle path, which is that of acceptance and understanding. In learning to accept and to live with contradictions, something new emerges: a third reality, which is beyond either.

The ability to understand is far more than the ability to see distinctions. We sometimes find it strange to observe that people who have caught a glimpse of the importance of complementarity still interpret certain situations in the way of either-or. I was thinking, as I was saying that, of what is called the Marxist philosophy. From the essential contradiction in the two ways of considering human society, a progress is possible, but for emotional reasons, many have departed from the true meaning of the principle and are convinced that one must prevail over the other, that it is an either-or. From time to time, some people begin to see that it is not like that.

The greatest need of the world is that people should be able to pass from knowing to understanding. It is certainly very important for us as individuals, and that is one reason why I speak about it here now at Coombe Springs. It has always been my wish to try to make Coombe a place where there could be real action. It does not by any means follow that I have always adhered properly to the principles which I myself believe in: it is not so easy! But if we are to have a real life we must be prepared to live without vagueness as to the reality of, and also the necessity for, contradictions. If we cannot face this, we shall tend to evade the difficulty by rejection of all that does not suit us. This leads to a false distinction between "we" and "they," because if it has to be either-or, then inevitably all those who do not share our own convictions must be wrong. But that way of living does not produce the means of changing anything in oneself. When we can take into ourselves this contradiction of opposing convictions and live with it, that itself can produce a change in us. And the change that will come is the supremely important gift of understanding. Those who understand do not believe themselves to be right and others to be wrong; but they do fully grasp and accept the real necessity for distinctions. That is why understanding means both tolerance and also effectiveness. Those who do not understand are usually both ineffectual in themselves and intolerant towards others. This would not happen if they insisted upon clarity and repented of the "sin of vagueness."

After-Lunch Discussion

Questioner. If I believe in aim, progress, self-development, then I have to say "this is wrong and that is right," and I must choose what is good for my progress and reject what is bad.

JG Bennett. Certainly. Complementarity does not exclude choice. The complementarity of aim consists in recognizing that not everything is possible at once. In progress, there is not so much right and wrong, as appropriate and timely and inappropriate and untimely action. What is right at one stage may be wrong at another. Vagueness consists in the failure to distinguish between what is possible at this present moment and what is impossible until conditions change. If we try to set up an absolute distinction of "right and wrong" we shall find that it is an obstacle to progress and prevents understanding. Even the aim we pursue cannot be something static and absolute; it is at any given moment partly visible and partly still out of sight. As we progress we see our aim differently.

Choice requires clarity and it also produces clarity. Vagueness and indecision are two wicked sisters that steal our birthright. Just because choice must come from clarity, it requires understanding of complementarity. If we see only "one side of the question" there is no real choice. True choice comes when we are most acutely conscious of the dilemma, which means to be in touch with both sides of the complementarity.

From the examples I gave you this morning, you can see for yourselves how contradictions make choice possible. For example, the contradiction between the inner and the outer life. There is no absence of choice here; but there is no supposition that the inner is right and the outer is wrong, although people sometimes imagine that is so. Again, in the question of aim it is possible to say "My aim must be something of my own, that I have chosen; this is what I want." It is also possible to say "My aim is to fit into the totality of things and really suppress myself and simply become a part of the whole." Now those are contradictions, yet here there is not that division of right and wrong. It is necessary that one should have aim and need for self-fulfillment, self-realization. It is also necessary that one should have the aim and purpose of fitting-in, of accepting to be part of the great whole. They do not agree; they do contradict one another. If it is just for myself, then I am rejecting the others, and if it is just for the others, then I am rejecting myself. There is contradiction, but that is the kind of contradiction that has to be accepted: somehow something has to be found which accepts this dilemma. But if you are trying to get somewhere, then it is obviously perfectly legitimate to say that there is a right way of getting there and a wrong way; there is a better way and a worse way. If I want to get from here to Edinburgh, I must not travel south, or I shall not get to Edinburgh; the general direction of my traveling must be northward. Since northward is right for getting to Edinburgh, southward is wrong. If you reflect on these things, you will see that is not the same kind of contradiction: there is no complementarity involved.

For example, one cannot have two aims. The aim must be one complete whole, but within that aim there can be a great deal of diversity. When you are defining a whole you say: "This is inside it and that is outside it." When you are defining an aim, you have got to be able to say: "This is inside of it and that is outside of it." What is inside can be very complex, and therefore understanding is needed before one can come to see it as a whole. But when one has done this a process of separation has occurred in oneself: we become aware of what is possible and practicable, what makes a consistent realizable whole. The contradiction here consists in what is inside and what is outside. If there were not a great number of things which are impossible for us, then we would not be human beings, or indeed creatures at all. We are the kinds of beings we are because each one of us is limited to a circle of possibilities. Outside this circle are a whole lot of things that are impossible for us.

What you say about aim is really connected with that: knowing one's potential, accepting it, being prepared to forego what is outside of it. That is the beginning of self-knowledge.

My life will only be a muddle and a chaos, if I am thirsting after things which are impossible for me and if I am neglecting the things which are possible. That self-knowledge is by no means easy to reach, and perhaps we are incapable of coming to it to the full in this life. Nevertheless, one process of our lives consists in getting to know what our aim really is so that the real meaning of our life will become clear to us. As we do this we also find ourselves being drawn towards these notions of complementarity, which we call, in the language of Systematics, the Dyad. If we reject those notions, then the notion of relatedness—the Triad—cannot come to life. If we accept them, they in their turn will draw us towards the threefold reality.

As you become conscious of the One which contains within itself all diversity, you become aware that out of this One has to come Two. As you become conscious of Two, you become aware that out of this has to come Three: that somehow there has to be some third element which has to reconcile the contradictions that you have to face. Out of that again will come the Fourth, which is the process of creating oneself, of making all this real.* This I think brings us to what you were feeling was somehow incomplete in what I said this morning: for when you come to the Fourth, the Tetrad, then there is an up-and-down direction which defines where we are going and the horizontal direction which is concerned with the means of getting there. The Tetrad is something knit, bound together. It is means and ends united in action.

---

* cf. *The Tao Teh King of Lao Tzu,* Verse 42: "Out of the Tao comes the One, out of One, Two and Three and hence all the myriad kinds of things."

9.
ON ASKING QUESTIONS

7 June 1964

WE MEN have the property to be able to ask questions. We even have the power of asking questions which do not arise out of simple curiosity, and therefore we should be able to divide our questions into those which are the same as animal curiosity—no more than the attraction of what is unfamiliar—and the questions which are asked because we sense the need for an answer. It is possible to carry questioning so far that man can come to his own ultimate realization. There are methods, particularly that taught by Sri Ramana Maharshi, with his: "Who am I?," or the Shivapuri Baba with his: "What is this Life?" in which the question is made the basis of the whole process of reaching final enlightenment. The Maharshi asserted that if we will persist in asking this question and rejecting all doubtful answers, we will finally come to know everything that can be known by man. This is taking the method of questioning to the extreme limit of importance in human life. Less extreme forms are the methods called Socratic and Cartesian; both of which are based upon determined questioning of our experience. Even if we do not follow the way of question alone, still questioning remains important for us. It is very useful for us to get into the way of stopping to ask ourselves the question: "What am I doing at this moment?"

There is another kind of questioning which is concerned with necessary knowledge. We need to ask ourselves: "Do I understand this?" "Do I know what is required here?," "Am I acting with the best understanding of the situation that is possible for me or am I just blindly going ahead?" That is a different kind of questioning because it is not a questioning of oneself in isolation but in relationship with the environment and the external situation. This kind of questioning is also a necessary self-discipline. We very often miss opportunities of changing the level of our activity, of bringing it on to a more creative line, by failing to ask ourselves the question "Is what I am doing really the best that can be done?," "Is there some more that I could know or understand about this that I am doing?," "Am I relying too much upon my own habits, upon my own fixed ideas of how this kind of question should be dealt with?"

Then there is another kind of questioning which really should more properly be called asking, that I have often spoken about, and I will only remind you of it here in passing. It is the asking for help from a source beyond our own powers, from beyond our own consciousness. Everyone should get into the way of relying with full trust upon the possibility of receiving help by asking for it. There is no doubt that help does come in this way, especially when one is in front of a situation where something has to be done and we have not got the power to do it. If, in such a situation, you ask yourself "Have I really the power to do what is required of me?" you see that we can only make a partial con-tribution ourselves, with our three human powers that I have spoken to you about so often: the power of presence, the power of wish and the power of thought. Even when they are brought together and we can say "I can, I wish, I am," they can never give us a complete answer to our problems because there always remains something unknown. There is always a defect in our ability to unite and hold everything together, and therefore we always need, in everything that we do, an ingredient that comes from beyond our ordinary self. To come to that ingredient, to receive it, we have to know how to ask, and we have to remember to ask when we are in need.

I am sure that we should, from time to time, ask ourselves the deep question I spoke about in the beginning: "Who am I?" "What is this Life?" You have heard, in the talks I had with the Shivapuri Baba, how he insisted upon these as the means of arriving at the knowledge of God; that one should just ask oneself continually: "What is this Life, what does it mean?"

We always have a certain limited understanding which can give us some kind of provisional answer to these questions; but we know very well that there is so much mystery, so much beyond what we can know, that the question can never cease in us. It is certainly a part of man's heritage—one part of the privilege of being a man—that he is able to ask such questions, even unanswerable ones. By that I mean even questions so great that they go far beyond the possibility of our understanding the complete answer. But this does not mean that such questions should not be asked—as long as we do not try to invent spurious answers to them. It is certain that men like the Buddha, Ramana Maharshi, or the Shivapuri Baba, whose lives have been based upon the asking of such questions, did come to an extraordinary realization and complete security from all the flux of life, just by the way of asking the ultimate question and being able to receive the answer. Sometimes we should do that, but more often, even quite frequently, we should ask in the sense of verifying: "What am I doing at this moment? Is what I am doing corresponding to the sense and meaning of my life? Am I even doing what I wish to be doing?"

Another part of the discipline of questioning is to be able to reject the kind of questions that we have no right to ask. The questions that come from curiosity or laziness, trying to obtain from outside ourselves what we have to find inside ourselves; or questions which simply amount to interference: presumptuous interference in affairs that do not concern us. All these kinds of questions we must learn to recognize and put away from ourselves so that we keep and concentrate our power of questioning—which is a very great power—to what really concerns us. Every unnecessary question deprives us of some of the power for asking a necessary one; but among the necessary questions there is a very big range: a whole gamut ranging from the immediate problems of our life here and now, to the ultimate question.

So I would simply say this, to recommend to you that you should bring the technique of questioning into your lives: not to an exaggerated extent; but recognizing what a powerful weapon is given to us by this means.

10.

THE THREE LEVELS OF OUR EXPERIENCE

5 May 1963

WHEN WE HAVE an opportunity of spending a day together like this we can use it to gain some understanding of something connected with our own natures, either as individuals or as human beings. This is not so easy under the ordinary conditions of life when, owing to habitual activities, our attention generally is much less available for this work of understanding. When, as today, we do something for the purpose of understanding ourselves and one another, then automatically more of our attention becomes available; and then we only have to decide how we will use it and the results will come by themselves.

It is important to realize that this presence, this availability of attention, is very much linked with our relationship with our own bodies. In our present conditions of life—what we call civilized conditions of life— there is usually a breach, a gap, between the activity of the body and the activity of our thoughts, as if we were living in two different worlds at the same time. If you just reflect on this for a minute, you will see how we forget our bodies all day long until they make some demand on us—for a call of nature or food—and we continue to live in the world of our thoughts, which really and truly is a dream world because it is not in direct contact with the reality about us. This makes it very difficult to understand anything, because the thoughts are often vague and undisciplined, the body is living its own separate life and the feelings are at the mercy of what affects them. Therefore, if we wish to attain anything serious in the way of understanding ourselves or of having a harmonious condition of existence, the first thing we have to do is to bring about a real contact between thought and body. This is done through a property or power of our bodies called sensation. We usually take no notice of this property, but if we use it to experience sensations, then we see that this is a very rich power. I am not only referring to the sensations that are ordinarily classified as the five senses, but all kinds of sensations such as the posture and position and movements and rhythm of our bodies, all the constantly changing experiences of our skin—which are mostly overlooked—and also the somewhat deeper experiences connected with the flow of blood through the veins and capillaries. All this is a rich world of experience which people usually disregard, or if they think about it at all they look upon it as something inferior that we share with the animals or even with the lowest forms of life. But that is just not true: the kind of sensations a man has are typically human sensations, and the human body is a different kind of body from any other body. It is therefore really necessary for us, if we wish to experience ourselves fully as human beings, to be aware of our own bodies through this power of sensation, which makes a connection between our thoughts and our feelings and allows us to recognize something that can be expressed in the words: "I am here, not just thinking of being here, I am experiencing my presence as a human being with thought and feeling and body." When that begins to come to us then we see how poor is the other condition where we are separated into dream thoughts and a body that is left to itself until it happens to be troubled in some way and demands something.

Now I would like you to pay attention today to the three levels of our possible experience: the three levels upon which we can live. These three levels I call the "automatic," the "sensitive" and the "conscious," or the automatic, the sensitive and the conscious ways of living. These are like three lives lived one within another. There is a very good description of it in one of the Buddha's sermons where he compares it to a bamboo and describes how, within the visible outer sheath of the bamboo, you find its strong wooden structure, and within that again there is the pith: its real life.

In the same way, with us, with our three modes of existence, there is first of all the automatic one, which goes on all the time from the moment of conception until the body has not only died, but even begun to decay. Automatic life of the bodily tissues starts before birth and continues for a time after death. In coma, in sleep, in states of dementia, always this automatic functioning continues, partly just to maintain the body in its existence—to look after the instinctive processes of breathing, of the heart beating and of the circulation and digestion and repair of tissue and so on—but also to keep the nervous system going. There is a certain rhythm in the brain connected with this automatic functioning, which can be detected with electrical instruments.

Quite a substantial portion of our lives—even of what we call our waking state—is passed on this level without there being anything happening upon a finer or more inward level. That more inward level is the one I call "sensitive." This is what is ordinarily called being awake, or conscious, and applies to seeing what we are looking at, hearing the sounds that come to us and being aware of what we touch. The "automatic" state is when we see without seeing, hear without hearing, think without thinking or without knowing that we think. In the sensitive state the immediate field of the activity is, we may say, "lit up." For example, I have been looking at this carpet. So long as I was looking at it just with the automatic seeing I did not see it. Although impressions were coming into my eyes and producing all the results as far as a certain level in my brain goes, I was not seeing. Then, in a moment, I saw and began to notice and be aware of the pattern of the carpet. At times we suddenly become aware of a sound which has been going on for some time without our hearing it. All that is connected with the sensitive state, or the sensitive energy. Beyond that again there is something within, which is not drawn towards anything, it is just aware; it is consciousness of the sensitivity. As the sensitivity is being sensitive to the automatism, so consciousness is being conscious of the sensitivity, each one within the other, like that simile of the bamboo.

This is not a new thing, this has been taught to man for thousands of years; it can be found everywhere, in all sorts of inspired writings from the sermons of the Buddha to the *Susila Budhi Dharma* of Pak Subuh—always attention is drawn to awareness of the different "withinnesses" and to the need to be able to distinguish the different degrees of withinness.

What I ask you to do today is to attempt to use what you have in the way of surplus attention—what you have in the way of an increased sense of presence as the result of being here and working together for noticing these different levels in yourselves. You may think it very interesting as an idea—but it does not do anything to us so long as it remains just an idea. When you really see it for yourself and have really understood these levels by direct experience, then you know that unless you are living on the level of consciousness you are not in your true human nature, you are not living as a man should live. When this happens, then one begins to have a real need, a real thirst to be conscious, not merely sensitive and, still less, not merely automatic. I consider it useful to take these opportunities to verify such ideas for oneself. You will find that you forget all about it—you may even let all the hours that we are here together pass without even thinking of it—and that will show you how much of your life is spent just on the automatic level. You are just ticking over, whatever you may be doing.

After-Lunch Discussion
Questioner. [inaudible]
JG Bennett. You must distinguish between the initiation of the process and the direction of the process. If you say you are directing attention towards something and withdrawing it from something else, what you are really working with is energy. You are inhibiting your sensitiveness to *this* and directing it to *that.* It is characteristic of the sensitive energy that it is directional; it connects us with something and at the same time disconnects us from other things. But you cannot initiate this process with sensitive energy alone. How then is it that it occurs to you to do it? What makes the break in the happenings that sets you free to take this in hand? At one moment your attention, your interest, is all held by what you are doing, more than likely just in an automatic state—as it has been with most of us at lunch today, with occasional moments of sensitiveness which we have either used, or not used. But what gave us the possibility of using it? Something woke up! That condition of being able to direct, being able to concentrate, is different from the direction of the concentration. So one can say that something has happened to our consciousness which was not in our control, not of our choosing. We can, if we practice, so prepare ourselves that we could decide that at exactly two o'clock or at such and such a time or exactly when I walk through a certain door, I will remember what I wish to do and will begin to direct my attention. But much more often it happens spontaneously without any assignable cause in yourself: you were at one moment asleep and at another moment you woke up. I am saying all this so that you can be sure of distinguishing between the fortuitous, or gratuitous, moments when we are conscious, and the use that we make of those moments. The exercise of the power that comes to us at that moment is our own affair.

Q. I am not quite sure what you mean when you say that when we are in the sensitive state we have the possibility of making use of it. What do you mean by "making use of it?"

JGB. It is not the sensitive state in itself that gives us that possibility, it is the consciousness that is behind it. "Making use" of the sensitive energy means to direct it where we want it to go. One of the clearest ways in which we can make use of this is in relaxing. When people are in an automatic state they develop tensions, and because of these tensions they begin to work with less of themselves than they might. They breathe with only part of their lungs; they are not in contact with what they are seeing and hearing—not in contact with their own bodies. At the moment of this presence of consciousness, we have the power to direct our sensitivity towards relaxing, and with that relaxation we come more fully into contact with ourselves. Waste of energy through tensions then diminishes, and so we feel ourselves more alive. Because of this we have more sensitivity at our disposal and therefore more what is ordinarily called "power of attention." This sort of thing is what I am referring to when I say that we can "make use" of it.

But the point is that you cannot make use of it unless there is something behind it to direct it. It is observable that consciousness can direct sensitivity. So that, for example, if I decide to relax, it directs my sensitiveness towards correcting my automatic energy and bringing my body into a more rhythmical, more open state.

Q. Is this then why our dreams are so disconnected, because we then cannot direct our sensitive energy?

JGB. Yes, that is right. What we call "sleep" is when the connection between the centers has broken, has been dissolved, and each center is really living its own life. This is partly observable in our dreams, and it is quite easy to recognize that the dreams come from the different centers. But because they are all separate there is no critical power: so one is not able to distinguish between fantasy and actual sensation. What people do not realize is that we often disconnect the centers in the so-called waking state. When the sensitive energy is present in our thinking we are aware of our thoughts and we call ourselves awake. But in that state we may not be aware of our bodies at all, so that as far as our bodies are concerned we are just as asleep as we were before. When the centers become connected so that the sensitiveness in the body, the sensitiveness in the mind and the sensitiveness in the emotions begin to blend with one another, that state is a state of harmony. One is aware then of one's own presence, one has a sense of being much more "substantial." When one is experiencing that state the usual state of disconnection seems to be very dreamlike and unreal.

When there is connection between the centers we are in a state of mastery which we can easily recognize. When we have this sense of connection with our body we have power over it. We can ask it to do what is required and it will do what we ask: that is, it will be genuinely obedient. That state where the body is genuinely obedient is possible only when we are actually related to it. As long as we keep the body outside and as it were repudiate it and do not care about it, it will not care about us. I think it is really an interesting and important thing to see how very little severity is actually needed to make the body obey, how very much the body will do for us by kindness which it would be very difficult to make it do by force. This relationship between us and our body can be very well compared to the relationship which exists between a good horseman and his horse. He is a good horseman only when he has his horse in hand and is riding it, and the horse knows it.

Q. Is there not a certain danger, if one has power over the sensitive energy, that one will overtax the body in a chemical sense, will burn up one's blood sugar at a faster rate than it can be released from the nitrogen reserves? Is there some sort of indication you can give us, of how to judge this?

JGB. Yes, I think there is. If something is going wrong somewhere, you begin to have a disagreeable inner taste—the beginning of an anxiety, or tension—which should be a warning to you. It is quite distinct from fatigue. Fatigue can be quite imaginary. For example, in building the Djami, when the concrete was being mixed and great physical efforts were required, people worked extremely hard at certain times and I sometimes saw that they were beginning to get into this particular danger; that is to say, they had such an enormous influx of sensitive energy due to emotional excitement and to many people working together, that they ceased to have any check on their bodies. As a result they were really in danger of seriously harming themselves through overtiring the body. This does not often happen, but there it was very clear. I then decided that every hour everyone would stop and sit quietly and relax for two or three minutes. Then this sort of overwinding of the flow of sensitive energy was cut, and the rhythm settled down instead of being self-accelerating. One recognizes such a situation by noticing the signs of a kind of unhealthy excitement. Once you begin to become aware of that, it should act as a warning.

On the other hand, what is called the "second wind" is quite normal. It happens when the sensitive energy is actually controlling the flow of the automatic energy. You cannot make strong physical efforts, like those an athlete has to make, with the automatic energy alone. The second wind is an extraordinarily interesting experience: you become aware of the sudden abandonment of the body's resistance and it suddenly becomes obedient.

Q. How does one deal with inertia, with the inability of the body to start?

JGB. Inertia is the other extreme from overtaxing the body's strength, and is, of course, a much more common problem for us. The difficulty here is not only to get the body started but to get all the other functions started as well. One sits down to do something which requires mental work and the brain is sluggish, the body lazy and the feelings quite indifferent. To alter the direction of the flow of the automatic energy, there must be some energy of a different kind, and that is just the sensitive energy.

There are many different ways in which we can bring about a concentration of the sensitive energy so as to start something off, whether it involves physical efforts, or mental concentration or the directing of the attention from one thing to another. The principle behind all of them is that we need some energy of that quality.

It is all these sorts of things that the alchemists were interested in, and the alchemical language is full of most subtle descriptions of the different kinds of sensitive energy and how one brings them to bear on a particular requirement. I am saying this because it is not something new or special; it is an ancient knowledge of man that to be able to control ourselves we need first of all to control our energies. If you can control your energies, you can control everything else. If you cannot, then everything is hard and has to be forced. A man who does not know that the engine can take a car from one place to another pushes it, and this is the way most people do things: they push their machine about like a person pushing a motorcar, and then it can easily happen that the steering wheel is out of reach.

Q. I have noticed that one loses energy in the presence of some people and they act as vampires upon one.

JGB. It is quite true; there are some people who have got into a very bad way of depending upon others for their sensitive energy and they do just take it from other people. There are also people who have such an ample flow of this energy that anyone coming near them is able to replenish themselves. There are so many different varieties of this kind of thing that one simple answer is not enough. The ideal person to deal with is the person who has all the forms of energy required and is willing to transmit them to people in need of it.

There certainly are people who are like vampires, who suck this energy out of others. Sometimes they can be very energetic people; it does not necessarily follow that only somebody who is very passive and short of this energy sucks it from others. There are some people who are bouncing about all the time, and everybody near them gets tired. We have to learn how to manage our own energies, that is the secret. We cannot do anything about other people.

Q. But is it not possible that one may dream about being free or being strong? How can one know?

JGB. It is quite true that one may dream about being what one would like to be, but the simple answer to that question is always found through one's bodily sensations. As soon as you bring yourself in contact with your bodily sensation again, you know whether you were really free or only dreaming.

11.
WHY WE HAVE A BODY

16 February 1964

LET US START today with an unusual question: "What is the point of having a physical body?" We can easily picture to ourselves that we could exist with some other kind of body, not subject to the conditions of this existence but with the same thoughts and feelings that we have. And as we live mainly in our thoughts and feelings, we can ask ourselves: "What good does it do to us to have a body?" Having a body lets us in for a great deal of trouble: the care of the body and its needs occupy at least half of our time. We have to spend at least half of our time in sleeping and eating and washing and clothing this body, and some of the time not directly occupied with that is occupied in earning what is necessary for its needs in the way of food and shelter and so on; so having to live in a body takes away a great deal of our freedom. It is also clear that the actions which take place in and through the body constantly distract our attention from our wish to understand the deeper reality; and also from our wish to be free and able to be fully ourselves.

We really have to make some effort to put ourselves, in imagination, into the position of being free from having to live in this kind of body made of physical matter. Some of you may have had the experience of getting out of this body, as I have,* and if so, you know how much freer and better off you feel and how reluctant you are to get back into it, as if it would be real bliss to go off and leave it for good.

Certainly, it is very probable that the body has to go through about an equal amount of pleasant and unpleasant experiences and it is very doubtful whether on balance it is more pleasant than unpleasant to be living in a physical body. One cannot say that it is for the sake of plea-

* cf. JG Bennett. *Witness: The Story of a Search*, Chp.1; and M. Grey. *Return from Death*.

sure that one is living in a physical body, nor can one say that it is necessary to have a physical body in order to be alive, because there is certainly something in us which is alive and does not require that it should inhabit this kind of body. So when you have discarded all the reasons which at first sight seemed to make it worthwhile living in a body and begin to ask yourself why we need to live in it, you see that it is not quite such an easy question to answer.

The answer is a very important and deep one. The body is an instrument which enables transformations to take place in us which are necessary for our freedom and for establishing ourselves with the possibility of existing in a different way. One of the reasons why a body can do this is because the physical body is related in a special way to time and therefore it is a very well-devised instrument for overcoming the problem of time in ourselves. Until we can overcome this problem of time, we are always undergoing a process of destruction. From the moment it is born, this body of ours is undergoing a process of destruction which is only partly compensated by its power of renewal, and we are inclined to think that the renewal mechanism that is placed in the body is just for the purpose of keeping it alive and active for the span of time allotted to each one of us. In other words, that we have this power of organic renewal simply so that the body can maintain itself.

But this is only part of the story. The real truth of it is that through this power of renewal of the body we can establish in ourselves a kind of renewal that no longer depends upon the body and then, when we discard the body, carry with us this means of renewal wherever we go afterwards. If we do not achieve this with the help of this body, it is not so easy. It can be compared with a workshop in which an apparatus is made. In the workshop of the body, a particular apparatus can be made by which man is able to renew his existence apart from and independently of the body. This apparatus of renewal is sometimes called the astral or *kesdjan* body, or "body of the soul"—not the soul itself, but the body of the soul. So if you look upon this body of ours as a workshop in which something is made which will be very difficult to make without this workshop to make it in, you will have a different attitude towards it. The value and meaning of a workshop is in what you can make in it, not just in keeping it tidy or going on filling it with more and more tools which you will never use.

Now what are the tools which are in this workshop? The one I want to speak about specially this morning is the tool that consists in the presence of rhythms in the body; processes that renew themselves at regular intervals such as our day-to-day existence, the rhythm of our daily life and also of course the rhythms of our heart beat and breathing and the rhythm of the digestive process. All of those are instruments for producing in ourselves this other apparatus that we require to be able to travel freely without being dependent on the process of time, as we are in this body.

These rhythms are all connected with renewal. As our heart beats, it is pumping blood around in order to renew the tissues. As we breathe, we are taking in air in order to renew the quality of the state of the blood. As we eat we are taking in the substances for the renewal both of our energies and also the tissues of our body. In our periods of sleep, a process of renewal and general regeneration of the organism takes place. Every rhythm is a renewal, like the swinging of a pendulum that renews its possibility of swinging by concentrating its energy into a potential form at the top of its swing. Every cyclic or rhythmical process is like that. It is very necessary for us to learn how to transfer this renewal of our organism into the finer parts of our being which are not automatically provided with them. For example, there is no automatic provision for renewal in our mental processes. They have another, very necessary, quality which is the property of spontaneity and freedom from the dependence on past and future, but they are always dependent upon accidental shocks to keep them going. We find this particularly in our wish to work on ourselves, to find reality, to make progress in our inner life. This wish, which may be strong at one moment, dies away and, as I said, there is no principle of renewal here that enables it to return constantly and keep us in the right direction. We depend upon some shock, some accident, some combination of circumstances to bring back this wish to us. The source of the wish does not disappear, because there is hunger and need for reality in all of us, but this does not usually translate itself into a wish that will lead us to act. To wake up, to act, we have somehow or other to find a way of bringing the principle of renewal into our wish, and this is just where our bodily organism must be used as what is sometimes called a reminding factor.

There are ways of getting reminding factors from the outside but they are precarious. The real secret of the reminding factor is in this physical body of ours; for the very reason that the physical body is equipped with a wonderful series of rhythmic renewals and we can link ourselves to any and all of these for whatever purpose we wish. We only have to learn how to do it. And once we have learned how to link ourselves with the processes of renewal in the body, then the renewals begin to come into other things, like our thoughts and our feelings, and can then maintain a direction and stability that they could not have otherwise. This is, as I said earlier, one of the ways in which this body serves as a workshop for constructing this other apparatus that we require.

I am proposing today to make an experiment with you by arranging that the big house bell be rung every quarter of an hour from eleven o'clock until lunchtime. I want you to take this as a signal for renewal in yourself of your wish.

You have presumably come here with a certain wish; but you know, as well as I do, that you will soon forget this wish, and that everything will then go in the usual broken-up way, because your thoughts and your feelings have not a principle of renewal, and your body will just go trudging along doing what is in front of it.

It is really necessary for us to bring our bodies into the service of our aim. If we try to do this with our thoughts and our feelings only, it is almost an impossible task, but with the help of the body it is possible. Something in you will be listening for that bell and that something is your own body. If you ask of your body that it should remind you of your wish when it hears the bell, you will see that it will begin to do so. I say "ask" because there is an intelligence in the body which we can rely on. We are inclined to treat the body as if it were a donkey that cannot understand anything; but even donkeys understand a good deal of what is said to them and our own bodies can understand a good deal more. They can be spoken to and they will respond; they will help us. In fact they will help us better than our thoughts or our feelings, because they are more reliable—if only we will let them do the work for which they are intended.

After-Lunch Discussion

Questioner. When I heard the bell, the very first stroke was sufficient to be a reminder, but then the question: "How can I make use of this?"

JG Bennett. I said it had to be a reminder to renew in oneself one's wish. There is not any need to make use of this. What we need is to be impregnated through and through with wish. If one is in a great hurry to go from just an impulse of wish to making use of it by doing something, then this process of impregnation cannot deepen in oneself. One should vibrate through and through with the wish for reality, so that this vibration is really felt in oneself each time one is reminded of it.

With that there comes a great thirst and need to find it, and from that one can begin to do things. But if one wants to do things as soon as one feels the wish for reality, it is like someone who wants to drive away in his car as soon as the first drops of petrol enable the engine to start, knowing that the car will very soon come to a stop again. It is not sufficient that there should be an impulse, we must be charged with this wish! Unless we are, we return into the state of just depending upon the pressures of the outside world to do things for us or to make us act. Most people live just in that way: when something has to be done, they do it; when it has not got to be done at this moment, they procrastinate and wait until they are obliged to act.

Or else it is simply a matter of habit: they always do certain things and they always will do them. There is no pressure in that.

Certainly, I do not mean that one can fabricate this wish out of nothing, but there should by now be some experience in all of us that makes us know the difference between the taste of living and the taste of not living. There is something in us which wishes to live, but that wish is easily dissipated and lost and has to be renewed until it is really so strong in us that we shall not forget it.

But you may all the same want to know what to do when you remember your wish. In that case I would advise you to remember the inevitability of your own death. If you remember that, you will see that something has to be prepared before that inevitable moment, and that will help.

Q. This morning I kept feeling that time was slipping away. I was missing opportunities. I felt that I should be able to use this time!

JGB. Yes, it is so, there should be in us a certain taste of time. This taste of time in us has a sort of bitterness of death about it and when we experience this taste we begin to see that something must be in us which is not the slave of time, or which time cannot destroy. Usually we are without this taste; time slips by just in the same way as air goes in and out of our lungs. Just as we have no idea what we are losing all the time by our way of breathing—how much precious substance is being wasted by not assimilating it as we breathe—so there is something precious that we allow to pass in time, which we do not notice.

Q. I think it is not so much the act of dying that a person is afraid of, as the feeling that they have not achieved what they hoped to do in life.

JGB. That is true, and that is why one should remember it in good time, while there is plenty of time to achieve it. It is perfectly true, this is the only serious thing about death: that things that have to be done before death cannot be done after death. There are various things of this kind that can begin to produce in us a certain concern.

Q. I have always understood that any kind of breathing exercises are dangerous. Can you tell us something about this matter?

JGB. Breathing is a very powerful thing and to interfere with breathing in an amateurish way is highly dangerous. The warnings are all against experimenting with breathing without knowing what will be the side effect. But this does not mean that breathing is not important. It is important, and if you have ever studied Gurdjieff's ideas you will know that for him breath is the central food for man. The food that we eat is simply to keep our bodies going, but from the air we extract the nourishment that is required for the inner body.

If one does not know how to breathe in the proper way, it does not mean that there is no chance of doing anything at all, because there are various kinds of exercises which produce the required changes in the breathing while at the same time adapting the other rhythms to the change; and then this sort of breathing change looks after itself. The results may be much slower and less noticeable than is the case with exercises which concentrate on the breathing only, but there is no danger with such a method. The real danger with breathing exercises is to pick out only the breathing rhythm in order to liberate some energies from the breath, which is really quite easy to do, but if there is no one at hand to cope with the results the consequences can be disastrous, as I have myself witnessed in more than one case. That is the reason why everyone who knows anything about it always gives warnings about unwarranted interference with breathing. But that is a totally different thing from saying that breathing is not of central importance. Without right breathing it is very difficult to obtain the nourishment required for a certain inner development in us.

Q. Is there any way of receiving guidance on the simple and safe technique to which you referred?

JGB. There are many people in this room to whom I have shown, for one or another purpose, techniques for breathing and for the extraction of energy from breath that are perfectly harmless. I have never known anyone who followed that sort of method in the way they were taught who has had any trouble. I do not say that they have always derived benefit, because it is something very mild and it is only under conditions where there is the possibility of much closer supervision and various collateral side exercises that one can push breathing exercises beyond something very simple.

Question: I went to lunch with somebody, and I had decided that I would leave at a certain time. But I was persuaded by my friend to stay on beyond the time. I stayed the whole afternoon! The longer I stayed, the more uncomfortable I felt in myself. All my small decisions had gone. I felt that this had happened because I had been trying to keep to my decisions. I disliked myself for this failure for a long time.

JG Bennett: You must make clear to yourself the distinction between proposals and decisions. If you fail to accomplish a proposal, it must not be a source of misery. But a decision must be something different for you. For your decisions, you must continue to keep account at night, and so on. If you had simply said to yourself: "I will get up and go at three o'clock," you would have been able to make a decision that would work for you. But when you don't do this, you are not able to have the necessary command over what you will do. This command has to be mobilized—and mobilized every time you make a decision. Each time you make a decision, there has to be a total commitment of yourself. Sometimes it seems to be taking a sledgehammer to crack a nut—but it is not a nut at all! The most difficult thing for us is to overcome this weakness in ourselves. It is not enough to feel miserable. It doesn't really do very much good.

Question: Is this the same as the penance of the Catholic church?

JG Bennett: Yes. Except that there it has become only pro forma. It should really be something that has a real significance for us personally. Preferably one should choose as penance for this kind of failure, something connected with one's own body. So you could go without something you wished to eat—or eat something you don't wish to eat, stewed eels, perhaps?

—Coombe Springs Group "S" Notes, 1964.

12.
INNER FREEDOM AND OBJECTIVE PURPOSE

2 February 1964

WE HAVE ALL HEARD the expression: "inner freedom towards life." There are various conditions in which we have to find this inner freedom, and the wish for it should be with us all the time. That is an aim to be aspired to, and we should always be trying to understand how this inner freedom is to be found and maintained in us. However, this morning I only want to speak about one or two of the kinds of situations in which we can look for inner freedom.

First of all, we have to remember that a great part of our outer lives is determined by the necessities of everyday life. We do not have outer freedom to reject the necessities and obligations of life. We are not free, for example, to refuse to sleep, to eat, to take the necessary care of our bodies; but, although we are not outwardly free in front of these situations, we can always remain inwardly free. Although we can be free, we seldom are and we can all recognize how much time, and mental and emotional energy we waste over things that, in any case, cannot be altered.

There is another kind of situation where we may find ourselves doing something which does not correspond at all to our own nature, and yet maybe it is still necessary and unavoidable. For instance, I may find myself obliged to do some task which I am not at all good at or which does not interest me, and in that kind of situation the possibility of inner freedom is much greater. Those situations—which on the face of it look like misfortunes—are in reality opportunities for maintaining the taste of inward freedom; and therefore one should never revolt against finding oneself in situations of that kind. I think you can all recognize that when one is in such a situation, it is possible to be more detached from the activity and to experience a state of inward freedom which can then become very satisfying indeed, so that a special kind of inner joyful state comes just from the fact that externally we are doing what we do not want to do and what is even inappropriate for us to do.

This can be increased still more when the external work we are doing is not merely inappropriate, but the result of our own mistake. It can easily happen to us (and it often happens to me), that through some omission or carelessness, I involve myself in doing something that is a sheer waste of time, that I ought not to be doing, and that I could perfectly well have arranged not to do. Then I find myself in a state of external absurdity; but because I am committed to it, I have to go through with it. In that kind of situation, the taste of inner freedom can be particularly strong. In proportion to the intensity of the external absurdity, there can be an equal intensity of inner peace and satisfaction because one is not affected by the absurdity of the outward activity. In fact such situations are of special value because they enable one to recognize the taste; and also what has to be done inwardly in order to detach oneself and enjoy this inward freedom.

Such a state is really much more difficult to find when we are doing useful, necessary things; and especially things which we have become habituated to doing and so can do with very little external attention. Although, on the face of it, such situations should be very favorable for inner freedom—because part of our attention can be withdrawn from the activity in order to taste one's inward state—the truth is just the opposite because, when an activity goes mechanically, by habit, it is very difficult to withdraw one's attention properly from it, and quite a considerable amount of self-training and self-discipline is required to do ordinary necessary things in a state of inward freedom.

Those are just some examples I have given you about the possibilities of enjoying a state of inward freedom; but the one I wish to speak to you about particularly today belongs to another category. It concerns the situations when we are *doing work for the sake of the Work*; that is, for an objective reason, external to ourselves. When I am doing something which is necessary for me, or an obligation of my life—such as taking care of my family or doing my professional work—then I am under the pressure of this necessity. But I can find myself in situations where it is possible to undertake something for a different reason; that is, either as an act of service which is not required of me, or, better to say, when I am doing something in the name of an aim or purpose that I feel to be objectively important, which I recognize and respect. One can also include that which one undertakes as part of one's own training, or one's own inner discipline. One will allot to oneself a certain amount of work to be done, not because one wants to, not because one has to, and not in the sense of this absurdity of which I spoke before, but simply for the sake of an objective purpose. In that kind of work one should try to keep one's motive quite clear in front of one; that is, that one is doing it for that reason: "In the name of Work," as I would put it. It is, of course, easy to get this mixed up with personal reasons. One may undertake some work with this object in one's mind and at the next moment begin to wonder whether other people will admire and appreciate what one is doing, or whether one will get some reward for doing it. One has of course to reject such things in order to keep one's attention on the reason why one is doing it, which is a decision one has taken with oneself alone: "I have decided to do this."

This is especially important to be understood when we have the sort of gathering we have on Work Sundays here. There is no reason for coming here on a Sunday when there are other things to occupy you— things which, from the point of view of your life, may be more useful than coming here. There is no reason for it unless it has that special quality of being a decision taken "in the name of Work." And there is very little value in taking such a decision and then forgetting all about it, and therefore it is necessary for us to bring this constantly before us: "I am doing this now in the name of Work."

But there is something more here which I wish to draw your attention to. There is much to be learned from doing something "in the name of Work," because then there is really both outward and inward freedom. I am not obliged to do it; there is no pressure upon me, and therefore in doing it I am acting freely: because it is from myself that I am doing it. Work of such a kind can give you this feeling of external freedom.

And how am I to have the sense of internal freedom? This comes from the way I do this work. If I remember why, or in the name of what, I am doing it—that is, in the name of objective reality, or truth, or God—then I must do it as well as I can. This means I must not forget. I must have my attention and my inward judgement clear, and then I begin to have a taste of what kind of freedom there can be when the outer as well as the inner are free; that is, when what I am doing externally is a freely chosen act and when my inner state is a freely chosen state. So I come towards this total freedom which is our objective, tied to nothing, outwardly or inwardly.

You have only about two hours of work in front of you before we have lunch. This is a very long time to maintain quality in the whole of one's activity, but at the same time it is not impossibly long. If we set ourselves to work in that way, that is, to regard everything that we are doing as something done "in the name of Work"—and that therefore must be done as perfectly as possible—then you will see that by choosing to work as well as we can, we can have a taste of inward freedom of a particular kind. This taste does not depend upon detaching oneself from what is outside—the detachment comes from the fact that we remember this is being freely chosen, and there is no reason why we should do anything at all here today, unless we choose to do it. Nobody will disturb us if we go and sit down and do nothing, or if we go away, or if we never came at all; it is wholly our own business what we do with this time. We are not with the people that we just happen to like, or doing the job that happens to interest us, or that happens to be necessary. We are here because we choose to be here.

After-Lunch Discussion

Questioner. Can one say that inner freedom is the presence in one of work which takes the place of what otherwise would have been just habit or routine?

JG Bennett. As I said this morning, conditions for inner freedom can either come about by a combination of circumstances arising accidentally or the circumstances must be created intentionally. Depending upon accidentally arising circumstances is like trying to make your living by picking up pennies in the street. We do pick up pennies in the street, but it is a precarious livelihood. In other words, things do happen to us that make us wake up inwardly and experience inner freedom, but this is uncertain. What we need are conditions intentionally created which will produce these circumstances sufficiently often and sufficiently strongly for this to establish itself in us. It is the intentional creating of such conditions that we call Work. The reason we call it Work is that they cannot be created artificially: they require to have an element of objective purpose. In other words, it is not sufficient to create conditions of stress that merely look like the conditions of stress which arrive by fate; those conditions of stress must be related to some purpose. Experience shows that created conditions which do not correspond to an objective purpose can only produce very transient results;

very soon the whole thing dies away and becomes a pretense. Therefore objectivity in activity is an essential element, even if the process itself is not aiming at that but at something quite different, like the attainment of inner freedom.

Just to make it quite clear by an illustration, if I set myself to perform some task, for example to learn how to do something which is going to require a refinement of my attention and a real inner discipline in order to achieve it, it will not give me very much if the accomplishment of this task has no objective purpose. In fact, all that it will give me is just that training. Supposing, for example, that I set myself to become a very good woodcarver with no objective reason for doing it. If I do succeed in becoming a very good woodcarver, if there is no other purpose in it, I shall be nothing else but a very good woodcarver. But if I set myself to become a very good woodcarver in order, let us say, to produce ornaments for a particular building which has objective purpose, then I shall not only learn how to carve wood well, but I shall also have something for my own inward freedom. Because when I am doing this work I shall be remembering that I am not just doing it for myself, and therefore I will remain free in a way that I could not otherwise. And yet I am doing it from myself; that is, I am obliging myself to learn a new craft. When the *Djami* was being built and we found that nobody knew how to work copper, some people went through a special training in order to learn how to do copper-working. This was very interesting for them and they acquired a particular kind of skill which they had never expected to acquire and which they would not lose. But the real point is that when they were sitting on top of the roof doing this work, they got something else besides knowing how to work copper.

Q. It seems then that this way of gaining inner freedom depends upon one being able to participate in an objective purpose, and as far as I can see, this is a most precarious thing.

JGB. An objective purpose is symbolized by *Noah's Ark* as the instrument by which one will be saved from the Flood. Nobody is interested in Noah's Ark if they do not believe in the Flood. If they believe in the Flood, then they participate in building the Ark and taking care of it. It was the building of the Ark that saved them, not the Ark itself, because only those who built it could get into it.

But what about the people who do not see the importance of serving an objective aim, or who cannot find one? They are in the position of the people of the time of Noah, and Noah stands for the one who has been made to see in advance what the purpose of the Ark is. There are always such people in the world, and part of their task is to transmit to others what they have seen. There are of course many things which have the appearance of being an objective purpose, such as the things that are done "for the good of mankind." But it only too often turns out that these things are either obligations that have to be fulfilled anyhow (which is quite a different thing) or else they are unrealistic because they have actually missed the point! Many people try to help others, but they do not see what the help really has to be, and many mistakes are made in this way. It must always be remembered that what I call here the objective purpose, or Noah's Ark, is something which is additional to the obligatory activities that are also going on. Noah and his friends built the Ark in their spare time, but it was a very prudent use of their spare time. They had to live. Nobody would keep them while they were building the Ark, so obviously they had to look after the necessities of their lives. But, as I said, they used their spare time wisely.

Q. Your answer sounded to me dangerously like suggesting something which I feel sure you do not intend to suggest. It sounded to me as though you were suggesting that only people who are in some movement of this kind have a chance of being saved and all the others are lost. I feel sure that this would be a wrong interpretation.

JGB. Yes, it is a wrong interpretation if it is taken to mean that Work is to be understood only as one particular kind of activity or, as you say, one particular movement, or collection, or society of people. It is not like that. The way in which the people of the Ark differ from the people of the Flood is simply this: that some people see and other people do not see. Many people can see if they are shown, but very, very few can see for themselves, and that is the only reason why what you call "movements" and so on are necessary. If anyone sees, they will do what is necessary. Sometimes people see, but they do not see in a way that could be communicated to anyone else. Nevertheless, such people do live their lives in such a way that they are Ark builders. Anyone who sees something connected with the obligation to live objectively rather than subjectively—that is, to live in terms of some objective standard rather than just in terms of one's likes and dislikes, habits and the rest of it—sees something vital. They may be of so many different kinds that you are quite right in saying: "Make sure that you are not suggesting that such people are any less engaged in Ark building than Noah's people." Of course they are engaged; but it is necessary not only to see but to *show* something.

If you ask "What is the point of having a place like Coombe Springs?" It is not that this place is for special people who are specially privileged because they see what nobody else sees and so they are saved where nobody else is saved. If any such idea crossed our minds we should be plunged below the level of the Flood! But a place like this can serve a very useful function in drawing the attention of people to these questions.

I have spoken quite a lot about objective purpose, but you must understand that the really important thing is freedom. What matters is that one should be free, and one of the conditions of freedom is that one should be serving an objective purpose. But, as I said this morning, even when we are committed to absurd tasks, it is very important to understand that this is no bar to being free. I find the contrary, that this is one of the situations where I experience most strongly the sense of freedom.

Q. I usually would get very nervous and in a flap about all the various situations that arose this morning; but it was most queer, because I actually seemed to want to get into a flap yet seemed quite unable to do so! It was a most strange experience and I could feel that it would be marvelous if one could do this in daily housework at home and so on. Is there any way in which one can encourage it when one is just away by oneself?

JGB. Yes, if you really are beginning to see that inner freedom is the most important thing, that everything else is built up on this, then your attitude towards everything that happens to you will be quite different. If annoying and irritating things happen, they will not annoy and irritate you because you see how very useful those things are for inner freedom. You will be far from wanting them not to be there, and then you will have that peculiar taste that you experienced this morning: that your whole attitude towards the situation is turned upside down. Once you come to understand that, your life becomes so much happier, and the whole of it becomes so differently interesting, that you cannot imagine how people can live in such a way that they object to unpleasant, or irritating or stupid time-wasting things happening to them. These things only have an unpleasant flavor about them if one has no taste for inner freedom. If one has a taste for inner freedom one welcomes them. That does not mean one goes as far as to provoke them artificially; but the sense of "this sort of thing is more unpleasant than that" totally disappears; and with that there comes an enormously increased power of enjoying everything.

Q. Is there not a danger of misinterpreting something as an obligation when it isn't one; in other words, of overcommitting yourself?

JGB. There is a danger, but if you begin to follow what I have just been saying, you begin to be less harmfully involved in what you are doing. You remain free in front of your external activities. With that, you find a more objective judgement appearing in you. When I say that these absurd situations are good for inner freedom it does not mean that we should cease to use our discrimination about not getting involved in them. But the point is that the inner freedom we can experience in such situations can be used to remind one; and particularly to enable one not to put oneself into that situation again. People who find themselves in an absurd situation through their own mistakes ordinarily become emotionally involved and upset—angry with themselves or with other people because this happened to them—and as a result, all the understanding which could have been acquired is wasted; and inevitably they will repeat the same mistake over and over again. But it should really go like this: from over commitment one falls into absurd situations; from absurd situations one is able to experience freedom; from freedom one is able to see more clearly what will happen and therefore one is able to avoid such mistakes on other occasions.

13.
GOOD WORKS AND PLUS POWERS

19 July 1964

IN THE WORDS "Good Works" there must be some meaning that we should try to understand. Now let us suppose that we are going to leave out all the meanings which deserve to be spoken of with some mockery: such as all activity that is done for the sake of impressing other people, for gaining a reputation, or even just for satisfying one's own uneasy conscience. If we also leave out of account all kinds of activities pursued for the good of others or for the good of some cause merely by imitation or habit; and look for Good Works in some objective sense, what shall we find then?

We obviously use the words "Good Works" in some way that distinguishes them from our necessary activities, or even from our obligations. They represent something extra that is done not from necessity but because it is right in itself. The obvious way in which one can describe good works of this sort is when they are in relief of the suffering of other people, or to give help to other people; and we tend to think their justification lies chiefly in this: that they are unselfish activities for the good of others. This is true, but it can be taken far too narrowly and we know very well that owing to our ignorance of what other people really need and what will be the results of our own activities, good works of this kind can often produce results quite opposite from what we hope for or intend. So certainly one cannot understand "Good Works" just in terms of the benefit of others rather than our own private benefit, or in terms of something which is not an immediate necessity. If you begin to see in how many ways one can misunderstand the idea of good works, you can understand that either there is nothing very much here, or that we miss what is most important.

There is a most important activity of man, which includes all kinds of good works, and that is an activity that is creative, by which I mean that it would not and could not be done without his intentional action.

Apart from a number of activities that are required to maintain the existence of our organism, we are compelled to do a number of things that take into account our relations with other people and our dependence upon them, our need for them and their reciprocal need for us. All these are just conditions of this kind of existence that we live here on this earth in this kind of body. We, all of us, have however, latent reserve powers beyond what is needed for the fulfilling of these obligations. Everything in man is made with a reserve over and above bare necessity. His body is made in such a way that practically all of his organs can work at a quarter or less of their possible output and yet maintain him in a state of health. His time does not have to be occupied wholly, or almost wholly, with the needs of his body, as it is with most animals, and this reserve of functioning and of time, coupled with an ability to see beyond his immediate needs, all of this creates for man a special situation we have to understand. With these reserves or "plus powers" something is required of us; and that is that we should put something into this world in which we live. It is this that in the end constitutes the "Good Works" about which we are speaking, so that there must be many different kinds of good works, according to all the different kinds of needs in the world about us.

There is an objective relationship here, not a private personal matter of our own whims or likes and dislikes, nor of the social conventions of the world, of the place and time in which we are living. Objectively there is something that is required from all of us: men, women, young, old. We can take this secondhand, just by doing the kind of things that appear to be desirable and are labeled as "Good Works" by the society in which we live, or we can try to understand objectively what is needed. This is much more difficult; and not everyone can hope to come to it—but we can at least put this in front of us. "Am I doing with my life all that is objectively possible for me and am I using my plus powers—all that is over and above the actual necessities in my existence—to the best objective purpose?" You see how difficult it is to answer this question, except by "No, this cannot possibly be true about myself." But I can also say to myself: "What can I be doing better, what is the real right use of my plus powers?" We know precious little about the answer and we have to turn to traditional sources, to people with special wisdom and experience, to try to understand better the world in which we live and what is required in it. In all this we human beings are really like children and we are just as much children today as we were a thousand, or ten thousand, and probably a hundred thousand years ago. Maybe far away in the future, races of men will come who will have grown up sufficiently to understand what all this is about and what is required, but as we are at present we can know very little. We should, however, not forget that, although we are ignorant of what our objective obligations in the world are, we should be trying to understand them better. We must not be satisfied with an animal existence. It is not sufficient that we should be taking care of our bodies, of our lives as family lives; something is required of us that is not required of animals.

Now there are certain things we can do, partly in the sense of trying to understand this problem better, but partly in the sense also of setting free what I call latent or plus powers, so that they can be used when the opportunity comes; and this must be understood to concern the way we act in the world around us. It is only indirectly and to a minor extent concerned with what happens inside us. It is what we do, how we live our lives, that determines whether or not we make the right use of these plus powers, not how good or how understanding or how kind we are inwardly. And really we have to go even further than this and see that there is in this use of our powers a formative action within ourselves.

One way of looking at "Good Works" is that they are an act of gratitude, or recognition, or repayment for the benefits we ourselves receive, an obligation of worship that we should be doing these, as it is said "for the Glory of God," or, "for the Love of God."

All this is excellent, but there is also the other way this needs to be understood, which is that because of our ignorance and because of the disorganized condition of these plus powers, something is required to make them available. If you look at and study life, you will see that our organic activity in regard to the needs of the body and our immediate life round us is fairly well organized in us, but when we get beyond that, to problems of understanding, or doing, or penetration into the needs that are beyond these immediate needs, it is all chaos. Very little is understood; even what has been taught us, what is handed down by tradition, is misunderstood. We do not know our plus powers. We do not know how to use them. We do not know how they are connected with one another. We do not know what connections they make between people. In all of this there is an immense amount of ignorance and imperfection. Something has to be done to get all this into order, to make it available so that it can be used.

Part of this work has to be done inside ourselves because undoubtedly self-knowledge and self-discipline are required, but part of it can only be done through action. In the long run, every power becomes available through use, not through disuse. If you have a particular latent skill, you will only be able to acquire the full value of that skill for yourself if you will patiently exercise it, and probably only with the help of someone who is an expert and specialist in that field. For example, if you have a latent power of being a good pianist, you will not, without much work, be able to mobilize that power. It is the same with all the powers that are not called upon for our everyday life. How then are we to find ways of developing and using, of learning the requisites for these powers—which you would call super skills? It is by "Good Works." It is by learning how to do things in such a way that these powers are called out, mobilized and required to work. If they are made to work they will develop. If they are merely looked at, jealously guarded, kept for inner and private experience, they will remain dormant.

With this putting to work, there comes a reciprocal action, a return upon ourselves. We change in the process: we grow up; we acquire understanding, skill, ability in dealing with ourselves and other people. Therefore, if we begin to understand this, we have to look constantly for ways in which we can set ourselves to work in that particular way, which consists in undertaking tasks, and doing things which fall outside of the immediate necessities of our life and therefore compel us to mobilize these plus powers. I must make it quite clear that by these plus powers I do not mean anything mysterious or strange, out of the reach of ordinary man; they are simply powers which become available to us to develop when our ordinary work is done.

As I have said so often before, we gather here on these "Work Sundays" to undertake various tasks together which are entirely voluntary, especially for those who come as visitors. A certain proportion of these tasks are related to the necessities of the place: we have to prepare food, and to serve it and clear up afterwards, and see to the needs of the children who are here—all these obligations have always to be fulfilled. What we learn in such situations as these Work Sundays is how to mobilize and use the plus powers, how to do something over and above what is necessary. But for that we must take everything that we do as a means: nothing that we do here must be to impress other people, or to satisfy our own uneasy consciences, because nothing will bring us rewards in the ordinary sense of the word. Nevertheless, if we do use these opportunities rightly, it will bring us rewards in an extraordinary sense of the word; that is, in the right development of ourselves and the right harmonizing of the powers that we have. This is why it is that the smallest work that is done for its own sake can be a means for a very big process in ourselves totally. By totally, I mean outwardly as well as inwardly. We really ought to learn how to discard these words "outwardly" and "inwardly" and think always of ourselves as total, whole people! In a normal man, in full possession of himself, there is not the separation of outward and inward. One of the results of working in this way is that we bring the different parts of us together and give them a chance to take shape. This is why I said it is not only a mobilization of our powers, but the development of ourselves.

After-Lunch Discussion

Questioner. In the ordinary way of things it is difficult to find someone who can tell us exactly what we can do and to commit ourselves to it. We must also be able to see whether there is a reasonable chance for us to carry it out; it is not something that we can take lightly.

JG Bennett. One always has to take the scale into account. What you cannot do on one scale, you can do on another. If we try to do things on a scale that is outside of our own understanding or our own powers, obviously nothing will come of it; or there will be so many factors out of our control that it will not be our doing anyhow. But if we reduce the scale, we will eventually come to a point where we can say: "This small simple thing I can do," and very often we find that even then we have undertaken more than we have bargained for; maybe we find ourselves again obliged to reduce the scale until something extremely simple is done.

As an example I can take what happened just now. Someone had the idea to increase the speed and efficiency in serving us our coffee by putting the saucers out first and then bringing round the filled cups. I objected, because this was not a hospitable way of doing it, and then coffee was served with the saucers, in the usual way. When you have in front of you the task of serving coffee, there is a decision to be taken which, on its own scale, is a real decision. Under some circumstances, if time were very short, it would be right to do it in the quickest possible way—if not, the quality of service to the people who are taking part in the meal becomes more important. One just has to be discriminating in front of such a situation. When one does, it becomes a different kind of action. It is the change in the kind of action which is important rather than the scale. If we learn how to do small actions with that kind of total assessment of what is required, it is not so very difficult to transfer it on to a larger scale. There is never a necessity, never any justification for saying: "It is too much for me, I cannot be bothered to take any care for this," because a small action can be done with all the qualities that are required. And this is not something that is static. If we begin to introduce, via discrimination, this quality into our actions, we begin to see more possibilities for doing so than we had dreamt of at first.

In the example I have just given you, there is no room for anything that can be called "Good Works" as far as the fact that coffee has to be served goes. Where something finer comes into the situation is in remembering that this is a meal we are all sharing together. It is not being turned out like a snack at a factory canteen. It is this additional quality brought into it that is a creative act.

Q. Why is it that we have always the tendency to keep dropping back from this?

JGB. The reason for it is that one can be an animal unintentionally, one can be a machine unintentionally, but one cannot be a human being—that means a responsible person—unintentionally. Therefore, as soon as our intention collapses, our humanness collapses also and we begin to have this divorce, this separation between quality and quantity, or between form and content. Everything begins to fall apart as soon as our intention goes; which really means that our human nature begins to fall apart from our animal nature. Our human nature just goes off into dreams and all that is left is simply an imitation human being.

Q. It is really dependent upon our ability to catch that moment of freedom between actions, because quite often I find that I have been thinking of that quality, but my attention just goes from one thing to another.

JGB. Now, this is important to understand, because it might seem from what I have been saying that you have to be intending at every moment. That is quite outside of our power, and people become disheartened or just incredulous when they misunderstand it as that. You may say, then, that we can surely live our lives quite satisfactorily without continual intention. This is true; the intention does not have to be conscious all the time. An intention can penetrate and persist for a considerable time after we cease to be conscious of it, providing it is a real intention. If you start a task and you intend to do this task in the way that we have been speaking about—that is, with a human quality in it—if that intention is strong enough, your awareness can become quite occupied with the job, and you forget all about it in fact. Yet you notice from time to time that you are doing it differently; and you even notice—providing the intention was strong enough—when you have begun to lose it. Then your losing actually becomes a reminding factor for you to return to the way you intended to work; your discomfort in not working as you intended seems to wake you up. We have to practice to become more and more sensitive to this, because it is a very valuable and necessary thing for us to feel discomfort when we are not doing things in the way we intend. >From that we remember and from remembering we renew. But if we become callous to this sort of discomfort, then the whole renewing mechanism breaks down and we just fall into the habit of doing things in a mechanical way.

Q. Many people feel that when they act with intention they lose spontaneity. I wonder if you could say something about that?

JGB. On the contrary, by intentional action we open the way to spontaneity. Our being sensitive to discomfort when we are not working as we intend, also enables us to notice spontaneously arising ideas, pictures, possibilities and so on. What is the use of spontaneity if it does not enter into our actions, and how can it enter into our actions unless we know it? If I am doing something intentionally, I shall find that quite spontaneously there will arise in me suggestions or ideas as to how I could do it better, and I will notice them because I am doing it intentionally; otherwise I should no more notice those than notice my mistakes. It is simply not true to say that intentional action is the enemy of spontaneity. It may seem like a contradiction, but the truth is that the more complete the intention, the greater the element of spontaneity that enters with it. If you look at the work of a really great artist, the intensity of the intention that he brings to his work is the condition which allows spontaneity to enter. Do you understand?

Q. Yes, but often people find they are really spontaneous only when they are working without any intention or picture in their minds...doodling in other words. Is this spontaneity?

JGB. Yes, this can be so, but there has to be selection all the same. The height of spontaneity is when you do nothing whatever except just throw things together and let them fall as they fall, like leaves in the autumn. Such a pattern can be very beautiful, but you still have to be aware, because out of twenty such attempts, one of them will have some special quality that makes it something worthy to be kept. Spontaneity without awareness is nothing, any more than intention without awareness is anything; because it simply turns into machine work.

Let us take musical improvisation. It is not true to say that when you improvise in music there should be nothing intentional about it. You have got to be able to see what comes by itself, how a theme will grow by itself and how you have to follow it. Out of what seemed to be merely an interesting theme, Beethoven could see spontaneously arising something which was really a divine inspiration. There was a transition from the one to the other, all by a number of spontaneous steps, but he was able to recognize them.

14.
THE POWER OF INTENTION

6 October 1963

THE ORDINARY STATE of man into which he falls by developing various habits from childhood onwards is a comparatively small part of his whole being. This small part is directly concerned with his day-to-day living and the greater part is either unknown or disregarded. Psychologists make a division into the conscious and the unconscious parts of man's life. This does not refer to the same distinction as I am making, and indeed would be a comic way of speaking about it because the disregarded parts are the place where the true consciousness of man is seated.

I want to emphasize the general disconnectedness of the ordinary state of man. One obvious form of disconnectedness is the isolation of man's thinking from his body: his mental images, inner talking, associations and so on go on without reference to his body, and his body—because it has its own mind, its own powers—lives its own life, separated from the thinking.

The feeling states of man are constantly changing without his thinking brain being able to adapt itself. The feelings constantly influence our thoughts and our bodily states and movements: but the influence is unconscious and indirect. The general disconnectedness of the three principal groups of functions—bodily, mental and emotional—affects both our conscious states and our unconscious workings. We are aware of contradictions and conflicts, of our inability to act as we wish to act, of our tendency to get lost in day dreams and fantasies. We can also easily verify the isolation of each group of functions from the other two. It is much harder to see what goes on behind the scenes in those parts of the mind of which we are not usually aware.

This condition of isolation of the psychic functions from one another is an abnormal state which can and must be rectified if we are to make spiritual progress. In the spiritually developed man there is a pattern, a structure in the whole of his being so that every part knows what it has to do and is directed from one center: his "I." This is the seat of his own will, which remains unaffected by anything that goes on inside him and outside him. In a true and complete man there is no division between conscious and unconscious parts because he can reach in himself, whenever it is necessary to do so, the parts of which people are usually unconscious. He is aware of his deeply hidden and disguised motives and the connections that bind him and relate him to other people, of which again the ordinary man is not able to be conscious.

Now our aim is to become such complete people that we shall be able to live with the whole of ourselves. This means that our nature must acquire a complete and harmonious structure that can work rightly at all levels, from the external, material, to the innermost, spiritual parts. Obviously we cannot achieve this just by wanting it, so where are we to begin?

It all starts with our intention. If we have a stable intention, then the fluctuations which cause the random connections between the different functions need not touch it. When we are able to hold on to our wish and the way in which we picture the reason and purpose of our life, then we shall not be disturbed whatever may happen to us. We may not, at the beginning, have a clear idea of it all, but our intention can be established. We should know how to return to this intention and feel that it is all the time accompanying us in everything we do. We shall begin to become aware of it whenever we act or think in a way that is not in harmony with that intention. Then something will begin to hurt in us and we shall return to actions that do correspond to our intention. And so, although the intention in the first place has no real power, as it is established and maintained in us it will begin to influence and change our lives.

I certainly hope and believe that all of us here have an intention—towards our own perfection, towards the fulfillment of our destiny, towards the task that we exist on this earth to accomplish. We are here, I suppose, because we want to make that intention more effective. It is true that all people in some form or another do have that intention, but very few are sufficiently clear about it to have it as something which accompanies them all the time. Only such an intention can produce a unifying action on the whole of our being because it is directed towards our bodies, towards our feelings, towards our understanding, towards our knowing, towards our actions with ourselves and with our neighbors, towards the performance of all our duties—everywhere this intention can accompany us and in that way be a factor of unification in the presence of the general chaos and disharmony which is in all human nature.

Now I do not believe that even the perfected man is free from disharmony and chaos, because disharmony is one of the characteristics of the universe in which we live. It is in the very nature of existence that there can never be perfect harmony; because perfect harmony in the sense that everything was just right all the time would bring the world to a standstill. If everything were just right all the time, there would be no reason for anything to happen at all and it would just remain for ever in a state of static perfection. Because there is disharmony there is always something to be done and therefore a meaning to our lives.

I am sure that even in the perfected man there is always the impossibility of being immutably perfect. He is perfected and yet never perfect. From the descriptions we read of their own experience we can see that, although such men have come a long way—perhaps as near as is possible for man to perfection—they are always acutely aware of imperfection and disharmony in themselves. It is sometimes even disconcerting to realize this and we ask ourselves how it is possible that a being who has reached such evident perfection within his own totality—in body and heart and mind and action and charity and so on—lives all the time with the acute sense of his own disharmony and imperfection. We ask ourselves if such self-abasement is not just imagination or even something morbid? No, it is not so; he sees things as they really are, he does not deceive himself at all, and it is certainly not a sign of a kind of false or forced humility.

I remember the shock I experienced in reading *The Sincere Narrations of a Pilgrim to his Spiritual Father*, where the pilgrim describes his conversation with a *staretz* who had evidently reached a high degree of spiritual perfection and who, for a long time, talked about his own imperfections and sinfulness, all of which seemed to be completely out of keeping with what he was and his way of life. The point here is that when man is intent upon the highest perfection, he becomes more and more sensitive to his defects and failings. To another they seem small: but objectively they are great for they are relative to his own state.

93

I say all this because it should not be our intention, or our hope or expectation, to reach some kind of static perfection where the need to do anything more disappears; but rather that there should be such a condition in us that we are unified into one whole and that we should have the ability to perform whatever actions are needed as perfectly as is necessary. At the same time we must live constantly with the awareness that the need to act and its motivation come from the presence everywhere of imperfections which have to be overcome. They have to be overcome and, although they can never be wholly overcome, they have to be lived with and yet never accepted.

So we have to understand that in a strange way we have to both accept ourselves and also reject ourselves. This is where our intention comes in. I see constantly in myself every kind of imperfection, every kind of chaotic and disruptive influence in everything—in my body, in my feelings, in my thinking, in my plans, in my relationships with every other person that I have to deal with. I am constantly aware of all this and I am aware that this cannot change and this is just how things are. That is what I have to accept, and yet, every single one of these imperfections must be rejected. If I see that there is some disharmony in my body, I must do everything I can to remove this disharmony, to bring my body back to harmony. If I see that my feelings are disturbed and troubled, I must wish and do whatever is necessary to have peace in my feelings. If I see that I am lacking in charity, I must do everything to rid myself of any uncharitable impulses in myself, and so on.

This is the strange paradox of our lives, that we have all the time to accept what we are and yet never accept anything we are. That is how our intention can become something which can be lived with and can really accompany us. If our intention is towards an impossible perfection, it will let us down; if it is towards something incomplete, something short of perfection, it will also let us down.

This is something that everyone can grasp from their own everyday experience, for everyone can see how difficult it is to bring ourselves back to accepting to bear what we are and what everyone else is. If we do not succeed in holding our intention in this way then we can topple into another kind of dualism or separation which is false and harmful for man; that is to say, man can excuse and put up with all sorts of defects in himself or, worse still, hide them from himself and refuse to see them—and yet at the same time he can have a strong desire to be different or other than he is. In other words, he can refuse to accept himself and at the same time put up an excuse for all his defects. That kind of inward discontent with ourselves is a very common thing, but it must be clear to us that hiding and refusing to face all the things that are wrong in us is silly. We have to be at peace with ourselves, we have to accept ourselves very deeply; accept this nature of ours such as it is, neither revolting against the fact that we are imperfect beings nor hiding or disguising from ourselves any imperfections which we do not want to find.

This work begins with being clear, not confused, about what we find in our experience. The confusion comes when we wish to change what cannot be changed and do not trouble to change what can be changed. We cannot change our nature any more than an oak can change into an apple tree. Each one of us is a certain kind of being; but we can and must work on our weaknesses and wrong actions and attitudes.

I am saying all this to you because I think it is not difficult for anyone to see what this means and to use what I have been saying to strengthen and clarify the intention that should accompany us in our lives. Intention is perhaps the first thing that really distinguishes a man from an animal, and when we live without intention we are not living as men. But we can have illusory, absurd intentions and we can have sound intentions that correspond to the reality.

My advice to you today is to set yourselves the task of forming an intention as to the way in which you will work while you are here. This is a kind of "miniature" intention, that corresponds to the larger intention of living the whole of our lives in a certain way. When you have decided this so that it is clear to you, you should return to it from time to time and see if you can make it "accompany" you in all that you have to do during the day.

After-Lunch Discussion

Questioner. When we meet or hear about people who have gone a long way towards being perfected, we are always impressed by their serenity. How can they always be serene and happy when they are also aware of their disharmony and imperfection?

JG Bennett. In a person who develops nearer to his real self, there is one place which is always unmoved and serene. Whatever the conditions of imperfection and disturbance may be in other places, one place is quiet. If one is engaged in some activity, the instruments that are being used become involved and therefore they cannot remain still. Things will go right and things will go wrong, but there still should be one place where there is no disturbance at all. The point is that this stillness is not a condition of isolation where there is no awareness of disturbance, because that would mean being completely shut off, in a kind of nirvana, isolated from everything, which is not what we really understand as the aim of our development.

Q. Then this means feeling unhappy on account of disharmony and at the same time being serene?

JGB. Being serene at the same time; yes, that is what must be achieved. The ordinary state of man is for happiness and unhappiness to alternate. He is either feeling happy and forgets that there is such a thing as unhappiness, or he is feeling unhappy, forgetting that there is such a thing as happiness. But as man makes a little progress, this swinging of the pendulum begins to give way to a state where he is always aware of happiness and always aware of unhappiness. He realizes that towards one side one has to be unhappy because of imperfection, towards another side one has to be happy because there is an ultimate right, an ultimate truth. It seems an absurd thing to say that there cannot be happiness when there is awareness of unhappiness. Nevertheless, everyone who has experienced really intense happiness has recognized that in such a state there is always a certain suffering at the same time; and everyone who has experienced intense suffering has always seen with astonishment that something else and very wonderful is present also. Therefore you can never say that Reality consists in excluding the one and keeping only the other.

Q. What would be important is what you do with your unhappiness, wouldn't it?

JGB. What you have to bear is not so much the unhappiness as to accept that life is like that and has to be like that. We must not even wish to do any thing about it. What you can do belongs to a different world.

Q. Do happiness and unhappiness belong to one's sensitivity or to one's consciousness?

JGB. There is an insensitive condition where there is no feeling either of happiness or unhappiness. Then there is a sensitive condition which is always divided into opposites, when one is wholly identified with the particular state that happens to be present—if pain is present one has no awareness of pleasure, if pleasure is present one has no awareness of pain, and so on. Then something can be added to that state of sensitivity where one is able to be aware of both poles together, which is consciousness. In other words, one can experience pleasure and remember what pain was, when there is pain one can remember what pleasure was. But there is something again which is beyond consciousness itself, a real stillness; where there is no involvement in anything at all and no experiencing of either pleasure or pain or anything of that kind. It is an experiencing of a totally different kind. Only then are these opposites quite left behind; but it does not mean that, if they are left behind, they are destroyed or cease to exist. They still remain in the place to which they rightly belong, and that is our sensitivity.

The nature of sensitivity is called polar. It gives rise to an enormous variety of positive and negative manifestations according to the different instruments through which it works. In the physical body there is activity and repose, there is pleasure and pain, there is desire and aversion. In the emotions, there is satisfaction and dissatisfaction; approval and disapproval; like and dislike; and so on. In the mind, there is agreement and disagreement; acceptance and rejection; yes and no.

As long as we are on the level of sensitivity, everything is colored in that way; but we can recognize that there is "something" in us which is behind that. Everyone knows that there are times when there is a consciousness that is somehow looking on at these alternations of pleasure and pain or whatever it may be; we can see the hesitations going on in our mind, hovering between yes and no, and be aware of them. Ordinary people do not have this observing consciousness sufficiently organized. It is more like a child looking through a peephole and seeing what is going on, not like someone who is really able to be present and by his presence influence those who are in the room. When consciousness really enters into us then it is like a good schoolmaster coming into the room and all the pupils feeling his presence and responding to him. That is how consciousness is when it takes over from sensitivity.

Q. It is said that the way to hell is paved with good intentions. Is it with the will that we should have intentions?

JGB. Yes it is so; but we must be clear what we mean by "will." At first it seems as if will is power; but will cannot act unless it has the instruments; and, if the instruments are not suitable or not trained, then the will is helpless. The saying that hell is paved with good intentions simply means that good intentions without training and discipline are a deception and lead man into a world of unreality.

The point that I was really wanting to make about intention this morning is that there is one place where it can enter much more easily than others and that is into our understanding, our mind. When I say "mind" here I do not mean just our thinking and talking apparatus but that which sees and understands. There we can have an intention. It is much harder to have an intention in our feelings because they are so unstable. I can intend something with my feelings at one moment and then somebody makes an ugly face at me and all my intentions have disappeared. When a man's feelings are trained in such a way that they do not lose their bearings when somebody makes an ugly face, then he can have such intentions, but until then it is only words, it is only talk. But, as I said, where you can really have an intention is in your mind, because your mind can see clearly and continue to see clearly that one thing is good for you and another thing is bad for you.

Q. It is very difficult to observe the different parts in us because they are so integrated.

JGB. The word "integrated" does not express it. It is better to say that they are intertwined or mixed-up. It takes very little to see that mind and feelings are not at all integrated. They are, to a quite considerable extent, intertwined, but intertwined is quite different from integrated. It means that they will act upon one another. Our thoughts, for example, will be colored by the state of our feelings, but that is not integration—our thoughts should not be colored by our feelings, nor should they be colored by the condition of our bodies. If you observe yourself you can see how what you think depends upon how your digestion is, whether you have got a cold in your head or not. Do not call that integration.

Q. No, it is not integration, but a relationship between all these factors of mind and emotions. Although in principle it seems nice to think that they are separate functions to be seen as having separate activities, it is not in actual fact so easy to cut them up as it were into their separate functions: they are like twine.

JGB. It is not so easy. But if you begin to see the consequences of this indiscriminate action of one part of us on another and how it makes us helpless to do what we really want to do, then you see that we must—easy or not easy—find a way of making the different parts of us each do their own jobs. There is an illustration, that belongs to really ancient wisdom, and which is quoted again and again. I remember Pak Subuh quoting it when talking in Sydney when we were there with him in 1958, in almost exactly the same terms as I have heard Gurdjieff quote it, and as it is to be found in the sacred writings of the East. This illustration compares man to a house in which there are many servants; each of whom is specialist for a particular job—the cooks, the grooms, the gardeners, the house-cleaners and so on. In a well-run house, each of the servants does his own job. In a badly run house, they begin to interfere with one another, and in a totally disorderly house they take no notice of anyone, each does just what he likes, putting his hand to what he does not know how to do. That is a picture of the situation which you can observe, but it is not integration. It can only be called muddle—mutual interference—and each part usurping positions that it has no right to.

Why does this happen? Because there is no master in the house. If there were a master, the servants would not be up to all this nonsense. But the master should not really have to go and see that the cook is in the kitchen, for example; there should be somebody doing that on his behalf, someone able to undertake that responsibility. This is the mind, and when I speak about intention, this is the beginning of the process of getting things into order. But even people who have followed such work as this for a long time and who have come to it in different kinds of ways, still need to remember that where we have full power to put things in order is in our intentions, and that we can bring clarity behind those intentions. Everyone is able to do that.

It is not so very hard to train one's body so that it will behave rightly and serve the master who is within; but very few people have power over their feelings and are sure that they will always feel what is important and not get drawn away by trivial things. The feelings are the hardest to manage, but they can be made to obey and some other time I will speak about this. Of course it is difficult and cannot be rushed, and it really cannot be done by force, it can only be done by all the different parts of us becoming aware of the absurdity and discomfort of living in that sort of chaotic way in which the average man lives. Nevertheless, the full control of our feelings is both possible and necessary for us. Only we must learn how it is to be achieved.

Saturday 14 November 1953: This morning as I was sitting on the floor eating a breakfast of hot milk, hard bread softened in the milk, olives and sheep cheese, my host Hadji Mehmed came and sat in front of me. Coughing all over me and my food, he told me once again the story of Saleh and the camel. This was in proof of God's omnipotence. Then he said, "There is no need to go so far. Look at the rivers; all the time they are pouring out water which if it were not taken away would flood the whole land. But God has made the sea to take all the waters, and has made it so that with all the water that enters it, the level of the sea never rises." Here I made a mistake and said, "Yes, it is wonderfully balanced. God has made it so that the sun lifts up the water and puts it into the clouds, from which it descends again as rain and fills the rivers." He was terribly shocked and said, "Never! You must not believe a thing like that. There is no such thing said in the *Quran*. God does not need the sun. He simply orders the sea to remain at the level He wills and it obeys him.'"

—from *Journeys in Islamic Countries*

15.
CONTROL OF FEELINGS

15 March 1964

IT IS SAID THAT we have some control over our thoughts and over our bodies, but that we have no control over our feelings. This is one of those half-truths that can be very misleading; and it can even be made into an excuse for allowing ourselves to have states of feeling that are undesirable because we are convinced that: "I cannot do anything about that," "I cannot help liking this," or "I cannot help disliking that person." It is just not true that we cannot help it all; only we must recognize what it is that we are able to do and what we cannot do.

Our feeling reactions are not controlled in the same way as thoughts can be, by the direction of our attention. I can choose some subject and direct my thoughts to that subject. This is possible because of the nature of thought, as its energy is very mobile and can therefore easily be shifted from one direction to another. But this very mobility of thought makes it unstable, so that although we may quite easily direct our thoughts to some particular object, we can never keep them on it for very long. Thoughts will always wander. This is also seen very clearly when we try to keep our mind empty of thoughts. Although it is not difficult to do this for a short space of time, it is literally impossible to do it for a long period. At the same time our minds can be emptied of thoughts by other ways; that is, there are various indirect procedures by which one can arrive at a state of blankness in one's inner attention.

Obviously our control over our bodies is quite different from our control over our thoughts. For example, although I can make my thought rise up to the ceiling without any difficulty, I cannot make my body do so. What I can do with my body usually comes about either through some habitually formed reaction, or by direction from my thought. The really immediate and direct control of the body is not such an easy thing, and we do not usually notice what is required for this until we set ourselves to learn some new skill or action where the body has to adapt itself to something it has not done before. I am saying this to remind you that, although we can do some things in the way of controlling thought and body, they are also subject to limitations.

It is the same with our feelings; we can control and direct our feelings within certain limits, if we understand what has to be done. For instance, we need not give way to our likes and dislikes; we have a certain power to refuse to let them dominate us. This means we can hold ourselves free from our reactions. But this is negative, it means simply a refusal to go with a reaction of like or dislike, or, as it is said, to be identified with our reactions. There is also a positive movement and we can learn how to make that movement and see for ourselves what it really does require.

There is a certain power in us which is best described by the word "trust." We can go in a certain way on trust or by trusting. If I trust in a power in myself that I shall be able to do something, then that trust will really enable me to do it, and that trust in one's own powers is something that we should develop and make stronger. It must be just right, because there is a false self-deceptive trust which makes us believe in ourselves where there is no ground for it; or we imagine that we can do things that we never do and then make excuses for ourselves and continue to imagine that we can do them. That kind of foolishness destroys real trust. Real trust is in the immediate action. At this moment, I know that it is possible for me to stand up and I trust in the power. If I decide to stand up I can rely upon my body to respond and obey the order to stand up.

It is also really as simple as that when it comes to dealing with our feelings. If we trust the power in us that says: "I will feel such-and-such," we shall feel it. The best way to study this and to exercise ourselves in it, is to take one particular kind of feeling and see that we really are able to evoke it, even if there is not anything there to stimulate it (because, as you know, nearly the whole time our feelings are simply reactions to some stimulation). As I said at the beginning, we say "I cannot help liking, or I cannot help feeling this or that," "I cannot help feeling angry when I see so-and-so." This means that we cannot help reacting to such and such a stimulus because we have got into the habit of supposing that our states of feeling are always dependent upon some stimulation that will produce them. We think that, to be angry, something has to make us angry; to be sad, something has to make us sad; to be excited, something has to make us excited. This is obviously not always true: because very often we are in a state of anger, and if we are noticing and observing ourselves, we can see that we are really looking round for something to be angry about, and anything will do to serve as an object of our anger.

Now the particular feeling that I am going to propose to take as an experiment today during the time that we are working, is the feeling of interest. About this also we tend to say "I cannot help being interested in such and such" or "I cannot make myself take an interest in such and such things," and that is quite true in a way. We cannot force our emotional states and we cannot produce them from our mental energy because this has not the power to produce images in the emotional center. At the same time, these images and these states will arise in the feelings if we have the idea and trust that the feeling that corresponds to it will arise in us. To verify what I am saying, you have to experiment with it.

For example, while you go about doing various things this morning, you may realize that you are neither interested nor not interested, or that your attention is half on what you are doing and half on some inward daydreams or something of this kind. When you observe that, you can decide that you will be interested and that you are interested. When you experience a feeling of this sort, it immediately produces a corresponding bodily state. You cannot have this feeling, or you cannot maintain it, if your body will not take the corresponding attitude, or posture, or condition. When we are interested there is a certain distribution of our attention and of our energies. If we are interested in something that we are looking at, the physical state of our eyes changes; our eyes open in a way that they were not open before. We notice things that we were not noticing before. If we are interested in an action, then that part of our bodies which is performing the action comes to life; we become aware of the contact, let us say, between our hands and what we are doing. This is usually almost imperceptible, so that people do not notice that a state of being interested is always accompanied by a bodily change.

In order to see this you have to observe more attentively, with more intention. If I say to myself "I will be interested in that carpet," I see the carpet at once in a different way, and I am not now just interested with my mind, by thinking about the carpet, I really feel this carpet is an interesting object. It begins to talk to me, it tells me how many people have trodden on it, how many lives it has been through before it came here, how it has become worn in the way that it is, how it has become stained in the way that it is stained. All that comes out towards me as I look at the carpet with a feeling of interest towards it, and none of these things came to me from the carpet when I was looking at it before.

I see somebody walking along in a particular way. When I become interested in the way he is walking, at once it begins to take on a meaning. I say to myself "He is walking like that because he intends to go and do such and such a thing; that is why he is walking a little more quickly than I would have expected him to walk." I notice things in this way because I have not only aroused in myself the feeling of interest, but my body also has responded to this. As I am speaking to you now, I take an interest in being interested. As a consequence I begin to feel differently the sound that is coming from my throat as I am speaking because this too has come within the field of my interest.

Interest is a state of feeling. It is not thought. It is just as much a state of feeling as being angry, or being astonished, or being pleased, or liking and disliking, and it is really not specially easy nor specially difficult to work at.

I have chosen it only because it is a very convenient state of feeling to use for this kind of study. Only, if you want to do this and learn from it something about the possibility of having the feelings that we choose to have; then you must realize that there is a difference between having the feeling of being interested and only thinking about it. You feel interest in your breast, but you think interest with your mind; that is, you have then only the thought of being interested. But you must also understand that you cannot have more than a passing moment of being interested unless your body cooperates.

To take another example, if you are angry and you wish to be in a state of calm, then your body itself must relax: it is not enough just to ask yourself not to have the feeling of anger. Or if, on the contrary, you need for a certain purpose to be angry and to manifest anger, again your body must play its part. But the chief thing I want to underline is that it is not such a remote or difficult thing as people sometimes imagine. It is only necessary to trust in yourself that if you choose to feel something you really can feel it. It is a very valuable hint that I am giving you here.

After-Lunch Discussion

Questioner. While you were speaking this morning, I noticed that when you referred to looking at things with interest, I became aware of the intensifying of colors in the carpet. They seemed to have a special quality, and the carpet *became* a carpet.

JG Bennett. It is quite true that when you look at something with interest, that something comes into existence for you. It begins to be what it is. As you say, the carpet became a carpet. Before, it was just part of your more or less undifferentiated stream of impressions. With your interest a connection is made that comes from the object as well as from you.

I want to repeat that what I am really concerned with is to point out that this is a voluntary power. It is not true as people commonly suppose, that we are only able to be interested in what happens to interest us and not capable of being interested in what does not appeal to us.

Q. I found I could not recognize what you said about the posture of the body in relationship to the establishing of an interest.

JGB. I did not mean posture exclusively, but referred to a certain change of state in the body that is recognizable. This is elusive, difficult to catch, because we are unaccustomed to observing the changes in bodily state that accompany changes in feeling. The point is that if we want to produce an intentional change of feeling we cannot do so unless the body is free to follow it. Some people go as far as to say that we can only act on our feelings through our bodies. It is not true that this is the only way: the real point is that the body is usually an obstacle, preventing us from acting on our feelings.

Q. I have often noticed, if I try to make small children think very hard, there comes a stage when they start moving around; and the harder the problem the more they move; and then their attention goes altogether.

JGB. Yes, this is not only true of children, but the habit is got in childhood, that is the trouble. In childhood one develops the habit of letting the body absorb the feeling state and then we are no longer able to control it, and with that we also lose control over our attention. Those people who attach so much importance to posture—like Ida P. Rolf, Moshe Feldenkrais, F. M. Alexander and others—have discovered something that is quite important in its own way, and that is the realization that we cannot change our ways of thinking and feeling if we leave our bodies to persist in their own habits. It is often much simpler to change a bodily habit than it is to change a mental or an emotional one. Therefore we can often liberate ourselves from emotional habits by working on posture. With children, the practice of stillness does seem to be important. When we had an experimental infant school here ten years ago, I used to watch how the children responded to what was called "the quiet exercise." It was really very striking and I think that it probably leaves a lasting benefit if it is done between the ages of two and five or so.

"If a new world is to come, we must first create it in ourselves. You may ask how the work of a few people can change the world. It has always been so. Ideas are powerful, not organizations. Nothing can be done by outward force; everything can be done by inner strength.

"Let me try to give you a picture of how such changes can come. Some of you no doubt are cooks and have had to make sauces. Suppose I am making some sauce, like a hollandaise, that is liable to demulsify, that is, the butter separates from the egg. This can be a terrifying experience if you are making a sauce for 60 or 70 people with pounds of butter and dozens of eggs. An inexperienced cook loses his head and beats the sauce violently—but only makes things worse. A good cook pours a little water at one edge of the bowl and stirs quietly until it turns back again, and then it spreads through the whole mass until the sauce is right again.

"The first time you do this, it seems almost miraculous. It is the same with the world. Everywhere people are stirring violently to get oil and water to mix. This cannot happen. The part of wisdom is to establish here and there centers in which right relationships can exist by the power of a common understanding of what is ultimately important. From such centers there can spread throughout the world—perhaps far more quickly than you might imagine possible—the seeds of a new world."

—from *Is There "Life" On Earth?*

16.
UNDERSTANDING AND HELP

6 June 1965

WE SHOULD KEEP in front of us that we are beings capable of growth,
development and transformation, not beings destined to remain such
as we are. The meaning of our lives is not to be found in what we are
now, but in what we can become. The conditions for this growth and
development are in part provided for us, but we have also in part to
create them ourselves. We are provided with nourishment of three
kinds: Nature gives us nourishment for our bodies; human culture
gives us psychic nourishment; and we are provided with spiritual
nourishment from a spiritual Source. But we cannot benefit by all this
provision unless a certain minimum cooperation comes from ourselves. We have to work in order to pay for and profit from the food that
is made available to us by the working of Nature, and this work, in one
way or another, has to be done. If we do not do it ourselves, someone
else has to do it for us, and we must not forget that in that case we are
in debt, because someone has done for us what we were required to do
for ourselves.

The same is true of our psychic nourishment. We can receive this
nourishment passively, by allowing other people to influence, encourage, support us, but if we do not make our own contribution corresponding to the nourishment we receive, here again we are in debt.

The same is not less true of our spiritual nourishment. This nourishment is being poured into the stream of human life and we can take
it out; but there is a difference here from the other kinds, and that is
that it is not possible for someone else to do the work for us, or only in

a very limited degree. That is, things which draw us towards a greater reality can be given to us, like psychic nourishment, through things that interest and excite us, but when it comes to the true spiritual nourishment, we have to recognize it, value it, take it in and make use of it ourselves.

All three forms of nourishment are for our growth: the growth of our physical body, the growth of our psychic body, the growth of our spiritual body. But this is not the whole story. There is also our will, which also requires something: it requires help, which is different from nourishment. This help firstly resides in the conditions which make it possible for us to begin to feel that we are able to meet the call and the hope of our life. It may therefore appear as a challenge, which even sometimes withholds the nourishment so that we are obliged to bestir ourselves in order to obtain it. So that sometimes this help appears to us as if it is something against our growth, as if it were depriving us of something that we need. This we do not understand unless we realize that, without this challenge, this other part of us—which is the part where our will must be present—cannot find itself.

There has therefore to be a certain distinction between the growth which comes from the different kinds of nourishment; and the strengthening of this other part in us. This part is strengthened firstly by overcoming difficulties and secondly by the clarification of what we truly wish for. What we wish for is what we serve. Wish is the magnet which draws us towards something to which we will give our service. Our service depends upon our understanding. The will of man, without understanding, is like a headless chicken. If we do not understand how to direct our wish, our desire to serve is drawn towards ourselves. It can be service towards our self-love or our fears, or habits, in which case that is where our wish is and that is where our will remains imprisoned. It can be as high as we choose to make it; that is, we can wish to serve the very highest and most perfect aim, that which is truly and wholly Right. But we cannot yet know what this is, nor have we the power or the means to serve it. Therefore all that we can do is to have an intention towards it. This intention is not nothing, however unsuccessful it is, however much we remain in ignorance and helplessness about it. We must never underrate this intention of ours; it is in our power to make it stronger. Again and again we should ask ourselves: "What do I really intend, what do I really wish that my life should serve?" And as it becomes clearer, a transformation accompanies it. That transformation is something other than growth, because it is transforming us from one kind of being to another. Therefore it is not just enabling us to develop our natural powers, or even our spiritual powers.

The possibility of being transformed is not offered to us in the way that nourishment is offered to us. It comes about because there is a higher will. When we have the intention to serve, we are getting connected with Something, or Someone, or we may picture it as a Will or Intelligence that we cannot yet know, but which is really there and, most important of all, which really does need us. Because of this we are given help, to which we at first are not able to respond, and sometimes it appears to us quite opposite to help. People often speak to me about things which appear to them to be obstacles, or events which appear to them to be failures, or states in which they think something has gone wrong with them, whereas it is possible to see from experience that, in many cases, what is happening to them is that they are being helped to make some step. But because they cannot yet understand, this help arouses in them revolt, despair, apathy and rejection. And yet these same people really intend and wish to serve; only they do not understand that help often comes in ways that we do not expect and cannot understand. With more experience, these situations or happenings which seem to us to be difficulties and failures, begin to come into a right perspective. We then begin to see that these apparent obstacles in the way are the very means by which this intention of ours can come to grips with our own need to relate ourselves to something higher. This is the second stage in understanding help. We still do not recognize its true nature, but we do begin to see for ourselves that what previously appeared to be failure and misery is really a means for us to make a step forward.

This help may also come to us in the form of joyful, blissful experiences which we are perhaps afraid of accepting fully because it seems to us that they are going to draw us away from our aim. We do not see that they are given to us in order to have a taste of what is a right relationship to something higher, which is certainly a blissful relationship. And so, as we reject suffering and failure and frustration, we also tend to reject the joys and the satisfactions of life. These can also be a form of help because they, as I said, are a way to get the taste of that state towards which we have to go.

For some people it is even sometimes harder to come to the understanding of this kind of help, and to see what it means, than to understand the other kind of help, that is, the opportunity of making the right use of our failures and sufferings. But one has to realize that this bliss, this satisfaction, whatever it is we may experience, is still only a means towards something, it is not to be taken as an end for itself. It is by passing through such experiences without identifying ourselves with them, that we can come to a third understanding. This is the beginning of true insight into the hidden pattern of Destiny. When we see how exactly timed and regulated the help is that is offered to us, we begin to have faith in the Intelligence that is behind it. The help that comes in this way is not always of a personal kind, we do occasionally get glimpses—perhaps in moments of special difficulty—when help comes that corresponds to our actual needs of that very moment. Even then, we sometimes do not even recognize what has happened to us because it appears to us as luck or accident.

I am saying all this to remind you that, in its early stages, help can reach us only with difficulty because of our own lack of understanding. We are cut off from it by all the wrong ways we have of thinking of almost everything that happens to us. Later, if our progress goes on in this way and we are not satisfied with growth and development, but really wish to be able to serve the purpose of our existence, we begin to develop the power to recognize help in a finer, more inward way, still not knowing where it comes from, but beginning to recognize what it is.

Beyond this there are, of course, further stages. Finally this relationship is seen and understood directly, and then man really knows where he belongs and who he is, and there is no separation between him and the Source from which he gets help. And then he is able to serve that Source fully, with everything he has, because there is no separation.

What I speak about now is the necessity of preparing ourselves to be able to recognize this relationship better. With people who are quite new to what we call Work, one of the earliest things it is useful to tell them about is the power of listening, to help them to see how seldom it is that we hear what is being said by another person. And this will lead to the realization of how little we hear of what is being said within us: how our capacity for hearing ourselves is clouded by our own habits. If you will practice listening, if you will practice simply observing and noticing what happens within you, you are already on the way to being able to recognize better how help comes to us. When you begin to understand how unexpectedness—disturbance of our habitual ways of living, sometimes unexpected suffering, sometimes unexpected bliss and satisfaction, new interests and so on—may be a means for us to understand differently and better what our lives are for; not just something to be borne because it is painful, or to be grasped after because it is delightful, then you will take another step forward towards deeper understanding.

What I advise, in our work today, is that when you remember it you should practice, as well as you can, the noticing of opportunities. Perhaps you will then see the difference between what I call help and the nourishment about which I spoke at the beginning. One should distinguish between what gives us energy for life, for work and so on, and what makes it possible for us to come to this inner communication with the Source of Help present in us. This is a very perilous thing. Therefore one should approach it first of all from easily understood outward things and not come too quickly to suppose that we can receive higher forms of help for which we are not yet ready.

After-Lunch Discussion .

Questioner. I have been coming here for a long time, but today I came across a part of the garden I had never noticed before.

JG Bennett. It is just a helpful indication. It reminds you that you can sit right next to something and not see it. It may help you to believe that what you want is nearer to you than you think and that *not being able to see* is the obstacle rather than the remoteness of what you are looking for. When you really come to understand, truly and completely, that this Truth we are looking for is closer than anything can possibly be, and it is simply that the capacity to see it is not yet formed in us, then, by that realization, it already begins to form. But as long as we think that it is somewhere else, that there are some external conditions that have first to be fulfilled, or that one day somebody will come along and tell us, then we have still much to learn. When you are really convinced that the truth is very, very close and that all that has to happen is that you have to have your eyes open, then it is a big step.

Q. You said this morning, one is perhaps rejecting help because it is unpleasant. Can you tell us how to conduct oneself in such situations?

JGB. It is a very good thing to picture to oneself that all the situations of our life are presented to us by the loving Intelligence whose purpose is to help us. For the time being, it does not matter whether we are convinced of this or not. It is good practice and can have a great effect on our lives if we go along as if it were so. I was thinking about this after I had spoken this morning, and the familiar picture of an ant trying to get back to its home came to me. It has obstacles in the way, and if you poke it with a stick to help it, probably the last thing it realizes is that a higher intelligence is acting. It is not bad to picture oneself as an ant and think that somebody with a big stick is poking at us to help us. In all ways of thinking of it, it is better to suppose that the things that happen to us happen with the intention of being a help, than to suppose that we are living in the middle of a meaningless, feelingless world.

Q. But the majority of our miserable situations are those that have been caused by ourselves! So how can we think that it is a good thing that has happened to us? It seems to me that we are in this state only because of something we have done in the past; we cannot blame anyone for it but ourselves.

JGB. One half of the story, as you put it, is true: that we reap what we have sown. Another part of the story is that in any situation there is always the possibility of profit. But the profit does not come by itself. If, in some foolish way, I have sown the causes of some unpleasant experiences, this I have got to reap and I have got to bear. But that is not the whole story, because from this foolishness of mine a lesson can be learned, and this possible lesson is something much more positive than that I should merely realize I should not have been so stupid. From this mistake, from this failure and the unpleasant consequences of my action, I may be able to make a step forward.

Let me take it the other way round: when pleasant and joyful experiences come to us, how do we take them? We do not usually think that we have earned them and that this is the fruits of our good actions: "I deserve this good bit of luck." We think it just happened like that; we may even have a kind of guilty feeling: "Why should I have had this bit of luck?" Or, more frequently, we do not connect it with anything and it never occurs to us to give the experience a meaning or to look upon it as a means for transformation. It is quite true that this could not have come to us unless our previous life had made it possible, but it came to us in that particular way and at that particular moment in order that we may be able to move to something else.

It is really hard for us, brought up to think that man alone has any purpose, to realize that there is a pattern and a meaning in everything that exists. It is sometimes said that to love nature is preparation to love God, but nevertheless, people usually think of the beauty of nature as something that has no purpose; either it just happens to be beautiful or it was created in order to cheer us up. But the deep purpose to be understood by us human beings is that the power of admiration should develop in us through the admiration of nature, and that we should, from that, go beyond and be able to admire what is not visible, not tangible. In the same way, when suffering comes, it is a means for our power of freedom to grow. When you come to see it more deeply, you will realize that joy and suffering are justly divided in the world; one has to have the one and one has to have the other. There is not the possibility in this world of having joy without suffering, and it is not possible either to have suffering without joy. One will come, the other will come; it has to be. All those things are only means to an end, but through these means we are prepared for that state where we shall taste the Reality. And yet, no law is broken; everything has to be fulfilled, all consequences of actions have to be reaped. The great stumbling block for many people is that they only see the law of cause and effect, or what is called karma—that one simply reaps what one sows and there is nothing more to it—and fail to see that all this is only a means, opportunities, not the end.

Q. Could you tell us something about "The fear of the Lord is the beginning of Wisdom?"

JGB. Some time ago I spoke about fear and its connection with sensitivity, and what you ask now is not irrelevant to what I am talking about today. Without sensitivity, wisdom cannot come. You can do many things with a stone, but you cannot teach it discrimination and wisdom. Why is this? Because its responses are not sensitive; it just has to be what it is. People who are insensitive are like stone's, they cannot be taught, because they are not afraid of ignorance. When fear, which is in all sensitive people, is transformed, then it opens them up to the awareness of destiny. In that transformation fear is converted into something different.

We must distinguish between subjective or imaginary fear and objective or productive fear. There is the subjective fear which is an inward slavery—the fear of people and of what people will think of us, the fear of the future and so on; all this is subjective. When you begin to be free from that, you begin to see that we are in the hands of very great forces and then, through the transformation of your fears, you begin to be able to be aware of these forces. When you are able to accept your condition and the destiny that is allotted to you in the great process, you cease to be afraid of it and your fear then becomes the means by which you can respond. It loses this character of subjective fear. But it still remains; it still has this property of making us more than ordinarily sensitive.

17.
UNDERSTANDING AND WHOLENESS

20 June 1965

THERE ARE RIGHT AND WRONG ways of bringing things together. The separate parts of a whole cannot work properly unless they are integrated into that whole in such a way that each part helps the other. This is obvious in the case of our bodies, for instance, which cannot work properly unless our hands and our feet, our minds and our hearts and the rest are all integrated into a living whole. It cannot be said that something is good for one part of the body and bad for another part, because everything is well or ill together. So it is with humanity: there cannot be something beneficial to one part and harmful to another part; but this is not so obvious to us because the scale is so great and our tendency is to see things in a narrow and limited perspective. But we must hold on to the idea that there is an integral whole to which we certainly belong and in which we must, and must want to, find our own place. But it is certainly also true that we do not know how this "body of humanity" is put together, and if we try to integrate it according to our own ideas, we may make quite monstrous constructions, putting the wrong things in the wrong places; like someone ignorant of the real structure of a human body would do if he tried to put the different members and organs together. Integration without understanding can be a very dangerous undertaking, and we have therefore to hold a balance between our feeling of the need for integration and all that threatens us from our ignorance. Through ignorance we try to put things together that will not work together; but we also keep things apart that need one another and cannot prosper without one another.

The same is true of our inner transformation. We are meant to be one whole. We must look towards complete integration of our nature—both the visible, outer nature and the invisible nature which is not yet realized in us. No way of life can be satisfying that does not look towards an ultimate integration, a oneness of our whole nature. And no private way of life can be satisfying unless it looks towards an integration of all human life into the whole purpose of existence, beyond human life. Nevertheless, we must be careful to remember that there can be a wrong kind of wholeness or false integration. Wholeness built on the wrong foundation can be disastrous. We must have the conviction that the only secure way of looking at either ourselves or at life together is that it should be towards oneness, towards integration, towards everything being in its right place and doing its right work. But, there again, we must not forget our own ignorance. If I try to put things together in myself without knowing how they work, I am like a blundering mechanic who tries to put the parts of a car together without even knowing how a car is constructed. This same principle applies therefore to the various techniques and methods that are required for this process of integration of ourselves. If they are not used in the right way, at the right place, at the right time, in the right order, they will not produce integration, they will produce monsters, or trouble, or at the very least a great waste of time and effort.

So, side by side with integration we must look towards science as the opposite of ignorance—science in the highest, fullest sense of this word, meaning knowledge of what is and what has to be, and knowledge, above all, of how it is all to be done. Those of you who sometimes visited Mr. Gurdjieff will remember how he did extraordinary things with people and behaved in ways that in an ordinary sense would look outrageous and then would turn round and, with a beaming smile, say: "You not surprised what I do such things? Why you think I do such things? Because I have science." He had science, up to what point one cannot know, but certainly science that we did not have; that is, the science of man and of his nature and how it is to be put together. It is very necessary for us to remember that understanding of this science is also a necessary aim for us. It is no use to hope for an ideal unless we also know how to work for the ideal.

In the history of mankind, there have been times when science is broken down into specialized knowledge and times when it is built up again into an integrated knowledge. There are cycles of concentration and of expansion, as everyone can see who studies history. And this is true not only in the outward life, it is also true in the inward life. There are times when the situation of the world is such that the outward life has to develop, as it has been doing over the last thousand years, and man has made immense progress in his science of nature and in his ability to work with the forces of nature. This was necessary to enable progress to be made for the human race as a whole. But during all that time man has been sorely lacking in the science of his own inner nature. He has not known either how he himself is to be integrated, or the ways in which human society should be integrated.

It is obvious that this is so, because all our attempts to integrate human society, however well-meaning and with whatever energy it was done, have failed because what is required was simply not known. It is easy to look back over the history even of this century and see that people just did not know how to build up a human society that is able to work in an integrated way. And it is also obvious that very little knowledge of the inner or spiritual life was available to people. For a long, long time we have been told what we have to do, how we ought to live, but we have not been told the way, the technique of doing it. This is because these techniques have been dispersed. Various groupings, the different religions of the world, various teachings have preserved bits of this knowledge here and there, but nowhere is there to be seen a total integrated science of man's spiritual nature. This is something each one of us can see for himself or herself. It does not require a great deal of reading or study, because it is obvious that if this science were available, we should, all of us—certainly everyone here—have gone to the source of it.

If you have come here today to take part in the work we are doing here, it is, I suppose, because you have some hope that there is some way towards this science, towards this knowledge, and perhaps here there will be a chance of finding something out about it. And this is true, we do have some knowledge here and some access to a more integral understanding of man's nature through what we are doing here. Only this must not be taken to mean that we possess all this knowledge or even an authentic fragment of it. We have little more than an indication that it exists and that there is a way to it. But if this way is to be found, we must hold on very strongly to this; that we want the whole, the total integral science, in so far known to man, of how man is to live; in himself and in community. This is what we have to look for, and nothing less than this. That certainly means that we will have to make sacrifices, that we will have to accept very much which at the present time we cannot understand. But, at the same time, we must be very careful not to think that we can build before we know how to build, that we can integrate before we know what is the structure that we are trying to integrate. Although we have studied very much here at Coombe and have access to traditional knowledge and even personal, direct teaching of very great value, it is still only the beginning.

What hope have we that this beginning will lead on to something more? It is connected with what I said earlier about cycles, about time. We can all of us see that here and now, in the middle of this twentieth century, we are in a different phase of world history from what has been current for the last thousand, or two thousand—or even more—years. We are at a time when enormous changes are taking place and we can also see that man is not prepared for them and does not know what to do about it. But we must also have trust that what is not generally known, is known somewhere, by those to whom this knowledge has been entrusted. You may have heard it said that at times like this, at times of great changes—really and truly revolutionary times—when the world is not moving slowly, step by step, but is passing through great convulsions—during such times a special work has to be done of collecting together again what has been neglected or misused, so that a new power, new knowledge, new conditions, will be available when the world is ready for them. Be sure that we are in just such a time as that!

At such times, all our attitudes have to be different from what they are in times when things are going forward more or less quietly, when it is sufficient to preserve what one has and sufficient also to be loyal to a narrow and even isolated society, without concerning oneself with the whole. Now it is different. All small loyalties, all readiness to sit on what one has, all refusal to share with others and refusal to admit that others have value that we have not got—are contrary to the spirit and needs of our time. Such attitudes may have merit and even do have merit at other times, but now they are great sins. Now, we have to overcome in ourselves all narrowness, all sense that "I have something which other people have not got," that "My particular group, my particular society, my country, my anything is somehow to be respected and valued differently from other things." And this is not so easy as it looks; it requires a great inner discipline to be determined to see what is good in what is not our own and to value and respect what we do not understand—even what we disagree with. Only in this way can we hope that we shall become connected with a more integral world than we have been up till now.

This does not mean, though, that we can take upon ourselves to pick up bits here and bits there and try to make a total construction. This is the awkwardness of it, that in spite of the necessity for integration, we still are faced with our own ignorance. We do not know how to judge what is valuable and what is worthless; what should be used now and what should be used for some other time; what belongs to the past and is no longer applicable to the present situation—all this requires knowledge we have not got.

How are we to face these big demands? Only by using whatever understanding we may have of the things I have been talking to you about earlier. There are certain things one can always do, and one is to rectify one's own understanding, to struggle against narrowness, against rejection, and also to struggle against cocksureness and the belief that one already knows something, that one is already able to make judgements. All of this is an inner straightening out, which every one of us can and has to do.

We have to hold on to this: there is nothing that any one of us knows that contains the whole truth or even one tenth part of it. Everything that we know is a fraction of the whole. Behind the scenes, hidden from us, is the whole real structure that we are trying to understand. We should have no doubts that the real structure towards which human life is moving is really there. But also we must be quite sure that no one we know has direct knowledge and understanding of this structure: no school, no teaching, no religion, no society, no way of life, no theory—none of them is even nearly complete.

You must also remember and really grasp, with regard to the techniques of our own inner work, that it is an immensely complicated thing to set to work to transform a man. To try to do this ignorantly will either cause destruction or be an appalling waste of effort and time. So that we should always be striving towards science, always hoping that we shall be able to understand more, or find someone who understands more.

[Mr. Bennett then gave explanations about the "stop" exercise.]

After-Lunch Discussion

Questioner. I found that, when you called "stop" this morning, somehow the state I was in was never particularly dispersed. But during lunch I woke up and saw that I had been daydreaming for a long time. This terrified me, because I thought: "Supposing I died while I was daydreaming like that, what happens then?" How does one wake up—or

can one wake up—if one dies in a state where one is completely identified with daydreaming?

JG Bennett. The greatest handicap we people live under, is that we
have got something in us which makes us forget that we have got to
die; and therefore we do not feel it necessary to be prepared. Of course
we can comfort ourselves by saying: "After all, death will not be such a
difficult step; things will go on more or less as they do now, and even
though we shall not have a physical body, we shall have something to
work with." But believe me, it is not so simple or so easy as that. If
something is not prepared, this very state of daydreaming that you
describe will continue. And if there is nothing prepared, there is no
escape. The state of affairs of those who have nothing prepared in them
is that they simply dream and dream until the energy for dreaming is
used up and then they do not dream any more and then there is nothing. So really and truly it is important that something should be
prepared.

If you cannot bring yourself to believe that it really is important that
we should prepare something before we die, then look at how our lives
go from day to day. Somehow or other, we have got to establish in ourselves this conviction that something must be formed in us. It is not
something which appears from nowhere because the material from
which it is to be made is already there. We have the material for a soul,
but this must not be an excuse for us to do nothing with that material.
People say "Either I have a soul, in which case it is all right, or I have
not got a soul, in which case it does not matter anyhow," and they
think this is an answer to the whole thing. It is nothing like so simple
as that. We have the material out of which this something permanent
is to be made, and this material cannot be destroyed by dying; it has
got to remain. This realization you have just described—of seeing that
one can be in a state where there is nothing at all except daydreams—
really must give you an idea of what it is to die without something prepared. But the very fact that you are able to see this means that
already something has started to form in you. That means that you
can have hope, but it does not mean that you can take comfort.

As I said at the beginning of my answer, it is a very remarkable
thing about man that he is usually protected from the realization that
he must die until he is ready and able to face it and ready and able to
do something about it. It can happen that this realization comes to
someone before he is ready for it, and then it is too much for him. So
that this protection, this shield that is put round the part of us that

really knows what death is, is really necessary. In the same way as it is necessary for a seed to have a shell round it to protect it before it is ready to grow. If it has not got this protection, it will simply rot away and be destroyed. So this seed of the soul in us has to be protected until it is able to germinate and grow. But at the same time one must know that this shell has to be discarded when the seed is beginning to grow. People who are not going to grow do not feel their situation because all they can see and know about is the shield which hides it all; they do not feel that they have got a seed in them that may rot, may lose its chance of life. This must not be taken as a special kind of kindness to man, to make life easy for him, but because this protection is necessary until a seed is able to bear the action of life. But once this begins, once you really begin to wish for life, then you have to be prepared to do without the shell which protects you from seeing the truth.

Q. What happens to all the countless millions who must die without knowing about this? Will they have another chance?

JGB. Who are they? If they *are*, they must have another chance. But if they are not, then *who* is to have the chance?

Q. That is a very fine distinction which I am not able to answer. I just think of the majority who may die in this grievous state because so very few are able to benefit from a teaching like you give. There must be, as I said, countless millions who die without knowing that there is such a possibility.

JGB. Why do you refer to me? Does not every religion give men the same hope and the same warning? No, it is not dependent upon the teaching I give or anyone else gives; something else is required. Teaching is only to awaken this life; no teaching can give this life. There is a certain inner attitude within people which decides whether they have a hold on life or not. If they have that hold on life, then you can say that such a person is, and he will have the chance to achieve what is needed. The reality of the situation is that it depends upon what we are. This is how we have to see it for ourselves-whether it concerns countless millions or not is beside the point. It does not matter whether somebody else is rich or poor, I remain what I am, my problem is my problem. This does not mean that my problem is one that I can solve by myself, that I am isolated from my fellow-men-very far from it. There is precious little hope for anyone to achieve life in isolation from other people, but it still remains true that unless I belong to life, life does not belong to me.

Q. If the seed shoots before the soil is ready, whether spontaneously or induced by anything else, does this mean that the germ suffers irreparable damage?

JGB. It is not quite like this. I do not want to speak in detail about this kind of thing because it belongs to another conversation; that is, about the destiny of people who start, and things do not develop as they should, and so on. You must recognize that this is all expressed very succinctly and well, in the Parable of the Sower and the Seed.* This parable must not be taken as an interesting picture; it is about how life really is for man, how it has been and always will be. The meaning of this parable will not change.

Q. I would like to know more about understanding things and doing things. It always seems pretty obvious to me that I do not understand enough to do properly what I am trying to do. It seems that understanding hardly ever fits in with the time in which we can do things. For instance, I do not understand how to bring up children, and by the time I may understand, it will be too late. And so also perhaps about death. I feel I might not have reached the right understanding when death comes. It seems not quite fair to me.

JGB. It is true, there is something wrong and unreasonable about life. Man is at the present time put in front of situations that are beyond him. And it is not just a matter of twenty years' time, it will perhaps be twenty thousand years—a long time, anyhow—before mankind will have reached the stage of maturity when the sort of situation that we are meeting with today will really be dealt with and understood. You must realize that this is not your private affair, there are a hundred million other parents who are in the same situation as you are and it therefore ceases to be private. The problem expands out from this to the whole situation of the world, in its politics, in its society, in its economics, in its population and so on.

On the face of it, it seems unfair that man should be required to do things that are beyond his understanding. But this is only "on the face of it." Deeper down, it is quite different. We are not left without help, mankind is not left to its own resources in the way it seems to be. This applies all the way from private affairs to the whole process of the life of mankind. If we really had nothing to bring up our children with except our own understanding of children, it would indeed be disastrous, because we can see for ourselves how little we understand of what is actually required. But there is something which makes up for this: children usually grow up so much more normal, so much more hope-

* Matthew 13,3; Mark 4,3; Luke 8,5.

ful than we have any right to expect. And this is not just for you and me, but, as I said, for a hundred million parents besides.

We must learn to trust that there is *something* that is wiser than we are. Just in the same way, when you open your newspapers or look at anything connected with the goings-on of mankind, you would say "These people here, living on this planet, are in for a very sticky end, and that quickly." But it is not true. It is not going to happen like that, because there is a greater wisdom that is acting in this situation, and acting in a way that we cannot understand. But it is acting.

When I said, a few minutes ago, that if we could see the purpose that we have to serve, and how wonderful it is and how great a wisdom there is connected with that purpose, none of us would hesitate, we would give all our lives to serve that, and we would do everything in order to be prepared so that we could serve it. But it so happens that this very thing cannot be declared, because this purpose would be ruined if it were turned into an ordinary formula as to how things should be done; a plan that could be described. It is the same with your life and my life, and the lives of our children; there is something there which is to be realized for us all. But the very nature of that something is that we have got to find it, that we cannot know it in advance. Because we cannot find it, we are all the time being helped, our mistakes are being put right. And you know well enough that you make mistake after mistake but because you wish for good, things go better than you have any right to expect; there is no doubt about it. Is it not so?

Q. Yes, but one still goes on worrying too much about them.

JGB. Yes, it is so. It is a very strange thing that we, such as we are-the minds that are listening to me speaking and I, speaking to you-all of this is on one side and, on another side, there is a wisdom that we cannot see. Compared with that wisdom, all of us are children, and that is why we are worried, we are anxious because we cannot see how things can work out. But they do. There is-we must really believe this-something to be trusted, and the more we trust it, the more it is able to help us. You know the picture Gurdjieff gives about man: "Like a fish. Fish is out of the water and fish knows that if it does not get back into the water it will die. A passing man has compassion on fish and wants to put it back, but when he picks up fish, it squirms out of his hands, because it just cannot trust the man long enough to be put back into the water." This is a true picture of our situation. We do not trust the higher wisdom that is there, behind the scenes, and therefore it is not able to help us as much as it wishes to help us. As much as the man can help the fish, he does help the fish; but if the fish persists in trusting its own capacity for squirming more than the man's capacity for throwing it into the water, it is likely to come to the end of its life very quickly.

Q. About this science of higher wisdom; it seems to be implied in what you are saying that there is, in everyone who is searching for understanding, the potentiality to accept and receive, to some degree, this science of integration. It seems a very remarkable situation that man always has the potential to understand this, but he is not always given the chance of receiving it. Is that the case?

JGB. You must realize that the great purpose is the evolution of humanity towards integration and consciousness, so that the human race will become one whole, able to serve a still higher purpose in the Cosmic Plan. This higher purpose must be more important than the transformation of individuals. In the working-out of history there are periods of development and there are periods of renewal. Development proceeds in relatively quiet conditions. Then there is no urgency and people are neither under the same pressure nor do they have the same opportunities as in periods of renewal. To us a renewal period may look like a catastrophe or, at least, a severe strain. At such times, far more help is given to mankind by the higher wisdom. It can be given because more people become aware of their need. Also more conscious, integrated people are required.

In ordinary times, comparatively few transformed individuals suffice to preserve and transmit the hidden science. In times of great stress, these people have to come out into the world—sometimes they even come into the open and are seen and known by ordinary people. For this, they have to be specially trained. It happens at such times that there is need for more people and less time for them to be trained, and therefore more help has to be given. At the present moment there is more need for people who can understand than there has been for a very, very long time. Perhaps never in the history of mankind has it been so important that there should be people who could really understand what is happening. And there is not very much time. It may well be that before your generation has completed its span, things will have changed very greatly in this world. How it will change and how successful the transformation will be, will depend on how many people can understand and co-operate with it. It happens also that all this is foreseen and provided for, even to the extent that a greater proportion of children with more capacity for understanding are born at such times than at other times.

Q. This is on the assumption that it is all governed by a wisdom and not left to blind chance?

JGB. That is how I see it. And more and more, as I grow older and come to see more things—not only in quantity but also in depth—the more sure I am that there is a purpose and a wisdom behind the historical process. Not far away, not on the other side of the next galaxy, but right here.

Q. Would you say that fear hampers us a great deal; that we cannot open to what you say because fear holds us back, in everything?

JGB. Yes, it is certainly true. But at the same time, fear can make us sensitive to what is needed, as I told you last time. When M. was speaking about waking up and seeing that he had been for a long time in a state of daydreaming, this is a frightening experience, but from that fear understanding can come. The thing is to know how to have clever fear and not stupid fear. Our trouble is that so much of our fear is stupid: about things that will not happen and that we could do nothing about if they did happen. If we look at ourselves, we can see that we are not menacing anyone, and yet we think that other people are menacing us, and so on. This all belongs to the kinds of stupid fears that we have to be free from. But this does not mean that one should not have a real, good, necessary fear. One should be fearful of one's ignorance, like A. was saying. This is a right kind of fear, but it can easily turn into stupid fear. My task with A. is to protect her all the time from turning a good fear, which is right, into a stupid fear which spoils everything for her.

Question: Could you say something about what our attitude should be towards failure?

JG Bennett: Yes. I must say something about this. To fail because you don't understand what is wanted, is bad. This is because we have an obligation to understand. To fail because of other obligations we have, which are of an objective character, is not bad. It is not good to make exaggerated sacrifices. You may well say: "How can I understand, if I don't understand?" You must learn to see that you can't understand by having things pointed out to you. I am saying all this, to show you one thing that we do have, that is within our power— and with respect to which we do, therefore, have an obligation—and it is this: We have it in our power to know what it is we want. To ask ourselves: "What is it that really matters to me?" With the asking, and the requiring of a sincere answer of ourselves, we will always make a step in our own understanding. By asking oneself this question: "What do I really want?" one inevitably brings all sorts of things into focus for oneself. Only when we avoid asking it, can we continue to live with our own contradictions and self-deceptions.

I'm talking about attitude. The one thing man can control is attitude—behavior, seldom. But a man can put away self-deception, with regard to what is really important to him. This is the very axis—the core—on which the whole is built up. If we are really clear about this all the other things will fall into place. We can't even hope to live according to our own attitude, but we can demand of ourselves that we should be really clear about what we want to come to in this life. Then everything we do has meaning in relation to that. If I am not real, then nothing else is real. C.S. Lewis' "solid" people are real. What will come of your life is not in your power, but it is in your power to wish to be something. We have always to remember this also: Nothing whatever can go on as it was. Everything has to change, otherwise it dies.

—Coombe Springs Group "S" Notes, 1964.

18.
THE TWOFOLD MIRACLE OF LIFE

4 July 1965

AS YOU WERE WALKING DOWN to the Djami this morning, you came through a living world. You saw plants and trees and birds and animals, and you felt more or less of a contact with this life that surrounds us. But what is this life? We may think about it, but with our thinking power alone we do not perceive the reality of it. An instinctive contact is needed with living things and with everything that bears life. By "bearing life" I mean not only living organized forms, like animals and plants, but also the surface of our earth, which has been transformed over thousands of millions of years to support life. When we look at the earth and at all that grows and lives on it, we see a process of transformation. As we see the process of life, we recognize that it is not simple change—like the changes of weather—but transformation in a definite direction. Life takes in the inert materials of the earth's crust and converts them into millions of forms. It does more than this, for it creates all over the earth states of sensitivity and responsiveness that are quite foreign to inert matter. We ourselves are altogether involved in these transformations. We could not exist without them and we know it. But we are far from understanding their full significance. We can perhaps come nearer to understanding if we apply the alchemical formula: "Learn to separate the fine from the coarse." All life is engaged in this separation. By "coarse" here we mean the inert materials of earth, air and water, on which life feeds, and by "fine" we mean the sensitive energies, in all their marvelous variety, that living creatures concentrate and transform.

When we really are able to look at life as transformation, to see the rising of quality in the materials of the world towards the finest experiences we know, we must also be very certain that this transformation goes on beyond us, and that we men cannot be the summit and the end. One very great service that science has done for man has been to show us that we are very small in the vast existing world and that our time-scales, our scales of magnitude, our possibilities of understanding, are very small compared with the universe in which we live. And this concerns not just this earth and this solar system, but immensities which are quite beyond our powers of picturing.

Nevertheless, science has not yet been able to show us that with this vast complexity of the universe there also go higher and higher transformations of substances to modes of experience and consciousness immeasurably transcending what we know. From the realization that we only occupy a humble place in the scale of spiritual beings, inevitably follows the question: "If there are higher intelligences, higher powers, greater and better than we are, why do they not help us, why do they not transform this earth and this human life on the earth into a more ideal world?" It is right to ask this question; we should even insist with ourselves upon finding an answer to it, because this must be the key to our hope of understanding the riddle of our existence.

We can, if we like, reject the very idea that there is anything higher and more powerful in this universe than man. We may say that we are now living at a difficult moment and that a thousand or ten thousand years hence man will have evolved to a point where he will, himself, by his own intelligence and his own unaided powers, have produced a state of affairs on this earth that corresponds to what we believe and feel to be the right world for man to be living in. I think those of us who are here could not accept such a glorified view of what man is and what he can accomplish by his own unaided powers. We feel compelled to face the more difficult question: "Accepting that there are higher intelligences, why do they not do more for us?"

Everyone knows that it is not so hopelessly impossible to answer this question and that the necessity to understand the meaning of our very development and evolution lies in the answer to it. But what I do want to say to you is that we should be aware of, keep in front of us, remind ourselves of the transformation that is going on around and within every one of us. We should remember to look upon ourselves as participating in what I am going to call a second life; that is, a transformation within a transformation, a life within a life, a growing within the growing of nature. The one proceeds visibly and maybe inevitably, we do not know; anyhow, it has been going on for two or three thousand million years on this earth alone. But we also know that there is, in us all, a second life or a second transformation. In one sense, we can look upon the visible transformation of life as the condition of this second one. In another sense, we can look upon this first life as a symbol and reminder, a paradigm, of this other life inside, of the second transformation.

This other life is not an inevitable part of the natural process of life, but is offered to us as a possibility, which we can accept freely or allow to pass us by. It must be clear to us all that the nature of this second life is that it is permitted, we are allowed to have it, it is offered to us, it is not given to us readymade and it is not forced upon us. As is said in Deuteronomy [30,19]: "Behold, I have set before you this day life and death, blessing and cursing; choose therefore life that you and your seed may live." This offer of life and with it the choice of life is the essence of the second transformation. It is very closely linked, certainly, with the notion of the presence of higher intelligences than man. Obviously, it contains the seeds of the solution of the problem of why these intelligences, if they are wise and powerful and also compassionate towards our human race, do not change the situation. This second transformation, this second life, is such a special gift that its potential must be carefully safeguarded by those powers that understand it. So they will do only what is unavoidable in the way of not interfering with our affairs. It may even be that they have no right to do more than is necessary to preserve our existence and our possibilities; but not to the extent of depriving us of the effective choice on which the second transformation depends.

I think all of us do know that the answer must lie in some such understanding of our situation. The more we are able to see what this second life is, the more we see why it has to be as it is; that is, a precarious thing that we are always in danger of losing and that depends on our incessant choice. When we begin to understand that, so many of the problems that confront us take on a different aspect, and that is why it is useful for us to keep it in mind.

One reason why I always wish that when we work together we should have the opportunity of working in closer contact with Nature is because Nature is both a reminder and a help to us in understanding our own place. What we do with plants and animals is not unlike what has to be done with us by the higher intelligences. We know ourselves that there are limits to the interference that is desirable in our dealings with Nature, or we ought to know it. Unfortunately, man at the present time has got badly out of step with this responsibility of his; but we should know and understand it in our dealings with Nature—and not only with living things, but with all natural objects, even the human artifacts that we have to deal with in our work. We should see that a certain relationship has to be maintained and try to experience ourselves also in a similar relationship with powers and intelligences higher than our own; but this requires from us a really deep humility about the human situation. It is not so easy for us to look upon ourselves as no more important to these higher intelligences than trees and plants and animals are to us, and perhaps even pots and pans that have to be kept clean and have to be used for certain purposes and are interesting to us just because of their use. As far as we are concerned we are, it is true, a special kind of pots and pans that can cooperate intelligently with their users. But we do not like to think of ourselves as no more than instruments whose existence is justified only by their usefulness. We do not want to face the possibility that this may be the true situation. We like to think that we are the masters of the situation, that we are using the world, not that we are here to serve and to be used. This is repugnant to us.

For some reason or other, men have, for several centuries, been more and more conditioned to think of themselves as masters—or potential masters—of the world, and not as servants and instruments. And, therefore, a considerable deconditioning process is required to accept that we are, and must be, instruments in the hands of higher intelligences, and that the best thing for us is to be able to cooperate willingly and consciously with those Higher Intelligences.

I suggest that for today we take as an exercise to try to see, as we deal with the living things in the garden, with inert objects, with human artifacts, or with the preparation of food, that all of this is part of the great process of transformation in which we are ourselves involved, not only in the dominant role, but also in the role of servants, of instruments.

I myself have found that when I set myself for a day or two to exercise my attention in this way—constantly reminding myself throughout the day that I am part of the transformation process—that my own sense of my existence changes. I become aware that I exist not less—in the ordinary way that people imagine they exist—but much more, in the substantial sense.

You can look at it in this way: supposing my hand were cut off, and supposing it could keep its own life as a hand, it would feel self-important, thinking "I can do something that nothing else can do." But we know how much more significant this hand is as a part of my body. This hand would certainly have to surrender something to accept to be reintegrated into my body. If it were quite ignorant of what it meant to be part of a body, it might be an almost unbearable sacrifice, having had the sense of freedom, of self-importance of being a hand all on its own. We have just this kind of illusion of independence, and fear of sacrificing and losing something if we were to be integrated into a living whole in which we should be merely a part. We cannot picture this to ourselves because we are so conditioned to the illusion that man is an endpoint of creation instead of a midpoint. You must remember that these things—which, as I am saying them to you probably seem quite obvious—are totally foreign, not only to our ordinary ways of thinking, but to our very feeling of what it means to be oneself. Therefore quite a considerable effort is required to bring oneself to the awareness that what really matters is that we are part of the process of transformation, not that I am I or you are you, as isolated individuals.

After-Lunch Discussion

Questioner. When there is a pressure of work, one tends to put one's attention on this instead of having some to spare for observing interactions between oneself and the job.

JG Bennett. We have to recognize the rhythm of the activity. If there is pressure, there will be a time when all your attention is needed by the job in hand, and in that case it is an obligation to put all your attention on it. But in the rhythm of every job there are pauses, either in the activity or in the attention that we have to give to it. And even if pauses do not appear naturally, they should be introduced, because we should learn to work rhythmically. Rhythm is an alternation of tension and relaxation, of intensity and letting go. If you find that you are doing something in such a way that you are in a constant state of tension in doing it—either physical or mental—this should be a warning that it is not being rightly done, because it is not more efficiently done by doing it in a constant state of maximum tension.

Our processes of transformation provide a certain quantity of the energy that has to flow into anything we do. This is partly accumulated and preserved, but partly it is being produced and drawn on as fast as it is produced. This also we have to take into account, as it puts a limit on the amount of attention we can give to anything, to the demands we can make on ourselves at any given time. On the whole—because they do not understand about rhythms—people tend to do things with a degree of attention that is not dictated by any intelligent appreciation, but just by the state of their emotions, feelings, excitement, or the lack of it, and this may be wholly out of keeping with the rhythmical requirements of the activity. There are people who always start off too fast and their emotional energy drives them to activity beyond what they are able to sustain, just at a time when it would really be much better to go slow and observe more carefully what they are doing. Other people get emotionally disturbed when they think they are not going to accomplish what they have undertaken; and then they also rush and do things in a hurry. This is what I mean by non-rhythmical, even anti-rhythmical work. If you work rhythmically, you will find that you can just precisely do this sort of thing: that you can, in the most difficult work, find times of relaxation. This will be to the benefit of everyone, and yourself especially. If you let your attention be withdrawn at the right moment, something of a more eternal significance enters into the job in hand.

Q. I find that what rattles me most is being forced to do several things at once; this makes me extremely irritable. So the only thing I try to concentrate on at such moments is to be calm.

JGB. Gurdjieff called a state of tension, when conflicting demands are made on us, by the name of Soliunensius. What you describe may be called a local Soliunensius, which means a state of tension that creates in us a desire for freedom. This desire for freedom is quite blind; it simply wants to break something and get free at all costs or, if it is not as blind as that, it reacts by irritation, by a sense of constraint—as you put it, "being forced to." It is really necessary to understand that this kind of situation can be used to very great profit indeed, because this thirst for freedom at that moment can be satisfied by inner freedom instead of trying to satisfy it by outer freedom. I can speak of this with confidence. From many, many years' experience of this particular action, I have learned how to use such situations so as to be able to be in a state of real detachment. The more absurd and demanding the external situation, the more complete the detachment. But there are certain reservations to be made about it. These situations are not to be sought after; one does not want to provoke them for oneself. Gurdjieff was a law unto himself. He brought impossible situations onto his own head by his own intentional actions, probably at all times of his life, and it was quite evident also that he really could be free in situations of extreme tension and absurdity. I have witnessed this many times with him. In his café in Paris, watching passers—by through the open window, he would not only allow himself to be exposed to the outward bustle and sense of urgency of Paris in the morning, but also even to the inner states of people. He really saw what could be read from looking at their faces. Once, for a moment, I could see what he was seeing. It became so intensely painful to see all these people in their highly subjective wrought-up states that I could not bear it. I had to shut my eyes and turn away. He simply said: "These are the conditions in which man can be awake." I now know what he meant because I have learned that outwardly disturbing situations are wonderful opportunities for being totally free inside.

Q. I accept this, but I cannot see how it is done.

JGB. It is necessary to understand the meaning of "Love your enemies." All these influences are your enemies, they are attacking you, they want to destroy your peace of mind. Instead of feeling that you hate them, you must feel that you love them. You can say to yourself: "They wish to destroy me, but I do not wish to destroy them because I can profit by this. This is what enemies are for: they are my best allies." When I see this, then I no longer have a feeling of irritation about all these disturbances. But I must be quite sure that I really feel this from my heart, that it is not just a thought in my mind—I cannot do it without a change of heart about it. When people allow their emotions to be negative while they try to be positive with their minds, they haven't a chance.

Certainly, one also has to help oneself by the physical relaxation of the body, because if you allow the tensions of the emotions to invade the body, then you have the sort of feelings that you cannot surmount. You may have enough control over your body to make it relax, but it is no use relaxing your body and thinking: "This is very advantageous, I must be free," and at the same time letting your emotions boil within you. To my mind, there is hardly anything in the world more profitable to us than the kind of attack you describe.

Q. Do you know any way to remember not to rush in on people when you should not?

JGB. You have only a limited power to deal with this, because your nature remains your nature. If you are impulsive, nothing will change it, you will go on being impulsive. You could, by means of a very severe sort of discipline, destroy your reactions, but this is not a good thing to do, and from that no real benefit comes. We have to accept our own nature and it is really a kind of self-destructive process to try ignorantly to change it. Therefore your problem is not yet to try and change, but how to learn how to deal with the situation as it arises. When there is a real need, then you have to take care. Do not try to do it four times out of five, because you cannot; but if you can succeed only once in five times in holding back some impulsive statement, it will do you a tremendous amount of good. If you succeed, it is not only that one time which will be different, but your impulsiveness will begin to regulate itself: it will begin to acquire a certain memory of its own. For that decision to be successful, you have to make use of your bodily sensation. For example, let us suppose that you set yourself, during the conversation, to be aware of sensation in your hand, or your foot, and not to let your attention stray away from that. When I began to speak to you just now, so that I could be clear in my explanation, I put my attention on my right hand, and the whole time that I am speaking now I am never ceasing to be aware of my right hand. As long as I am aware of my right hand, some of my energy of sensitivity is withdrawn; and therefore I may not speak so quickly, or so coherently, but I have some degree of control over what I am saying. Do not try this often; try it when it matters to you, when it is important for you not to say the wrong thing.

19.
THE POWER OF THOUGHT

18 July 1965

TODAY I WANT TO SPEAK to you about one of the uses of our "power of thought." By this I mean the power of forming mental images, the making of plans, connecting ideas together and all the inner and outer conversations that we hold with ourselves and with other people. All of these activities come from the availability in us of a certain substance or energy of thought—so that we can speak about thought-energy. We find that we have a certain power of using this energy to produce thoughts and mental images. The special property of this energy—to distinguish it from other energies of our bodily life—is that it is able to go outside of our own bodies, out of this present moment, and connect us with the past, with the future, with remote places. We are therefore able to form mental images of what is not present here and now, whereas we are not able to have sensations of what is not present here and now. If I touch the arm of this chair, I have the sensation of contact with it, but I cannot have sensation of contact now with the arms of chairs that are in some other place now or that were anywhere yesterday, or will be anywhere tomorrow.

This power of getting out of the present moment by the power of thought is one of the most important and characteristic powers of human beings. The same power may exist in animals, but it is certainly very much weaker in them. For example, if I plan to go for a walk, I can form the prior mental image of myself walking and enjoying the countryside, of when I will turn round and come home. But an animal which has the impulse to wander has no such power of presenting itself with a mental image of what it is going to do and what is going to happen.

Even in human beings this power is usually very poorly developed and the importance of it is not really understood in educational procedures. It is developed in a lopsided way mainly connected with verbal images, verbal signs and so on. The power of forming real mental images of something not present and of forming mental images of actions that one is going to perform is given very little importance. And yet it is the means by which we can extend, expand, our experience of the present and project our decisions—our acts of will—outside the present. If I merely say to myself in words: "I am going to do such and such in two hours' time," I may forget, my whole condition may then be quite different from what I anticipated, and I may simply not do it. But if, instead, I form a clear mental image of what I am intending to do in two hours' time—even if the conditions are unfavorable to doing it—the mental image will "meet me," as it were, will be waiting for me at that point where I projected it, and it will remind me; it will even oblige me to do something about it, because there is that kind of power in mental images when they are really coherently and intelligently made.

The exercise I want to suggest to accompany your work during the day is to practice—to test out for yourself—what this can do for you. I suggest we should pause for a minute or so every half hour and "meet ourselves." It is now twenty minutes to eleven. At eleven o'clock we shall all be somewhere or other. Some of us just do not know where we shall be then, except that we shall be in this body and not in some other body, and somewhere in the grounds or the buildings of Coombe Springs. But we must have some sort of picture of the surroundings in which we shall be, prescribed according to the work which has been allotted to each one of us. So to some extent you can make a mental image of yourself in twenty minutes' time. We can remind one another: anyone who happens to notice that it is eleven o'clock can stop and remind those working nearby in order that this should not become an effort at remembering the time. You then pause for a short time—half a minute to a minute—connecting yourself back to this moment that we are sitting here together now, and also making a new mental image of yourself in half an hour's time, and so on.

The point of this exercise is that you should try to verify for yourself this power of making mental images of oneself at some other moment from this present moment, and see how far it is possible to experience this encounter or meeting between that part of you which has gone through time with your physical body and the part that went, ahead of time in a mental image, to another moment. If you do it in that way, you will find that you bring into existence a chain of moments, strung together like beads on a string. Each such moment is a moment of return to a sense of your being one whole.

After-Lunch Discussion

Questioner. What I was at the time did not really correspond to what I had visualized.

JG Bennett. Probably you did not take "unexpectedness" into account. There is a constant flux of our experience: thoughts, sensations, states of feeling are fluctuating the whole time. Into this flux unexpectednesses are constantly entering; some from outside, some from a chance association in the mind and some also from a conscious source. One thing that this exercise can give is to make us very conscious of this fluctuation; because you see that in one sense you find yourself again, but what you find yourself in the midst of is not the same inner state, but an inner state that you had not foreseen; that you had not foreseen even a few minutes before. It helps you to recognize also the distinction between the constant fluctuations of our psychic states and the possibility of having something else which remains still, and so can be connected from one moment to another. You cannot connect the constantly fluctuating state of the activity of your mind, because its very nature is to be in a continual flux; but when you connect yourself in the way I asked you to, you separate something from this flux, and that something can also separate itself from the present moment. Projecting one's mental image forward and backward in time also gives one a chance of seeing that time is not an independent reality, but a measure of our inner state.

Q. Can one in any way alter the future by doing this?

JGB. Yes, one can do so. Through this kind of work you bring yourself closer to your own pattern; that is, what happens to you corresponds more with what you are, and meaningless accidents do not happen so easily. When you do not use this power at all and your mind is wandering in idle images without any purpose in them—daydreaming and so on—you can attract to yourself things that you do not want, which do not correspond at all to your destiny. That state of daydreaming, of idle mental associations, is a very vulnerable state; because when you are in that state you have nothing of your own to meet what is happening, and therefore accidental impacts will turn things in a direction you never intended. This is why some people can get so easily emotionally upset, or make mistakes that they would never otherwise make. It is just that they are not there to meet the situation. The use of the power of forming mental images does not mean that things will happen just as you want them to—at least, not yet— but you will be freed from quite a lot of the stupid, unnecessary things which are such a waste of time.

Q. Could it be preferable for some people to make a different kind of image than a visual one?

JGB. Yes, a mental image does not necessarily have to be a visual image. A mental image is any kind of mental construction. It can be a mental construction of posture, of how one will be sitting, or a mental construction of the thoughts that will be in one's mind, or a mental construction of one's relation to one's environment. Our mental activity has many different varieties of content and we can take any that happen to be easiest for us to construct. If you want to develop a weak power, for example if you are weak in auditory memory—at remembering sounds—then you can work to use this power to improve your ability to remember sounds. What is significant is just the one thing of connecting one moment of time with another moment of time and seeing that this is possible in spite of the fact that our mental world is in a constant state of flux!

Q. If you make a habit of this mental exercise, could you actually change the material world around you?

JGB. I did not say "make a habit of it," I said "make a practice of it." I remind you of this distinction because a habit is something mechanical; we lose control over our habits. If people do carry this sort of exercise into a regular discipline with themselves, it is true that through this they begin to control their outward lives. Things begin to happen to them in a more orderly way. They live more according to their destiny and less according to chance. But it does not mean that this is enough in itself, because the whole process of the transformation of man is something complex that has to be balanced. If someone were told to do this and nothing else—just for the sake of control over the material world—they might very well come to grief in their moral character. One cannot work on one thing only: one has to work on the whole. That is where the wisdom of our work resides. But what you say is true, that if this power is really systematically developed by someone, they begin to be able to control material happenings.

Q. An oculist told me I would go blind in a year's time. I did not react, I did not despair, I just accepted it and it fell into its proper place. I would not normally have reacted like that. Later on it was denied by the hospital.

JGB. Our reactional self, that is, the part of us which reacts to like and dislike, pleasure and pain, enjoyment and dissatisfaction and the rest of it, is always working on one level in us, and it is really mainly connected with the smaller incidents of life. When a bigger shock comes, very often this big shock goes right through this reactional level to something deeper in us, because it is coming nearer to ourselves and then it is more like an awakening of our conscience. Most people notice how strange it is that one will be upset and unable to control one's feelings about something small; and yet one will be able to be calm and master of oneself when it is something big. This is because, as I say, the big, powerful shock goes right through the shell of these ordinary reactions to something deeper in us. Of course, if there is nothing there, then it knocks people over and they have no resistance, but if there is something inside, then that is what meets the shock and they are not touched by it in the way they are by smaller things. When this happens to people they think: "This is wonderful, I really have some inner freedom," and then somebody frowns at them and they become angry and irritated. They continue to react to small things. This should make us realize that even big shocks do not transform people. Transformation is a process that requires time, conditions and technique. There are different techniques and methods for becoming master of our reactional powers and knowing how to use them positively than those required for meeting bigger things. This experience you describe is quite an interesting and important one because it shows you that underneath your reactions there is something else which is more stable.

Q. Could you explain a bit more about these levels?

JGB. Around our real self there is an outer shell which is quite mechanical, like when you withdraw on touching something very hot. There is no feeling about it. It is just an automatic reflex, the way in which the nervous system is conditioned to work. This is the outer shell that is sometimes called the *material* self. Inside that there is something more sensitive, which is polar; it has likes and dislikes, because it experiences the two sides in everything. This second shell I call the *reactional* self. Then there is a third self inside that, where our "character" resides, and for everyone this third shell behaves according to their own nature, whereas in the second shell people are all more or less alike—all have similar reactions of like and dislike, yes and no, activity and passivity and so on. The third shell, which I call the *divided self*, begins to show a pattern. In there, you begin to see what people are really like—as if you were taking off a mask and seeing what is underneath. Still further inside is what I call the *true* self, the real person, and if the shock is big enough, it goes right through to that real person and everything is quite, quite different.

You can read all about this in more detail in my book, *A Spiritual Psychology*. The problem for us is to bring all four selves within the consciousness of the true self and so gain mastery over them. What we have spoken of today is only one of the steps on the way.

20.
INNER HELP AND INNER FREEDOM

4 October 1965

THOSE OF YOU WHO have read the book *The Sufis* will remember a lit-tle dialogue where a would-be pupil asks the Master to teach him and he replies, "Can you learn to allow me to teach you?"*

I want to say something today about this "allowing something to be given to us." We all need help and we should also be convinced that help is available to us, partly because experience has shown us that, when we really need it, help does come; and, partly, because this is in accordance with the justice of things. Justice requires that nothing, neither people nor the world itself should be left helpless in front of what has to be done. We, therefore, should believe that what we have to do and cannot do by ourselves, we can be helped to do. The example I quoted of the teacher and the taught is an illustration of this situa-tion: we need to learn something and there is someone to teach us. What is missing is our ability to put ourselves into such a relationship with a teacher that we can be taught, and in a wider and greater sense put ourselves into such a relationship with life that we can receive the help which is always available, always offered.

How does this help come to us? Sometimes it comes through some outward instrument, some person we meet or something we happen to read about or hear said, apparently accidentally, which throws light on our problems. We can receive help in many such ways, providing we are able to be attentive at the moment and notice what is offered to us. If we are not attentive, the most valuable advice or hints as to how to

* "The Teacher, the Teaching, the Taught." Idries Shah. *The Sufis,* 1964, p.352.

solve our problems just go by and are wasted as far as we are concerned. So the ability to catch on, to make contact with what is offered to us, requires that we should recognize help when it comes from some visible source. But such "visible" help coming from outside is precarious; for not everything or everyone can be a channel for transmitting help; and it does not always come at the right moment.

The inner help, which comes from the invisible part of our own nature, is always available; but it is more difficult to accept. For nearly all of us, it is more difficult to allow ourselves to be helped from within, even though this help comes from our own hidden reality. I think we all have evidence to convince us that there is, within each one of us, a Reality beyond our own thoughts and feelings, even beyond our understanding, and almost always beyond our own consciousness. That is why I call it hidden.

What is hidden is not necessarily unfelt. In some ways we can be aware that there is a hidden reality behind our ordinary current of experiencing, behind the stream of awareness which we call our inner life, but which is really only just below the surface of the outer life. The true inner life, the true Inner Self, is almost all the time hidden from us. But this does not mean that it is absent or only there sometimes. Its very nature is that it does not come and go like our thoughts and feelings do; it has a very different and far more stable quality.

How can we learn to allow ourselves to be helped by this hidden Self? I said earlier that probably every one of us can remember times in moments of desperate need, when help has come unexpectedly in the form of seeing a way out which we could not have thought out for ourselves. Maybe we did accept that this vision of what could be done in that situation came to us from this hidden reality in us; but we forgot that it could come and be accepted by us only because at that moment we were really aware of our helplessness, really desperate, so that our resistance to receiving help had broken down. But this resistance quickly builds up again as soon as the desperate need passes; and, because of this, we live the greater part of our lives without calling upon the resources which are inside us.

Why we live in this usually foolish way is not very hard to understand: it comes from a fear that we shall lose something if we ask for help, that we ought to be able to rely on our own strength. Some people I know who are in a very poor way, whom I have tried for years to help out of their difficulties, have nonetheless remained without the help they asked for and never could understand why. In truth, the only obstacle to their receiving help, either from me or—what is much more important—from within themselves, was that they just could not bring themselves to admit that they needed it. Because of a quite false notion that they ought to be able to manage by themselves—that one more effort, one more try, would enable them to succeed—they refused to accept their helplessness, when it was obvious, to everyone except the persons concerned, that they could not solve their problem without help.

The kind of help that we can give to one another is very limited, first of all, because it is limited by our own understanding and our power to communicate. But behind this, as I said, is our inability to allow ourselves to be helped.

Going back to the dialogue I mentioned at the beginning; suppose there is a young man who really believes that he wants to be taught and cannot see that the difficulty for him is that he will not allow himself to be taught. He will protest against the suggestion that he believes he knows everything, or that he is able to judge what is right and what is wrong for him. He will say that he is asking to be taught without any reservations, and yet this is all self-deception, for in a very short time, when he is exposed to the conditions of receiving some teaching that could be useful for him, he rejects it.

So it is with most of us. You only have to see how difficult it is to believe that what I am saying now applies to you. You may see that it applies to someone else; but you will be very unwilling to admit that you reject the possibility of being helped, that you think that you can do without the hidden resources that are behind your own consciousness and beyond your own understanding.

We cannot do much to reason ourselves out of this situation. A little good can come from using our common sense and admitting to ourselves that if we can see that everyone else needs help, then probably we must need it also; and if we do not receive help, it may well be because we will not take it, as we see happening with others. But when we have done all that reasoning and perhaps have convinced ourselves, we forget it again when the occasion for receiving help comes our way. We never can foresee the form in which we shall either need help or have help offered to us, and therefore, when the moment comes, we fail to see that what we had understood earlier applies to this particular moment.

There is a way in which we can increase our receptivity or readiness to allow ourselves to be helped, and that is to use the method which I have so often recommended in relation to many of our problems, which is to practice it in the very small moments of life. What we do a hundred or a thousand times in small moments we shall find ourselves able to do when a big moment comes.

You have to picture for yourself, represent to yourself, that there is within you a source of help that you yet cannot know or understand. And whenever you start any kind of activity, or as often as you can remember it, ask that this invisible power within you should help you to accomplish this task in the right way. Let us take as an example your own conviction that we should not be doing everything only because we are driven by external circumstances or by habit, by the pressure of public opinion or all sorts of motivations that have nothing to do with our own reality; that we should be doing things because it is right to do them, not for praise or blame or for the hope of some reward, but just because they should be done. We wish to be able to live our lives on that basis, but we know we cannot do this because our own tendency to rely upon praise and blame, upon visible fruits of our actions, has become so strongly ingrained that they always press themselves upon us. If we realize our state of inner slavery, we can ask for help every time we have to act. When we start a new action, we can simply ask that our inner reality should direct our actions and not the trivial part of ourselves that is usually in command.

We can say to ourselves, in starting some activity or having to face a situation, something like "May I be directed rightly," as a sort of short expression of all that I have just been saying at some length. With practice this need no longer be said in words at all, it is just an inward pause, remembering that there is a source, a hidden resource that can direct our actions according to what is right, and not only direct it, but also when necessary give us strength to do it, give us the energy which perhaps we could not summon up by our own effort; or set us free from some emotional involvement that would make us act helplessly and perhaps foolishly instead of intentionally and wisely. This inner reality is not emotionally involved in anything, it has no desire for reward, nor does it fear blame, and it is to this that we turn in that momentary inward orientation towards the new action that is about to begin.

If we practice this, in whatever form it may take for us, this reiterated practice will gradually develop in us an ability to receive help which will make a very great difference to our lives, of that I can give you my assurance.

I suggest you try to put this into practice this morning.

After-Lunch Discussion

JG Bennett. Did any of you become aware of anything happening when you tried this exercise?

Questioner. I understood that what you spoke about this morning required a different kind of effort from the one I am used to making; because when doing a job I do try and pay special attention to what I am actually doing. I had always accepted in principle that you must do a job in the right way; but I had not seen what you said about letting yourself be helped. This morning I began to realize that something more was needed than I was giving to it, but I could not see in which direction to look for it.

JGB. Not something more, but something different is required. Both effort is needed and help is needed. One is not "more" than the other, but different and complementary. It is quite true that one half of our transformation depends upon the way we do things intentionally; that is, the quality of our intentional actions. But what this can give is limited, whereas here you have something of a different kind acting in a different way. You probably realize that this is connected with faith. Now faith is not a power that we can control, but a vague feeling that we can bring into focus. We cannot force ourselves to believe that there really is a higher consciousness or conscience, or higher part of the self, or a hidden reality in us. We may have heard about all this, and even vaguely believed it to be true; but we have not learned to rely upon it, and here it is necessary to do something that I call "bringing it into focus." In some kind of way inside yourself you agree that it must be like that: you must take things in that way; not to take this higher part of yourself into account is obviously foolish. When you come to look at it in this way, it is the beginning of some kind of faith in the reality of the higher part of yourself. When that faith is given a chance to establish itself by repetition, you will see for yourself what it can give you. At first, what happens when you do what I called "allowing yourself to be helped," is not the kind of thing that you expect, and therefore I asked: "Did anyone see anything?"

Q. I was doing a job with a wheelbarrow and I got it done satisfactorily, but I found it difficult to connect myself with anything else, so I cannot say that the feeling of being helped was conclusive.

JGB. It is quite true that in this work, as in everything else, you cannot draw general conclusions from single instances. I have given you nothing more than perhaps enough encouragement to go on trying. I can say for myself that after many, many years I can no longer doubt that this is the way to make life easier for oneself; this is the way to avoid unnecessary forcing of things. I used to think it was necessary and unavoidable to force oneself to do a job better by finding some way of reminding oneself not to lose touch with it. A great deal of this is really unnecessary. I say "a great deal" because it is not true that it is *all* unnecessary. As I said to L. just now, we always have to use intentional effort for some part of our activities, but there is a certain reconstruction of our nature which cannot occur solely by willing to make efforts ourselves, to act rightly in the light of what we know. We are always coming up against situations where we neither know what to do nor how to do it. No one can help seeing that there is an enormous region of actions where we have to either guess, or go by rule of thumb, or try to force things. This region contains many of the most important and difficult situations where we desperately want to do the right thing and do not know how to start. I say to you that this region becomes clarified, and life becomes much easier when you really get yourself into the way of trusting that there is something in you which is wiser than your ordinary self.

Q. Recently I found myself in a difficult situation at school and I knew I could not solve the problem by myself, by thinking it out. I just sat quietly for a moment and I found myself repeating "I don't know," and I just left it at that. But this was in effect a cry for help and later in the day I spoke about my problem to a colleague who was able to help me.

Q. Would you tell us the difference between projecting yourself outwardly to a power that one knows is there continuously and asking for help from something in yourself. This is something new to me, and today I tried to project myself inwardly and found it is the same thing as addressing myself to an outward power.

JGB. You address yourself to the sort of help that you picture as being outside you, but when the help comes, where does it come from? You do not see words written up in the sky telling you what to do. The answer comes from inside, doesn't it? Wherever the source of help is, the channel by which it reaches you is inside, and that is important to realize. Of course, it is true that really there is no outward or inward—these are just figures of speech. If I say behind, or deeper, or outside or inside and so on: I am simply groping for a way of trying to say something which can convey to you what is real for me. But I must say truthfully that the least appropriate thing of all is to say it is "outside." One cannot say that it is "somewhere out there" when one knows that the solution of a problem, or clarity about a situation wells up somehow into one's consciousness from some source, which is unmistakably more within one's own consciousness. Because it is more within, one cannot see it until it has welled up and until it has shown itself.

If you find, like H., that, after asking for help, the word somebody else happens to say is just the word that you wanted to hear—in that sense you can say it comes from outside. But this is not the whole story. If it is not mere accident, there must be some connection between what you ask and what you receive. This connection is hidden. It is hidden because it is "within" the consciousness of you and the other person. That person may not even know that the word he or she said is just the word you needed to hear. Therefore, you begin to see that of course the source of help is everywhere, not located, and that "outside" and "inside" are only figures of speech. But nevertheless, I do think we should accept that there is present within each one of us a finer level which we cannot ordinarily reach, through which higher influences can touch us when we open ourselves to them. In other words, one can say that in one sense the source is not located anywhere; it is everywhere, inside, outside, behind, in front, above, and any word you like, but in another sense there certainly is also something which is personal to each one of us, that is of a finer quality than our ordinary experiencing. But this something which is too fine to enter into our experience is always there, ready to help. And in that way one can, I think, make a radical distinction between a personal source of help and a supra-personal source of help. In Gurdjieff's language there is the "higher emotional center," and the "higher mental center." It is said that the higher emotional center puts you in touch with the truth about yourself—it is your own source of truth—and the higher mental center puts you in touch with the Universal Truth, the Truth of all Truth.

Q. Were you talking to us this morning about the first one?

JGB. Yes. People who are ignorant of this terminology nevertheless often have some sort of inkling of all this, but they think that one can always ask for help from that One who is universal and beyond; to God himself. But the roles of these two sources of help are different in our lives. If we put it in religious language, we can say that one corresponds to what our guardian angel does for us and the other to what God does for us. The guardian angel, or the higher emotional center, or the higher self, are there to give us immediate and personal help. There are many ways of describing it, but almost universally a distinction is made between the higher personal reality and the higher universal or supra-personal reality. For me, there is no question about it, my whole experience confirms that there are these two and that our relationship with these two is different. What I have been talking about today is this particular act of allowing oneself to be helped by opening ourselves to communication with what we call the higher emotional center. This is quite different from anything we can do by means of our own efforts, but it is also different from the salvation that comes from God alone.

Q. Would it be right to say it is the same thing as surrender?

JGB. To me, the word "surrender" implies something rather too passive. I often give the example of a blind man who wishes to cross the road. He accepts the offer of your hand and trusts you to lead him safely across. You cannot say he has surrendered to you. That picture of putting out one's hand to someone whom one trusts, because that person can see what we cannot see, as nearly as possible represents what I mean. There is in each of us a *someone* who sees what our ordinary self cannot see, and it is really then a question of how to put our hand in the hand of an inner friend.

21.
SECOND TALK ON FREEDOM

1 November 1964

I SUPPOSE THAT WE ALL want to change the level of our own living, to be able to live in a different world from that of the natural human environment; a finer, more perceptive world where we are nearer to the causes and meanings of things. In some way or another, we have some aspiration towards a different life. If that is so, we have to ask ourselves what are the conditions for this aspiration to be realized. It should be clear to us that if we wish to live in a different medium we shall have to be able to adapt ourselves to the conditions of that medium. For example, if I wish to be able to spend a part of my life in the air, I shall have to learn how to fly. It is no use my thinking that it would be "very nice" if I were able to fly; there is a practical requirement: which is that I must have the means of flying.

This we have to face, possibly more seriously than we do. The world that we aspire to is certainly a world in which there is greater freedom, in which man has more power to determine the course of his life, to choose what will happen to him, than ordinary people have. He is able to be connected with other people and other events in ways that ordinary people cannot; he can see what ordinary people cannot see. If he is to have all these privileges, he also has to fulfill certain requirements.

We are concerned that all of you who come here should have the opportunity of doing various things that have a real meaning in the preparation for being able to live in that different way; various exercises, various forms of self-discipline, demands upon oneself. But, at the same time, there is something that can be called "learning how to live according to different laws." This world that I am speaking of is not a world very far removed from our own. There may be people among us who already live in it, but it has some very important differences, and one is the inner freedom that enables one to choose what one will do and how one will do it.

In order to have that freedom, without which one cannot live in that world, one must set oneself free in certain ways. Much can be done in that direction by our own efforts, but a higher action, beyond our own powers, is needed to free us from certain bondage in us that is so intimate that we cannot cut ourselves loose from them by our own unaided efforts. For example, I do not think that anyone can cut himself loose from the bondage of his own egoism and self-will, just by wishing to, because even his wishing will come from his self-will. Therefore, something higher than oneself and higher than one's own egoism is needed if one really is to be free from it. Those of you who were here two weeks ago have heard me speak about the help we can call upon when we are helpless. But there are intermediate freedoms that are indispensable if we are to enter into and be able to live in that other world, otherwise we may find ourselves with the means of entering into it, but not the means of living in it because our actions would quickly exclude us from it again.

Now one of the essential freedoms, that really does belong to that world and does not belong to the world of ordinary people, is freedom from like and dislike. People who are content to live in the ordinary world are entitled to have their likes and dislikes, their prejudices, and be influenced by all these things. They are entitled to say: "I like whom I like, I dislike whom I dislike, I would not be true to myself if I did not recognize my likes and dislikes." They even believe that strong likes and dislikes are a mark of the self-respect that every man should have; but it must be understood that if they speak like this, they are not free people. Because, if they can only like what they like, and dislike what they dislike; then they are bound: they are slaves of their likes and dislikes. People who are subject to that slavery cannot live in that other world; although they may be excellent people for the purposes of this world, where everything is ruled by forces of attraction and repulsion or like and dislike.

There is no commandment to man: "Thou shalt be free from likes and dislikes;" but it is one of the inexorable conditions of the laws of the world that we want to enter. There is no such rule; but, as in this world also, you cannot enter certain places without a ticket of admission. There is no moral principle involved in liking and disliking; people can be very moral and yet be slaves of likes and dislikes. But it must be quite clear that they cannot have the same opportunities as free people have. If I wish to enter the world of freedom, I must learn to be free. It is no use imagining that one can enter and then will be enabled somehow to live according to the laws of that world; because, if you are not already prepared for that, you will not be able to. You may, as I said before, be allowed in; but then you will begin to approve of this and disapprove of that. You will then quickly discover that the scenery around you has changed, and you are back again where you were before. That other world is an objective world where one can neither deceive nor be deceived.

We are rational beings able to use our reason, and our reason should tell us that one cannot live in a world of freedom unless one is free. Our reason must also tell us that to be subject to like and dislike is not freedom; to have prejudices is obviously not freedom. But then people do not call their own likes and dislikes prejudices; it is other people's likes and dislikes that are called prejudices! Our own likes and dislikes are called "sincerity" or "honesty." But the name does not change the reality of it.

I have spoken to you about this because the freedom I speak of is within our own power to achieve. Man is not compelled to be the slave of his likes and dislikes any more than he is compelled to be free of them. This is one domain where man has a remarkable degree of freedom, much more than in many other domains of our experience and action.

We have to ask ourselves whether our reason is convinced that without freedom from likes and dislikes we cannot have any higher freedoms. If we become convinced of that, then this conviction must be established in our understanding; then our whole inner attitude must be linked to this, based on this. We must then set ourselves to learn how to remember persistently to put aside in ourselves all impulses of liking and disliking, of approving and disapproving, of judgement and the rest. Of course, there is always a tempter's voice in us that tells us that if we do this sort of thing we shall become weak people without any stable points of view, without personal opinions. That is not true. It is a lie from the Father of Lies, that is, the Devil. Likes and dislikes blind us so that we cannot see the objective situation. When you see the objective situation, you do not like it or dislike it: you only see what has to be done about it.

We know well enough from our own experience that if we speak or act from our subjective feelings and judgements, prejudices and the rest of it, we provoke similar reactions in other people. And we also know that the words of someone who is—even perhaps only temporarily and relatively—free from his subjective feelings and judgements have a very different weight for us. We therefore must understand that the fear that we shall become ineffectual if we become free, is a lying fear.

Some people also think that, far from it being morally wrong to have likes and dislikes, it is a duty, it is morally right to have them; that one should like good people and dislike bad people. Why? All are human. All have the same human soul. Why should he who is bringing retributive consequences on himself—in this world or another—for his bad actions, be disliked, and he who is earning rewards for his meritorious actions be liked?

It must also be remembered that living, as we mostly do, on the superficial levels of our own natures, the characteristics in someone else which appear objectionable or lovable to us may not be those of the real person at all. This other person we cannot see and meet as long as we cling to our subjective feelings about them. Of this also our reason can, and must, convince us.

Once our reason has truly convinced us that likes and dislikes belong to the lower world and to the lower part of our own nature and that freedom from likes and dislikes—impartiality—belongs to the higher world and to the higher part of our own nature; we can begin to do something about it. Every time we see these impulses in ourselves, our eyes can begin to train themselves to look with impartiality, not prejudice; our ears can become trained to listen impartially and not with like and dislike. This is in our power, this is something that can be practiced always.

After-Lunch Discussion

Questioner. I noticed this morning that there is in me a tendency to see the humorous side of things. There was no quality of separation about it, nor of being involved, but just seeing how funny it was.

JG Bennett. This is one stage in liberation, and it is a genuine stage. It means that something in one is being released instead of being dominated by one's own prejudices. This energy cannot yet flow into understanding and therefore it flows into either a sense of the comic or, perhaps, simply a more joyful sense of relief that these discords or worries that are apparently weighing on people are really only illusions.

Q. I can recognize what has just been said, and I think I sometimes make an error by taking a too relaxed or easygoing attitude, particularly towards a new job. I tend to think: "Everything will be all right," and that's all.

JGB. This is connected with another stage where there is a release, but not yet the necessary perceptiveness and wisdom to know what to do with it. Just from sheer enjoyment of the state of being released one begins to imagine that one is safe. But that sense of being free is accompanied by the hazard that it is not yet a complete freedom; and therefore it can turn into heedlessness and carelessness. One does not judge or discriminate properly because one feels: "Things are all right." When one feels like that, it should be a warning, because there is always something that we ourselves must do in every situation and heedlessness leaks away our power to do it.

Q. Yes, I do recognize the risk you speak of. I have often wondered why a bad state can come so quickly after a good one. What is the best way to deal with this flow of energy and freedom, what positive thing should one do?

JGB. One must learn how to blend it. When this is set free it cannot remain inactive, and therefore it must connect itself with something. It may just result in overactivity: one begins to talk too much, or to be excited, or to do things too fast; and then there is that danger of heedlessness, which can lead to all kinds of mistakes. In order to blend it there must also be some other kind of energy that is able to blend with it, and this is where understanding of presence is essential. It is very difficult to get beyond the stage of having a release as a result of seeing that we need not be caught into likes and dislikes, or tensions. Because of this, work such as relaxing, or the awareness of one's own presence here-and-now really is a necessary thing. If we take the analogy of making bread: the flour is like the energy released from the act of putting away the impulse to judge, to like, to dislike, to approve, to disapprove, and so on. But the flour alone will not enable you to make bread; it will blow about and be useless unless you mix it with water to make the dough, which will afterwards be able to go through all the processes of leavening and baking and so on. It is necessary to understand that our transformation is a process in which we are like raw stuff that is not yet able to be eaten. We have to be converted into edible food.

Q. This morning I had the energy and I had the presence, but is there not something else to add? Something like the remembrance of what one is? I felt some such need to see more.

JGB. Yes, we have to ask ourselves what, in the simile of the bread making, corresponds to the action of fire, to the baking. What you are saying is true, that this is a way of exposing ourselves to reality. Sometimes we feel unable to see more because we cannot find this reality to bake us, although we may have something which is connected with it.

To take another illustration: suppose somebody has trained to be a musician, and a time comes when by everything that he has been taught and all his hard work and so on, he is in a position to be able to perform in public. But something has not happened yet; he has not really gone through the kind of death and resurrection which is required to be a real artist.* Maybe some day he hears a real artist playing and then he experiences a sense of nothingness in front of the playing of that artist, in spite of all his own excellent technique and his mastery of his instrument. If he is fortunate enough to have this revelation of himself without any feelings of jealousy or envy but with the realization that this other artist has a creative quality in his work which he had no idea of, which he had perhaps never been able to perceive before, then he will see, and with that seeing the quality of his own work may be transformed. It does not mean that this seeing has always got to come about by perceiving something objective outside of oneself, like the example I gave you. It may be some kind of inward seeing that makes him realize: "There is here, hidden in me, something so different in its quality from anything I am now, that what I am now is nothing." This then begins the "baking" process.

Q. I realize that there is such a thing as slavery to one's likes and dislikes but is there not a use for them in forming one's judgements? If one has judged rightly in the light of one's own aesthetic or moral likes and dislikes, is one not justified in feeling pleased about it?

JGB. I did not say that likes and dislikes must disappear or be suppressed; but that if we are slaves of them, then we cannot call ourselves free. Impartial approval or disapproval is a very different thing from like or dislike; and it is certainly most necessary for our judgements. There are also quite legitimate enjoyments that we experience in our bodies and our minds.

Freedom is not the same thing as elimination. We are not required to eliminate any of our natural functions. There is a subtle self-justification that says, that because good and bad taste are necessary, like of good taste and dislike of bad taste are also necessary. We should be

* cf. JG Bennett. *The Dramatic Universe, Vol. III*, Santa Fe: Bennett Books, 1998, p.109ff.

able to see through this kind of self-deception. The impartial sense—to know that one is able to act without being the slave of one's likes and dislikes—gives a certain kind of satisfaction which, within limits, is legitimate and good, but only within limits. Because it is still on this side of the real barrier of our egoism, satisfaction can easily turn into a kind of pride in being unaffected by these things. In the long run something much more fundamental and different has to happen to us, and this is the separation of the "I," that experiences and decides, from the functions, which only react.

"It is very like a person who complains about money burning a hole in his pocket. He cannot bear the discomfort of having money in his pocket when things are in the shops. It is true that if we begin to do things which accumulate energy in ourselves there will be a very strong impulse for that energy to flow into habitual channels that have been formed over many years, and indulge ourselves in some particular kinds of manifestations that we justify and even look upon as necessary. For example, people very often think it is not only justified but praiseworthy to worry, and that a person who does not worry is hard-hearted and careless and does not take life seriously. In the same way, people sometimes say that if they are not angry they will become helpless victims of everyone else, who will take advantage of them if they do not stand up for themselves. They do not understand that they are merely in the habit of manifesting in this way, and that even if some of the things they fear were to happen, the price they are paying is the price of the possibility of their own being."

—a fragment

1. JG Bennett.
In his study at Coombe Springs, circa 1960.

2. Olga de Nottbeck. "The human recorder."
A long time close associate and dedicated assistant to JG Bennett.

3. Stop Exercise. Women.
Sunday Work Day at Coombe Springs

4. Stop Exercise. Men.
Sunday Work Day at Coombe Springs.

5. Movements on the lawn at Coombe Springs.

6. The Bridge at Coombe Springs.
The illustration used on the original *Sunday Talks* booklets.

7. The Djamichunatra at Coombe Springs, 1958.

Coming up the path are Pak Subuh and a party of Indonesians.

8. The Djamichunatra meeting hall at Coombe Springs.

9. The Djamichunatra meeting hall at Coombe Springs.

10. Frank Lloyd Wright and JG Bennett.
Discussing the Djamichunatra during building works, 1957.

11. "St. George and the Dragon." Paolo Uccello. See page 269.

12. "The Angelus."Jean-Francois Millet, 1859.
"A summons to prayer." See page 184.

INTRODUCTION TO PART 2

PUTTING TOGETHER THE TALKS that appear in the second half of this volume has proved very much a task of recovery and reconstruction. Apart from "Pentecost" and "The Source of Help," none of these talks has ever before been edited for final publication. "In the Beginning." which treats of the first words of Genesis, is the first such freshly published talk. But included here, too, are a few talks which, though given at Coombe Springs, belong to a different era or audience from those of the first part of this volume. Thus although by its original spelling (Hasnamuss) of the title word it must date from perhaps as early as 1949, the penultimate talk, on Gurdjieff's notion of "Hasnamuss" in *Beelzebub's Tales to His Grandson*, is included because the unexpected reappearance of long-missing final pages seemed to make editing the whole of publication worthwhile. Also discovered at the last moment were the exercise given and the complete after-lunch discussion session for "Death and Rebirth." Moving on to his encounter with Idries Shah's book, *Tales of the Dervishes*, the talk entitled "The Second Domain" reveals Bennett tackling, with one of his provincial groups, an interpretation in terms of Gurdjieff's cosmo-psychology of one of its more inscrutable Sufi stories, attributed by Shah to the "Sarmoun Sufis,"* Yet other talks, dating from a slightly earlier time than most of those in the first part, were originally addressed to Subud members urgently desirous of understanding what was happening to them by virtue of the Subud *latihan*. Indeed one such—"Understanding versus

---

* Bennett discusses Gurdjieff's three-month visit to a "Sarman" monastery reported in *Meetings with Remarkable Men* in his own book, *Gurdjieff: Making a New World*. Santa Fe: Bennett Books.

Knowing"—was very probably suggested by a remark, to Bennett about his own understanding, made by Pak Subuh. The superb talk, "Wholeheartedness and Courage," rescued from oblivion and republished here, communicates the impact of Bennett's meeting with the Shivapuri Baba in Nepal, and was clearly transitory and exploratory—looking ahead to later Work Sunday talks.

Some of these later talks, such as "Two Lives" and "Being Realistic," were clearly experiments to see how much material people could typically take in and use in just one Sunday morning of work and theme study. Their theme sometimes derived from his own work around that time on the last two volumes of *The Dramatic Universe*. Not all these experiments proved successful, for Bennett was an incurable optimist and made great demands on his audiences. Nevertheless they formed a foundation upon which he was later to build when further developing his "thematic technique" for use at Sherborne in the 1970s—his final experiment, for which he brought to bear some fifty years of accumulated experience.*

—Ken W.F. Pledge
London, July 2004

* cf. JG Bennett. *The First Liberation: Working with Themes at Sherborne House,* Santa Fe: Bennett Books, 2002, chap. 1; and Allen Roth. *Sherborne: An Experiment in Transformation,* Santa Fe: Bennett Books, 1998.

22.
IN THE BEGINNING

Easter Sunday, 18 April 1965

THE FIRST WORD OF THE BIBLE, in *Genesis,* translated "In the beginning," is *Bereshyt* in Hebrew. It is spelled with the six Hebrew letters: *bayt, raysh, aleph, sheen, yod,* and *tav*—and it tells us "This is how it all started, this is what it is all about." Next comes the word *Bara*—spelled *bayt, raysh, aleph*—which has not only the sense of creative act but also has in all languages (which shows it must be very ancient) the notion of bringing forth, of bringing to birth. The letter "B" with which these words start is also the second letter in most alphabets (the first is Aleph) representing duality, or two-ness. So the world already begins in a state of division, and we cannot look further back to an origin when all was one, because this is incomprehensible for us. We are here in this divided world, separated from the Source, and we have to remain separated from our source as long as we are in this world. This is, no doubt, why the Bible begins with the Hebrew letter Bayt of Bereshyt—not with Aleph.

From this already present separation from the Source, there is a progressive further separation, division, multiplication—as is wonderfully described in the first verses of Genesis, in the ten Acts of Creation. But that is also shown to us from everything we have learned from science and the observation of the history of this Earth of ours: there has been a complexification of something that was already separated when it started. And this separation, of course, enters deeply into our own human nature, because everyone, whether he has religious convictions or understanding of any kind, cannot help feeling and being aware of the dualism and the division of his own nature between what he is and

159

what he would wish to be—between what he is able to be and what he needs to be. Or between some unknown, higher part of himself that he just dimly senses, and the other part of himself—all too obviously separated from that higher part—with which he has to live.

The great manifestation of separation is death. This separator from the body—and also from our dearest companions and friends—is for us all the one certain fact of our life. Therefore we should not forget that we do live in a state of separation—always dying, always losing—losing the moment, losing our own selves. This is perhaps above all what Gurdjieff emphasized and brought home to us when he said that man cannot remember himself. What does it mean, that we cannot remember ourselves? It means that we are condemned to this separation; that even if we find ourselves, we have to lose ourselves again.

All this is symbolized in this first word of the Bible—*bereshyt*. From this two-ness, from this duality, come the many, represented by the letter "R" or *raysh,* the second letter—and syllable—of the Bible. After that comes the promise of return, because in both *bereshyt* and Bara the third letter is Aleph. So it is certainly a very strange message that seems to be given at the beginning of the Bible. "You appear as two and you are condemned to go into the many, but you can return to the one."

This return must be a reunion, a reuniting of the separated parts, and this is the significance of resurrection as distinct from liberation (which is another conception, but only a partial one, of human destiny). Up to a certain point, liberation is necessary because we are caught into the multiplicity—caught into the outgoing stream of things—and from this it is necessary to be able to stand apart, not just for the sake of being free, but in order to come to the next step, which is a step of union—of reunion! The Resurrection is both a symbol and an act of reunion. The soul and the body are separated, and it is not enough that the soul has been set free and is able to go into a different state of existence. In order that the reason for existence should be accomplished, it is necessary that these two should be reunited. Therefore, in the resurrection, there is symbolized a reunion of the altogether different principles of man's nature: his perishable body and his immortal soul.

If one stops at the notion of liberation—the soul separating from the body, discarding this world, going into a different state of existence—then no purpose will have been accomplished, because this existence would not have been transformed. The reason why the Two was the start of it all will not have been understood and realized. The notion of "liberation"—the separation of the selected or chosen part from the other—is of course again represented in the Bible by the Exodus: by the Jews going out of Egypt. Chosen to go out—not to remain permanently in the emptiness of the desert, but eventually to reenter and take possession of the Promised Land, to become reunited with the land that was promised to Abraham. All that is symbolized in this story. Liberation is not the completion. It is the *reentry,* the *reunion,* that is the completion of the story.

In all this rich symbolism of the Old Testament, there is so much to be understood about the role of Pharaoh, of Moses, of Joshua, and of Aaron in the Exodus. And of the *reestablishment* in the Promised Land, that, of course, one would have to talk for a long time. I am only speaking about it because in the New Testament, in the resurrection of Christ, the manifestation of the same separation must again be a "liberation" first and a "reunion" afterwards. And this liberation, which ends the involvement in multiplicity, should be—and has to be—a voluntary act: "Thy will be done"—"If it has to be, let it be." But not only that; there is also the Christian notion (which is connected with many ancient traditions) of willingly entering into the uttermost depth of the multiplicity, to undergo a state of separateness represented by the outer darkness of Hades, where separation or isolation—atomism—is pushed to its limits. After entering into this atomistic space of complete disintegration, there must still be the will to come back, to return, to unite.

I sometimes picture to myself—and, it seems to me, am even experiencing—the extraordinary condition of complete disintegration: when Christ enters into this state of ultimate separation and then returns rising through the different stages of reintegration to come back; reunites with the physical body and then carries through the whole process of reunion all the way back to the Source—having covered the whole range from the atom to the Source, from the infinitely many to the One. All this is represented in the Christian account. But in this process it is necessary, at the midpoint—because it is indeed really the midpoint that is represented by the bodily resurrection—to find again this nature and this condition. Otherwise, that which is finally reunited is only a shadow of what it was intended to be. I mean by this, that if one conceives of the reunion—the coming together—only in terms of the higher, or immaterial part of the self, this is not the reunion of a complete being.

How strongly this is emphasized in the story of the Exodus and of the conditions in the desert! For in spite of everything that is given, this is not complete until that particular geographical place has been occupied by the people to whom it was promised. And in the same way, however contrary to reason and however absurd it may be, it still must be that man, in order to be complete, must repossess the conditions of existence which belong to him as a man. Otherwise this is only liberation and not reunion—not reintegration.

All this was very strikingly brought home to me by the talks of the Shivapuri Baba (which you can read in *Long Pilgrimage,* the book I wrote about him) where he criticizes what is called *Nirvikalpa Samadhi.* Nirvikalpa Samadhi is regarded by some Vedantins as the ultimate aim, the final liberation, the achievement of final union with the One. That is, Nirvikalpa Samadhi means that state of bliss in which all differences disappear—"Nirvikalpa" without any distinction. But the Shivapuri Baba says, "No, this is an illusion. This is not the resting point. This is not the end. This must be rejected. One must go on to the conscious, substantial and active union with the Source." Not just the "liberation from" but the "unification with." Not just losing oneself in the whole, but finding oneself. But to find oneself one must be a completely integrated whole, and that is the purpose of our work—what we are here for. This is why it is not sufficient that we should look for experiences of liberation, of bliss. And why also we cannot just be satisfied with right actions—with doing our duty—because beyond both of these two things, it is necessary to come to the effective integration of the different parts of our own nature. And that is the whole process: that is the resurrection in which we are all perpetually engaged.

In one sense, the resurrection belongs to a certain moment; in another sense, it is timeless and must be in us all the time. There is, of course, a spontaneous resurrection in us every time we awaken. Every time we come out of the sleep of ignorance and begin to see "Here I am, why am I here?" we begin to set ourselves again to the work. This is the most intimate and direct proof of resurrection—which Nature is also showing us everywhere—around us now in the spring at Easter.

After-Lunch Discussion
JG Bennett. [In answer to a question inaudible on the tape.] You have left out something that really links the two together, and that is the theory of the two deaths—the first and second death. Without that, nothing of it makes sense. The first death is connected with what I was saying this morning. This death is a separation of the soul-stuff from

the body-stuff. When that happens, the soul-stuff, with whatever degree of coherence it has acquired, goes into the soul-stuff pool. It will always have some degree of coherence, except in infants, whose self—identity—remains unaffected by it all. I mean by this that their destiny stands outside of this. But if there is some degree of coherence, then there is still something there, but it is within the soul-stuff pool. With that degree of coherence it is possible to have communication; possible for certain experiences to happen, of various kinds.

But the second death is a different one. The second death is when the will separates from the soul-stuff (if that has become strong enough, so that the will has a vehicle) and this becomes an independent soul. Not everyone comes to achieve the degree of integration that will hold it together at the second death. I must say here that this is not my own theory. I have just given it a certain shape to fit it in with a lot of other things. The second death is the decisive one which decides whether there will be a reintegration of—the formation of—a complete independent, free being; or whether the different parts will be dispersed. If that degree of integration is not attained, then the different parts will be dispersed.

Then another question arises. What happens to a partly integrated soul? Probably some kind of timeless existence—therefore it is not a question of how long it lasts. There is probably something that corresponds to the "end of the world," when the soul-stuff pool undergoes a total transformation into something else. Then this situation is different. That is all beyond anything I have attempted to clarify for myself, but I do have vague ideas about it.

You put three questions: Firstly, not everyone acquires a soul. Secondly, there is the soul-stuff pool into which half-formed souls enter. And thirdly, in some sense, those who are dead do not cease to exist and some kind of contact is possible with them. And you said "Do not these three theories contradict, or are they incompatible?"

I think it is not so, because the soul-stuff pool is not amorphous. I am sure of that. I am quite certain that within it there remain structures, and these structures are people.

Questioner. I would like to ask about the difficulty of "going back," which seems to me more difficult than separating.

JGB. I spoke of returning, not of going back. There is a psychological account of this given in Gurdjieff's "Science of Idiotism" in what he calls "to consciously descend and consciously ascend." There are twenty-one gradations of "Idiots"—of identity, of kinds of beings. This gives you the picture of the going out and the returning, but it also adds something more, which is very important, and that is that there can be a kind of false returning, a returning which has not got the potential for totality.

This is what Gurdjieff was anxious to get over to people with his Science of Idiotism: that every kind of effort produces an integrative effect—a soul is made whenever there is an act of decision—something is integrated. But integration by itself is not enough. Integration has to be such that it can reach completion. If integration has failed to go to the limit before it is undertaken—if a soul fails to go to the limit of nothingness before it integrates—somewhere or other it will get stuck. The idea behind this is what I spoke about this morning in connection with the word *Bereshyt*. It is the notion that from simple separation into two there has to be an ultimate descent into complete atomism, completely disintegrated, with complete loss of identity, in order to come back in such a way that there is nothing left of the other process; so that the process of integration is integration and nothing else. That is what Gurdjieff tries to convey in his Science of Idiotism. Otherwise you may come to the stage of being an "Enlightened Idiot" who knows everything and, as far as knowledge is concerned, is complete, but cannot go further because his knowledge is built on a mixed foundation: partly going down, partly going up, not pure going up.

You say, "Is not the return difficult?" The return would be impossible if there were not the *principle* of return. This is what we experience in ourselves, as I said, in waking up. Whenever we come out of sleep, something impossible has happened. We did not wake ourselves up! Therefore, every time we remember ourselves, this is evidence that going up is possible. Why is it so? Because we did not do it! In other words, something has been given to us which we did not produce for ourselves but with which we can do something. And that is what makes this going up process possible.

I made a distinction between separation and division. Disintegration is separation in the sense of being set free from multiplicity. We are involved in a process that breaks us up and eventually will break us up into fragments. This has got to happen: "like"—"not like." We can set ourselves free from this process of disintegration by one kind of action. We can also reintegrate by another kind of action. So I said today that there is liberation and there is unification. They are different things; and people make a mistake if they think the whole story is simply liberation—simply to get free from multiplicity.

Q. Yesterday I had one of those samadhi-like experiences of being aware of the wonder of the world; in which everything was full of inner life. Yet in this state I was able to do nothing. I was unable to direct my thoughts. I was unable to have any sense of intention or decision. I realize that there is a difference between this and unification. But how does one do this? I could do no more than try to get present in my body—which seemed to help a little bit; but it failed altogether to get me out of this state and come back to the world again. Is there any method of going from this sort of state to a more active state?

JGB. You mean without losing it; because obviously you got back into a more directed state. You exactly describe what is called in Sufism *hal* or "state." It is necessary. There is nothing illusory, or deceptive, or undesirable about it, and through *hal* you become liberated, as you say yourself. In that state of liberation you see oneness, and even experience it, but you have not got complete truth, because you cannot do anything. The first requirement is that you should not forget this and you did not forget it. In other words, you did not think, "This is the end. This is the final goal. There is nothing but this. If I could always be like this, this is all I ask for." It is always tempting to say that to oneself. This is not what I spoke of this morning—Nirvikalpa Samadhi—but it is a samadhi. It is a samadhi, one can say, "of Nature."

What enables you to hold your own in this kind of situation is first of all what in Sufi language is called *ilm.* Gurdjieff called it "science" or "knowing." There was something in you which knew this *hal* was not the whole story; therefore your *ilm,* or knowledge, remained independent of your *hal.* At the time of an experience, to know what this experience signifies and what its limitations are, is a very big thing. For that there must be in you both *ilm* and *hal.* If there were only *hal,* and no *ilm,* you would believe in the *hal*—be entirely taken by it. There would be nothing else but that.

But knowing that is still not the whole story, nor is having the experience the complete thing. Because even these two together—as you yourself could see very well—do not give you back your will. This is one of the conditions of *hal,* that we have to give up our will to have it. In order to keep one's will—which is what your question is really about—one must be connected with a source of will, not simply with a source of *hal* or a source of knowledge.

One can look at it this way. There are three sources: there is a source of knowledge, of *ilm,* of science; which may be traditional, or the result of somebody's own discoveries. Whatever it may be, if it is true, valid knowledge, it is called *ilm*. There is a source of *hal*, which is to say that certain energies become available—they can either be released from within ourselves or through contact with some source of energy—which will bring you into this or that *hal*. And there is another thing.

There is also a source of true "doing"—"action"—"work." It looks as though this third source is the only one that matters, but this really is not right, because everything works, everything in the world has to do its duty whether it likes it or not. But in order to play his part, man must also have insight and knowledge. Therefore, he needs both *ilm* and *hal*, as well as this other, *amal' in 'haqiqah*, or work in truth. Only when you are aware of and accept to be linked with that—are serving and engaged in the true work—can you say you have this third one. When you have that one, the other two are both brought into a right relationship. (I say that because I was tempted to say that they are subordinated. It is really not a subordination.) That is how what you ask about is explained in Sufi terminology, but one can obviously express it equally well in other ways.

23.
SPIRIT, MAN, MATTER

Pentecost, 2 June 1963

TODAY IS PENTECOST, the day on which we commemorate the visible, tangible and audible manifestation of the working of the Holy Spirit in the disciples of Christ. I put it this way to emphasize that the theme of Pentecost is the working of the Spirit in the material world through human agency.

According to our Christian belief we are related to God in three distinct ways that correspond to the three Persons of the Trinity. We are here to study man in the hope of understanding better the processes of our own spiritual development and we are not experts in theology; so we shall turn our attention primarily to the psychology of Pentecost; that is, to the place which the direct experience of a spiritual action should occupy in our understanding.

As I reminded you just now, there are three ways in which man is related to God and to each of these three ways corresponds a deeply significant group of personal experiences. If we could understand these experiences rightly, we should come to the point where theology and psychology meet. In other words, we should see how knowledge of man leads to knowledge of God. I shall speak shortly of the three relationships before returning to the main theme of the Pentecostal manifestation.

There is first of all the relationship of Sonship. When we say the words "Our Father," we claim that God is our own Father, not just the Father of all mankind, but your Father and mine as individual human beings. We are given the courage to make this claim by the fact that it was enjoined on us by the founder of our religion, and therefore, as

Christians, we are entitled to say "Our Father." The overwhelming significance of this notion is too much for us to take in, but we can understand something of the meaning of it if we ask ourselves whether there is in man—in you and in me—something which is different from what we see in the world around us. There is something different, and that is our "I." "I AM" is the name by which God named himself when he answered Moses out of the bush. Moses asked what he should tell the children of Israel when they asked him the name of the God who had spoken to him. The answer was, "Tell them 'I AM' has spoken to you."

If then we are able to say "I am," it must be because there is in us something that is begotten in us by God. This relationship of Son to Father has come into the clearest and strongest significance in Christian belief, although man, whenever he has become aware of his "I" has certainly always felt this relationship.

The second way in which we are related to God is through the double nature of man himself. We ourselves are divided between the material and the spiritual, between the natural and the supernatural in our nature; and this division is so deep that it seems as if it could never be bridged. Indeed, it cannot be bridged because if we try to mix the spiritual and material, we do not arrive at something new, we only have the mixture. There is nothing halfway between spirit and matter. However finely matter may be purified, it remains matter; however much spirit may have taken form, it still remains spirit.

We are sometimes aware of this duality of our nature; of something in us which cannot put away the material because it is itself material, and something in us which cannot put away spirit because it is itself spirit. In Christ, we have before us the meaningful reality of the notion of man and God as one single divine person. But we too are spirit and matter in one single human person. This does not mean that Christ bridges the gap between God and man because this gap cannot be bridged, but it does mean that the opposition disappears, and we see instead that matter and spirit are complementary; that is, necessary to one another.

Matter would be meaningless if there were no spirit—that is, if there were no values—and spirit would have no place of action—it would be helpless—if there were no matter in which it was able to work. It is just because they are so completely different that they are so completely necessary to one another. It is just because the two natures of Christ are completely different and can never be confused that Christ is both God and man. This particular mystery of the separation of opposites is resolved, not by finding something which irons it out, which will smooth out the contradiction, but in accepting wholly and entirely that it has to be so.

If we can become aware through the experience of "I" that there is something in us that has come from God, in another sense we can realize through the division of our own nature that in God himself there must be the two natures of the Son, which can never be separated. This is the true meaning of complementarity.

We men find the division of natures in ourselves very hard to bear. We wish that we could put aside the material part of our nature to become wholly spiritual; or we find it impossible to respond to the demands of our spiritual nature and wish we could completely lose ourselves in our material nature. But there is no peace in either direction; there can be peace only by the full acceptance of this necessity to be two and not one. That is not by any means the end of the story. The lesson of Pentecost is not that we must return to the One but that we must find completion in the Three.

There are many other stages in the realization of the unlimited wealth of experience of which we begin to have glimpses, but at least one thing should be clear to us, and especially today, that there is no need to be distressed about the contradictions of our nature. In fact, the sharper these contradictions are, and the more strongly they are felt, the more are we able to be open to another influence. We discover that it is possible to make a real act only in the moment of impossibility. When we are not aware of contradiction, things may seem easy; but, in reality, there is nothing to be done because we are bound to be going with the stream with which we happen at that moment to be identified. When we feel contradiction—which really means feeling the impossibility—then there is something to be done. This is one of the lessons we learn little by little. When we learn it, we no longer wish to be shielded from the sufferings of contradiction, because we know it is only through them that we are able to rise to a new situation.

At such moments we are entering into the third relationship with God. It is above all the relationship of love, and all true love comes out of the meeting of opposites. That is why the greatest love of all is that which unites God and the creation. In the third relationship we experience God in the person of the Holy Spirit. In some ways, this is the very essence of all relatedness. Some theologians have gone so far as to say that the Holy Spirit is relationship. The very nature of the Holy Spirit is to relate. It is said that we are related to one another in the Spirit.

169

Through the Spirit we are related to our own acts. We are able to be men and women because the relating power of the Holy Spirit enables us to be one person without losing our threefold nature.

This third way in which we are related to God is what we understand by the love of God, that makes it possible for us to be what we are, to do what we do. God's love gives us not only our own "I" but also gives this "I" the power to enter into the world and to act in it. If that power were not given to it, the "I" would be a helpless spectator of what is happening in the world—and we know that sometimes our "I" feels exactly like that. The meaning of the Holy Spirit is that it enters and gives the "I" a power which it does not possess of itself. It is an enabling, a permitting power, and this is why it is called "reconciling" or unifying.

In Pentecost, there is the completion of the revelation—not by Christ somehow showing that this division or separation of his own nature into man and God is somehow overcome and turned into something else, but by the manifestation of a third and completely different power of God; that is, the power that can enter into everything high or low, large or small, strong or weak. When that power enters it transforms, as is described so vividly in the story of Pentecost: the coming of the Holy Ghost and the transformation of the disciples, followed by the conversion of hundreds of people.

Such a transformation happens psychologically in ourselves when we see the necessity somehow to be able to bring together this "I" which has in it no division, and this nature of ours which is divided into the material and the spiritual parts. That experience of the love of God entering into us comes to us when we realize that we have to live with the situation in which we are; and not merely to live with it, but to work in it, to transform it both inwardly and outwardly. That power does not come from our own "I," nor does it come from our nature; it comes from the love of God which is the working of the Holy Spirit.

We may not be religious people, or have had anything that can be compared to the experience of Pentecost; nevertheless, all of us should be able to recognize and be confident that there is the Holy Spirit and that it is through this third relationship that we can accomplish anything at all.

I have spoken to you in this way because my own belief is that until we recognize these realities in our own experience and see them working in our lives, they will remain as something outside of us, something we call "mysteries." They are only mysteries to the mind which thinks in terms of logic, expecting everything to make sense according to logic. They are not mysteries to our own immediate experience.

After-Lunch Discussion

Questioner. Could you enlarge on the two lives we lead which you spoke about this morning?

JG Bennett. One life goes from past to future. It is conditioned by all the influences which have acted upon us in the past and which are connected primarily with energy exchanges through hearing, seeing, touching and the rest of it. This includes not only the life of our physical body, but also our thinking which works in the same way by exchanges of energy, by a line of causal influences, so that we tend to think along a line. Our feelings, by which we react to what is happening to us, are of the same nature.

The pattern which we are destined to fulfill belongs to the second life, and that is the life we enter into through becoming conscious of it. We sometimes see these two lives connected, as for example when we experience things that matter—values and purposes, the reasons for things. There is something which cannot be reconciled between the way the inner life works and the way the other—the time-life, the material or causal life—works. For most people the value-life is like a dream, and their contact with it is almost solely in their imagination. Yet some part of that life really does influence us all. Everyone is in contact with values which draw them on to action. These values are not all of the same quality or on the same level. This is different from the life which goes from past to future, conditioned by the properties of matter and energy.

The value-life is not conditioned in that sort of way. It has its own laws, connected with quality, not with quantity. From the outside it seems as if quality and quantity can be fitted together, but when anyone tries to do it in any field whatever, it cannot be done. In art, for example, the artist himself knows that however much his values, his vision, enter into his work, a complete fusion of fact and value is never achieved. He has always a feeling that what really matters most has had to be left out. Yet it is not lost, because it is just the other—whatever it is—which cannot be made visible in the work of art that gives it life. There is something inexpressible in every expression, and a work of art is beautiful just because it cannot be as it ought to be.

The same thing happens with our behavior: however perfectly we may try to perform any act and the closer we get to it, the more do we become aware of the unbridgeable gap between what we actually do and the quality that we are trying to bring to it. This is true with everything we touch. Whenever we try seriously to bring the ideal and the actual together, only then do we understand that they can never be made to coincide. The point is that we ought not to see this as failure, or a reason for distress. To live and bear with the incompatibility of the ideal and the actual belongs to the very essence of our human life. We have to live in two worlds, one conditioned and one unconditioned; or, we can also say, the material world and the spiritual world.

We can also see the dilemma under another aspect; that is the distinction of form and content. That which has no form cannot be known; that which has no content cannot be felt. Therefore form and content are necessarily joined in all experience, but they can never merge. Content is never form, form is never content. The clay of which a cup is made has nothing in itself of cup, and the form of a cup has no cup-like powers unless it has the clay to hold them; so the clay out of which it is made and the form which the potter puts into it are necessary to one another. One can say that form without content is helpless, but content without form is meaningless. All philosophers have approached this problem and it has always seemed as if some way must be found of getting out of the dilemma. The search for a way out reached a peak at the beginning of this century, when it was assumed that anything that contains a contradiction must be unreal. The truth is exactly the opposite: without contradiction there are no realities.

Contradictions are not an end but a beginning. They are like the male and the female gametes from which a new life can be conceived; but they are not themselves the new life. The dynamism of life requires more than contradiction.

Herein lies the secret of Pentecost. The disciples had been made aware of a tremendous secret which was still hidden from the world. They had been commanded by the Risen Lord to bear witness to his Resurrection, but they could not put away the fears and the bewilderment that shut them away from the world. The upper room had become their world and prayer and supplication their only recourse. We can picture the sharpness of the contradiction of the urge to go out into the world and the urge to hide away in secret prayer. The world which knew not the Resurrection was more than ever an alien place to be shunned.

When seven weeks had passed from the Resurrection, the small community in St. Mark's house were gathered together, symbolizing the acceptance of the contradiction of the inner and outer lives. Then came the inpouring of the Holy Spirit and the birth of the Christian Church. What had been turned inward burst out in the dramatic manifestations of the gifts of tongues, of prophecy, of healing, and the announcement to all Jerusalem of the secret of the Resurrection. The disciples became apostles; the followers became leaders, prayer and supplication gave place to evangelical ministry.

In this event, we see the transformation of the dyad into the triad. The complementarity of the Gospels expressed in such words as "I and my Father are One" and "My kingdom is not of this world" was transformed into the dynamism of the newborn Church of Christ. The mutual rejection between the world and the chosen of the Lord was the manifestation of a dualism henceforward to be replaced by the acceptance of the world as the place of salvation and even the means of achieving it. Through the coming of the Holy Spirit, the world itself is transformed and its contradictions are transcended in the doctrine of *total salvation.* By "total salvation" I mean the belief that all man's powers, including those of his physical body, are to be purified and made whole. The doctrine of the perfect man as the union of body, soul and spirit would have no meaning if there were not a spiritualizing action able to redeem and transform every part of our nature. It seems to me that this is the message of Pentecost and that it is, more than ever before, important for us all today. Mankind can never return to the ancient divorce of mind and matter and must pass on towards a vision of total redemption, total transformation. This is the vision by which, in the long run, all humanity will be united in common action and common faith.

Q. When you feel uplifted in a situation, that seems to be the only moment when something has come into the baser nature.

JGB. Yes, that is what I was saying this morning. It is in the moment when we experience contradiction that it is possible for us to act. If we become aware of what we call the "baser" things at the same time as that which is drawing us in the opposite direction, then only do we have the possibility to choose. If you are only aware of the spiritual reality, there is nothing to do but to enjoy it. If you are only aware of the material reality, you go with the stream of events and your own reactions to them. It is only when you are aware of the two that you can choose the action that is right at that moment. The psychological experience of such a moment is the transition from contradiction and suffering to a state of relatedness and stability.

24.
THE SOURCE OF HELP

Pentecost, 17 May 1964

WE HAVE A POWER OF REPRESENTATION which we sometimes call visualizing, or making mental images. I prefer to keep to the word "representation" because the word visualization suggests a visual image, and a visual image is formed from what we have already seen, or heard. If we speak of "mental images" they can come from sounds we have heard and pictures we have seen, or from ideas that have already occupied our minds. But the power of representation is not limited to this. It is given to us to make a bridge between the visible and the invisible, between what can be brought into mental images and what cannot.

Today is a very good time for speaking about this subject, because it is Pentecost. Pentecost evokes the idea of a "source of help," an idea which is more ancient than Christianity and more universal than religion. The idea has been presented to mankind under many forms and this diversity of forms has been the cause of confusion and conflict. Unfortunately, we cannot picture to ourselves a source of help that has not a form, or a place, or a time when it works or a time when it does not work. For example, we are given images of what happened at Pentecost—of the tongues of flame, of the sound of wind rushing and the Spirit entering into the disciples and giving them the gift of tongues and the power to perform miracles—but these are only pictures, images; little more than bridges between the visible and the invisible.

All of us are concerned in the possibility of contact with a source of help, whether we have a Christian faith or whether we have not—I would even say whether we have any religious beliefs or none at all. When moments of terrible need come, everyone calls for help. Those who have been brought up in some religious belief will call for help in terms of their own religious teaching or training in childhood, but they do so because something deep down in them knows that it can be done and is to be done. Everyone who has experienced it, or who has shared such experiences with others, knows that help does come when there is this moment of dire need, and it does seem as if it happens irrespective of the beliefs or lack of beliefs of those who ask for help.

But there is another way in which we tend to ask for help which—if one expresses it crudely—is asking for help that things should happen as we want them to happen, irrespective of whether this is how they have to happen or should happen. It really amounts to the prayer: "Oh God, let my will be done, whether it is yours or not." Strangely enough, even this prayer is sometimes answered and when this happens, it is often terrifying in its results. Such consequences are explained in a simple form in children's fairytales when wishes are offered to people. For that reason, there is a certain protection against the indiscriminate use of our power to ask for help and to receive it. Because on account of our unwisdom we would ask again and again for what seems to be the best immediate thing for us; which may really not be the best at all.

But, although we do need this protection, and although there appears to be a great uncertainty in the way this calling for help is responded to, it remains true—and it is a very important truth—that there is a source of help accessible to everyone.

It is claimed by people that this source of help can be reached only through this religion or that religion, and that those who have not got a particular set of beliefs or practices cannot ask and receive help. This is not true. Help is open to everyone, and our power of representation enables us to strengthen our grasp and understanding of its reality. We have to represent to ourselves and accept the existence of a very subtle power that is able to accomplish miracles. In spite of its power, it never thrusts itself upon us, but rather keeps in the background. We can even go so far as to say that it is a very "timid" force. It is timid in the sense that if it is rebuffed or neglected, it withdraws, but if it is encouraged and believed in, it comes closer until it really begins to transform our lives.

Most of us have seen people—and very often the simplest people—who live their lives with complete confidence that they have access to this source of help whenever it is necessary. It really does not matter that one person represents it according to a particular image of this religion and another of that religion, because the image does not in any way determine the reality. The strangest thing of all perhaps is that these various images and pictures are all true and genuine, even when they seem to contradict one another. This shows the immense power of adaptation of the source of help. It can present itself to one as a child, to another as an overwhelming power, to a third simply as an inward confidence, to another as an inner voice. We can—and in my opinion we should—have our own clear representation of this source, and we can do this without attributing to it any form or image. We can say to ourselves that beyond all form there is a Reality. It is only beyond in the sense that it is more complete, more universal; it is not beyond in the sense that it is farther away.

In truth, nothing is closer to us than this source of help. It is pervading our own nature; it is working in us constantly in some ways that we do not understand and in others that we take for granted. No one can fully grasp how the forces of life are adjusted and adapted through the presence, within, of this source of help.

To picture this source in any specific form, such as in a religious form for example, can be for many people a serious obstacle. There is no reason why we should not make this representation without form, we can think of it as a very subtle pervasive energy that enters into everything, adapts itself to everything, but will only intervene or act when it is permitted to do so, or asked to do so, and can only do so if there is something in us which is of the same nature as itself. We have to learn to trust it and adapt ourselves to receiving it. Our bodily organism, for example, receives this help constantly, because it is so constructed that it is able to call for and receive it whenever it is unable to cope with something and this happens more often than we realize.

One can think of the analogy of a pipeline constructed from a natural spring right into a house, which would enable people to draw from it directly by turning a tap instead of having to fetch the water in buckets.

There is in us the possibility of that kind of a construction by which the flow of this power can be made permanently available, whenever it is necessary, even in the smallest things. But it is a construction, not (as is the physical body) one which is already made that way. One way in which this is constructed and built up in us is by the regular practice of connecting ourselves with the source. Only we must always remember, as I said earlier, that it is highly dangerous to connect ourselves according to our own whims. If we are tempted to ask for what we happen to want or believe to be right for us, we can be tolerably sure that our wisdom is not sufficient to know what is really right in any serious matter. Life is very complicated and there are many unseen factors.

There is one way in which this asking for help is always legitimate and always safe, and that is when we ask for it for the performance of our duties. It often happens that people find it difficult to do a task which they see should be done—maybe because they are tired, or they think they have not the necessary intelligence or training to do it. In reality, we can do things that not only appear to be, but really are, impossible to accomplish by ourselves, providing we are able to contact the source of help. I believe that carrying with one the representation of the intimately close presence of this source of help does serve as a reminder. It does to me, and if I forget and try to do things by relying on my own strength, then I quickly feel the pinch.

This power of representation of ours can therefore link our everyday experiences of life with the invisible spiritual world because it is not limited to the visual or tangible. It is not even limited to the imaginable; we can represent to ourselves something that we are not able to imagine.

In all that I have said so far, there has been no direct reference to Pentecost, but you will certainly recognize the connection. The Holy Spirit is called, in Greek, *paraclete,* which means, literally, "one who is called in to help." Thus we have at the very core of the Christian faith the belief that God in person is the source of help upon whom we call. Throughout the New Testament the role of the Holy Spirit is shown as that of the unseen helper in whom the disciples were to place their trust. If this was true then, it was true before and after: there is one source of help that stands beside and abides within us. All that we have to do is to learn how to ask and to receive the help that is offered.

In your work today, I want you to remember this, especially at moments when you feel yourselves lost or bewildered.

After-Lunch Discussion
Questioner. I want to realize the force you spoke of this morning, but I find it very difficult to do when engaged in outer work.

JG Bennett. You can observe it when there is the necessity for a change of quality in what you are doing. Even in doing manual work we can always observe our own reactions to it. If we want to benefit, to profit by what we are doing, we have to bring something to it, some intention to increase the value, to make something better out of it. We have moments either of discouragement, or inattention, or carelessness, when we lose this demand on ourselves to be doing our best. If you intend to be doing a certain piece of work as well as you can and you realize that for some reason you are not, that is the moment when a change of quality is wanted. It is at that moment that you get this help if you really want to keep the quality up. In that way we can keep our life process real or more alive. I do not mean by this that it is possible—and if it were possible that it could even be right—that everything should always be done at the maximum intensity. This would be quite contrary to nature, because nature works all the time in rhythms of relaxation and tension.

Therefore, it is not a question of always doing everything at a high tension but of learning how to make this rhythm of life—and of all kinds of activity—have a quality that both brings something into what we are doing and also brings something into ourselves. It is not possible to describe it by saying: "This is the quality that we are looking for," because it is a direct, an immediate thing that one experiences—one cannot describe it in terms of something else. But once you begin to look for that, then you very quickly see that you need help. If you are not looking for that, then you do not feel the need for help and you do not get help, because help is to enable us to live according to the right quality.

Q. If what you described this morning is true, how is it that things are not better than they are?

JGB. Some sad and difficult situations are necessary. People can be put into such situations because, through the way they bear them or respond to them, they acquire something that is necessary. So it cannot be said that all suffering and all difficulties are wasted, because it certainly is not true. But there is a great deal that is not necessary. People suffer where they could receive just this very help I am talking about, but they do not receive it because they do not have the faith to ask for it. Then it is really their own fault or the fault of someone who has deprived them of their faith. Even necessary suffering, the suffering that has to be borne, can be very different with this help; so different that you can see people whose lives are very hard and yet have something peaceful and joyful in them. If you see such people, you can be really sure that they have found the way to draw on this help.

Q. But surely those are the exceptions ...

JGB. Why is that? It is because people have become so accustomed to treating man as if he were self-sufficient, or thinking that we can look after ourselves, we can cope with life. Such people try to cope with things by their own strength, and when their strength fails them, they have nothing to turn to. It can be that they have never been in the presence of someone who believes in this help, that they have always been with people who do not believe in it and who have lost the power to believe in it.

Q. During the war there must have been many who had this faith and yet were killed. What happened to them seems quite arbitrary.

JGB. We cannot answer the question whether there is objective justice or not. We ourselves cannot experience compassion for the cells of our own bodies, which we sometimes heedlessly destroy by the million when we want to accomplish some aim which is important to us. We also destroy immense numbers of insects which may interfere with what we consider is good for our own plans. On a bigger scale, may it not be that there is some higher purpose which involves the destruction of millions of human beings? If I cannot feel compassion for the living cells of my own body, why should a consciousness immeasurably greater than I am feel compassion for me, if I am destroyed?

Whatever our feelings or beliefs are about this, we must realize that those sorts of question—that kind of mental experiment—bring out that we cannot possibly know how things are on a scale unimaginably larger than our own, and therefore we are not in a position to answer these questions at all. But what we can say—and this is quite irrespective of scale—anywhere and everywhere we can find that help which can transform an apparently destructive and wicked situation into something that is creative and beautiful. That is quite unrelated to these questions to which we cannot possibly find an answer.

Q. Does it apply to the hideous circumstances I've been referring to?

JGB. Of course it applies, but it applies to those who *ask* for it.

Q. Can there be some who asked and did not get help?

JGB. No, I do not think so; I think they have always received it. The only direct evidence we have is the testimony of those who survived and who have said this very thing, that they were helped to get through it by a source that was not their own strength. There is a wealth of agreement and testimony as to there being something that could be called upon. You may say, is it not just those fortunate few who did receive this help who survived? I do not think so; we also know from accounts of people who died that they were able to die in a heroic way that was extraordinarily unlike their normal nature, because something was given to them. But we cannot have answers to all such questions, because we cannot bring within the compass of our understanding the whole working of the universe; there is infinitely much that is beyond our understanding.

"It is very hard indeed to understand that when we are washing a cup we are not merely making a clean cup; we are actually doing something that is giving that cup its due. We are giving it its place in the real world because we are able to do so. If our attention goes off—if we have no care for it—then we are really denying it. We are casting it out. Everything that we don't care for we are casting out. This doesn't mean that we have to give things a false place or give ourselves a false place. All these events which are taking place here in time and space are all ephemeral. They pass. They have only a momentary hold on reality and we mustn't identify with them or rely on them or expect something from them. It is what we give to them that matters. What is hard to see is that every task that is well performed, every act that is caring for something—and not just people, but anything whatever that is treated in accordance with what it is—is creating reality. Without that, these things are all shadows: there is nothing there. But we also are in the same situation."

—from *The State Of Work*

25.
DEATH AND REBIRTH

16 May 1965

TODAY I WANT TO SPEAK ABOUT the idea of resurrection: of the body dying and being raised again from the dead. It is a wonderful idea, but it seems to belong to another world than ours. It is possible to take it literally, and possible also to take it in some other way; but it is not usually taken as concerning us immediately—as a significant factor in our everyday lives.

In the form in which it appears in Christian doctrine it seems perhaps even more extraordinary than the bare notion of resurrection alone. The Death, Passion and Resurrection of Jesus Christ seem a unique event: so extraordinary and so incomprehensible that it seems to be something which we can only look at from afar, not something concerning us personally. Yet in reality all great notions reproduce themselves again and again on all scales; so that if we cannot understand something on a very large scale, we may be able to see and understand it on a smaller scale nearer to our own experience.

Sometimes people have said, of course, that the very idea of death and resurrection is no more than a relic of an ancient fertility cult—celebrating the spring time and the arising of the seed from its apparent death in the earth during winter time. This kind of attitude is quite mistaken. I mean the either-or attitude that *either* death and resurrection is a sublime notion belonging only to theology and concerning God, *or* it is something concerning Nature only, and just a way of representing to us what we see going on all about us in the spring. This is wrong. We are all part of one single manifestation. There is, in the way this world is made, a principle of dying and being born again which runs right through the whole process of the world. The world does not go continuously from a beginning towards an end, but is constantly dying and constantly being renewed.

This constant dying and constant renewal takes place in us also, and we have to come to understand it most intimately in our own experience. Everyone who begins to study and know the transitoriness and impermanence of his own inner states becomes well aware that our own experience is one of recurrent dying and rebirth. We lose ourselves. We disappear entirely from the scene into the mechanicalness of our behavior. Mind, body, feelings—all become dissolved into an automatism. And then, at a certain moment, we awaken out of this. We become aware of ourselves again—aware of the world around us. And this awakening is really a rebirth—a resurrection—as truly and completely representing this universal cosmic idea as the great things that are taught in religion, or as what is going on around us all the time in Nature.

We do not have within us a principle of stable existence. What we find in ourselves, on the contrary, is a principle of renewal, of return, of being lost and found again. This principle we can really only understand if we experience it in ourselves; and we know its taste as the taste of rebirth: whenever we come back from a state of oblivion, of forgetfulness. This happens, over and over again, to such an extent that we become accustomed to it and cease to see how important it is—and how really wonderful it is—that we should be able to come back again after having been lost.

For it is nothing that we ourselves do. We become, as we say, psychologically "identified"—with our feelings, with our thoughts, with our activity—and we ourselves are lost. In that state of being lost, there is nothing that we can do to find ourselves. And then it happens! We suddenly see that we are back again and alive—seeing, feeling! Something is there again in us that, a moment ago, was not there. Someone has come back who had gone astray or gone to sleep.

We might perhaps expect this awareness in ourselves of the return to also bring with it the awareness of the taste of dying: of what it is to lose. But I think everyone who has seriously tried to understand this process in themselves knows that we cannot be aware of the moment of losing—this moment when we disintegrate, lose possession of ourselves and just disappear into the automatism of our activity. For this is the moment of our nothingness, when there is no one there to see what is happening to us. We are not even alone, because there is no one to be alone.

Out of this strange state, when there is nothing there except a machine—thinking, talking, acting, behaving and nothing else—there reappears awareness of oneself: "I am here!" It is truly a resurrection; a real rebirth. This rebirth can be helped by a call; portrayed in the picture of the resurrection of the dead by the imagery of the "last trump" that sounds when the dead rise up. It is like that when "something happens" to us from outside—or perhaps from within—and our inner dead state wakens.

We must not be frightened as we come to see this; although it is really a terrifying thing that we have no power to keep hold of our own life—of our own existence even—but that it has to be renewed and given back to us, from something that does not come from ourselves. In fact, most people are not frightened of it at all and never ask themselves the question: "What kind of existence is this that I have? Who can I be if most of the time I am absent or asleep?" Therefore there is for them no sense of fear at losing oneself, nor wonder at finding oneself. Yet even when this begins to overwhelm us and we see the helplessness with which we fall into oblivion, at the very moment when we are most trying to hold on to ourselves—to our own presence—we must learn to trust that there is also something else that calls us back. And if it calls us back from this sleep that minute by minute overwhelms us during the day, and calls us back from sleep at night, then it will call us back too from the last sleep into which we shall enter: The sleep of death.

But how can we learn to be more alert for the "sounding trumpet" summoning us to awake? There are various practices for this, and what I said at the beginning I want to remind you of now. We must not divide our experience into the mysterious and remote—which we regard with reverence and awe—and the immediate and obvious that we take for granted. The whole of it is wonderful and all of it manifests the selfsame principle of death and renewal. Therefore if I say to you that we have various simple means by which to remind ourselves, you must understand that on the one hand these are quite simple, practical and ordinary things—but on the other they are also representative of something much more than that. They are also symbols of the Great Cosmic Process of dying and being born again to which everything that exists in the universe is subject.

Most of you are already familiar with the particular practice that I want to tell you about, but to those unfamiliar with it I will explain further. It is called the "stop" exercise and has been used for thousands of years in certain Eastern Communities which are relatively little known in the West; though it has been incorporated into certain Western practices such as the bell of the Angelus. This used to be a reminder for people all over the Christian world, but this use has now been forgotten. It had that purpose of reminding one to return, of being a call: a summons to prayer.*

This particular exercise too has that quality. It comes at an unexpected moment not of our own choosing, and one purpose of this is to remind us that the moment of return also is not of our own choosing. We have to be ready for it even though "we know not the hour" of its coming. Another purpose is to remind us that at the moment of reawakening—the moment of resurrection—we see! This is why it is often called the "moment of truth" in which imagination and delusion are stripped aside and we see how things really are with us. This we are taught is what will happen with us at the moment of return. It is almost universally taught, in all religions, that this will be so. That there will be a moment of seeing when it will even be impossible for us not to see. And for that moment we have to be prepared, so that this seeing will not destroy our hopes. That is the second purpose: to accustom oneself to seeing oneself impartially, not as one chooses oneself but as one will be shown—as one will be made to see.

The exercise is carried out in this way: that someone who has the permission to do so, or takes the responsibility for doing so, gives the signal by calling the word "stop!" In our case I will be doing it during the day, while you are at your different works and activities, or at meals, or at any time. When you hear the "stop!" called, you should immediately arrest all that you are doing. Stop your body just as it is, if possible without starting or jumping—because there should be a state of relaxed, alert readiness in us all the time, so that this is something for which we are prepared. At that moment of stop, you turn your attention wholly towards your inward self—not looking outward, and certainly not looking around you. For that reason, one should hold one's eyes just where they were at the moment of hearing the call. And also one should arrest one's thoughts and just see: see who, what, and how one is at that moment. As if at that moment I am shown to myself: to see who, what, and in what state and how I am. This seeing—this

* "The Angelus," wrote Millet in 1865, "is a picture which I painted while thinking how, in the past, when working in the fields, my grandmother never failed, when she heard the Angelus, to makes us stop work and pray for 'those poor departed,' with our caps in our hands."

inward seeing of oneself—is maintained until there is the call to continue what one was doing, and then one returns into the activity just as if one had not been interrupted. It sometimes happens that people may hear the first call to stop and not the second call to continue, in which case they remain for a minute or so and then release themselves from the stop. Or it can sometimes happen that you do not hear the first call, but you do hear the second, in which case you just disregard it. Wherever you may be, if you actually do hear the call to stop, then you should stop. At first it is not easy, at first one starts or jumps—or even turns to look round—but this must be overcome as quickly as possible, so that the stop is really a stop, and one does not add—after the moment of stopping—involuntary motion, tightening up, taking some sort of posture, and so on. It can sometimes happen that when you hear the call to stop the body is not balanced—you may be running or leaning over or something and you cannot stay just as you are—and you will fall. Have no fear. If you fall in that way, you will not hurt yourself. And as you fall, you stop where you fall.

After-Lunch Discussion

Questioner. At the time of a stop I had an idiotic expression on my face. Did it just seem that way, or was it really idiotic?

JG Bennett. What about your thoughts? Were they also idiotic? I suppose all our thoughts will be idiotic at the last trump, so you needn't worry! One of the things the stop exercise really can do for us is to show us the difference between the imaginary picture we have of ourselves and how we should see ourselves if we were just suddenly caught and made to look.

Q. You mean you would possibly look even better than you thought you did?

JGB. I hope so. The truth is that you are accustomed to certain postures, certain facial expressions and so on, that you associate with yourself. You do not ordinarily notice all the transitions between these, and when you are caught with a stop you find yourself, very often, at some transitional moment that you have never known yourself in. So even if it is not objectively idiotic, it still seems quite strange and absurd because it is not what you imagine.

Q. I noticed, in the first stop you gave, that there seemed to be a great deal of time to see all sorts of alternatives—to consider the effects on other people if one fell or straightened oneself, whether one should do or not, and so on. None of all this could have taken more than a split second and yet it seemed as if there was all the time in the world to make a choice. And yet I felt that there was no choice at all—that what happened, just happened—and yet there might have been.

JGB. It is not so much time, as speed. The perceptions of our different parts have different speeds, and when your attention is suddenly forcibly drawn into the speed of perception of your body as distinct from the speed of perception of your mind, it suddenly appears that there is a great deal of time. People notice this at moments of accidents. Any kind of shock can suddenly switch perception from one center to another, producing this change of time, or change of speed.

Q. But would that affect choice?

JGB. It does not do so objectively. It appears as if you had time to choose, but your thinking part has not really the time to do anything about it until it passes through the mind at a different rate. It is not really to be understood in terms of thought. If you look at it more carefully, you realize that during that apparently long time you are not thinking, you are seeing. And you see much more quickly than you can think.

Q. Yet I noticed that each stop seemed to be over very quickly.

JGB. A long stop exercise is not useful to people who are not used to it. They do not know how to make use of it. That is why I finished the stop quickly, because it requires special training to be able to keep oneself immobile for a long period in the state of unmoving seeing. For this you must know how, with the help of the stop, you can pass into a different state altogether.

Q. It seems to me it would be easier if the stop were a little longer. There was hardly time to see anything.

JGB. And your mind was not wandering during that time?

Q. No.

JGB. That is good. One reason for that is probably that it is new to you, and so you could take it in a fresher way.

Q. I noticed the position I was in, but I could not notice anything else. What should I do about this?

JGB. This means you have really had produced in you the state of separation required, but that is because you have enough experience to make it possible for you. We ordinarily have the illusion of "someone there" in us because we are identified with our thoughts and feelings. If this illusion is arrested we see there is only a consciousness of what is going on—a presentation—but no sense of "I" at all. When it comes like that—just noticing, with no sense of "I"—that is real separation.

186

Q. Is that connected with self-remembering, because I had the same sort of experiences when I could not remember myself in my ordinary life?

JGB. When we speak of self-remembering, we speak of what can be remembered. In the first place one can be said to be remembering all this: the tangible, visible, perceptible part of oneself. But if there is real separation it appears as something wholly external—"not-I." This is the paradox of "self-remembering," that it is at the same time awareness of "not-self." "I remember myself yet I know that this self which I remember is 'not-I'."

Q. Could you go back to what you were saying about death and resurrection? Would you say something about what we can do and cannot do? It seems as if we fall because tremendous forces work upon us. When I was half the age I am now, I was caught on the edge of a pit into which I could have fallen, and there would have been no return. Many millions of people who have lived like me at the edge of a pit must have fallen in. What causes their falling?

JGB. Our part is to hear the call. To be able to respond to it, not to make it. We cannot call ourselves back. Lazarus could not resurrect himself, but he was able to hear Jesus saying "come." There was something formed in Lazarus which, although he was dead, enabled him to hear that he was being called. Had he lacked that something, the miracle would not have worked. So when you ask what we can do and cannot do, that is the distinction. We have to prepare something. We have to equip ourselves to be able to respond, to be able to hear and so on. But we do not know what comes from the other side to call us.

Q. During the morning there were odd moments when I seemed to "come to" spontaneously anyhow, but they gradually wore off. In speaking about it now—after the event—I can only be imagining about it, but what is one to do when these moments actually arise?

JGB. The first thing is that we do not notice how significant these spontaneous returns are in our lives. There is a curious question here that should deeply preoccupy people: "How can it happen—when I am in a state of inattention, dispersed, and do nothing about it—that into that state attention enters, and I see and notice? How?" I remember when I first became aware of this, how strange it seemed to me. "Why should I ever wake up? Why should I not continue to be a helpless automaton?" I could see that I constantly fall into these states of empty automatism. No one there. Nothing. "Why do I come back? How is it possible?" As soon as I realized that the idea that man is conscious is an illusion and that I was not conscious except by moments, the astonishing thing was not that I am unconscious, but why should I expect to be conscious, what is it that makes me so? How do these moments come? I saw that it is possible to have some artificial means of remembering if I make what is called an "alarm clock." Some signal will come to me which I have arranged. When this signal comes, either I see, hear, or touch something that reminds me, and that will wake me up at this moment. But I also knew very well that anything of this sort soon loses its efficacy. Another mysterious thing is that this does much less for me than these spontaneous—truly unearned— moments. And then one comes to see for oneself that something is constantly being given to us which not only do we not earn, but that we cannot earn. By no way we can think of, can we earn the reawakening. The simple and most undoubted psychological fact is that there is no way by which we can assure for ourselves that we shall wake up or have these moments of awakening that come, as you say, spontaneously for a certain time, and then diminish.

What is one to do when these moments actually arise? We must learn from them. For they are real evidence that we are dependent upon a higher power—that our possibilities do not come just from ourselves. We cannot manufacture them entirely from what we have. We cannot do without this something that is given to us. When you realize this simple thing, that you cannot even come back to a state of attentiveness by anything that you do, and that this has to be given to you, then you begin to ask "How much more also has to be given to us?" And you see that the whole process of our transformation all the time depends upon giving and taking—upon receiving something gratuitously and for our part making the right use of it. When you see that beyond possibility of doubt in small things, then you begin to realize this must be so in bigger things. And therefore you begin to become convinced of the undoubted fact that we have possibilities. It also means undoubtedly that there is something higher and bigger than we are that gives us these possibilities—that they do not just arise out of our mechanicalness. This argument—put forward just as an argument—is not convincing. It is the experience—when you see this happening in yourself—that is convincing.

Q. What is it in us that sees during the stop?

JGB. It is your mind that sees. We have no other instrument for becoming aware of things but our minds. Mind can become aware of emptiness as well as fullness. It can be aware of presentations from outside, but it can be aware of and see the inner condition too. This is really a tautology: the mind is the instrument of awareness and awareness is the property of the mind by definition, so I am not saying much by saying that.

Q. When I first did the Stop Exercise years ago, I hated it. I was really frightened of it. And then two or three years ago I had an experience in Subud when we did a test. I don't know if it had anything to do with it, but then you straightened this out for me. I can take this exercise now as I hope I should be taking it. Is there any connection between that?

JGB. Oh yes, certainly. I am even very pleased from what you tell me because it shows that this has really been a profitable sequence of experiences for you. If you had never seen the terrifying side of the Stop Exercise and been afraid of what it shows to you, you never would have taken it seriously. On the other hand, if you had not also seen that dying and being born again are so intimately connected with one another that they cannot be separated, then also you would not have been able to get beyond this feeling of terror. When you do get beyond, you see that the whole purpose of it is to prepare us so that this dying and being born again will become more and more natural for us. You have to go through it over and over again, in many, many forms. And it has to become so natural—so much in the course of things—that when we see this death taking place, we must willingly even cooperate with it, with full confidence that this death will mean something new being born. But this has to happen many times.

Q. "Time of death and time of darkness." Do they mean the same or not?

JGB. Death is more versatile than just darkness. There is more than just annihilation in death. Yes, this darkness is one kind of dying, and if we take it rightly, out of it something new is born. This is why we have to learn not to be dismayed when things go dark for us. It is a lesson that has to be learned because if we are not ready, we shall try to escape from it instead of going through it.

Q. I found I had a strong impulse to giggle when the stop came.

JGB. All the other different parts of you respond at different rates to it, and your feeling-reaction comes afterwards, so that you have either a feeling of absurdity—of being ridiculous—or, as you say, of wanting to giggle or laugh or something, to relieve this energy that is suddenly released. This is really only a matter of practice and experience. After a time these reactions cease and you can really stop. And it all stops.

26.
DHARMA

4 August 1963

Our attitude towards life is very different according to whether we believe and accept that there is an objectively right work to be done in the world which concerns us all, or whether we believe that our own spiritual fulfillment is something which is personal for us and entirely our own private affair—in which case our eyes are more or less turned away from the world except as a place to be lived in: to be enjoyed or disliked and so on but essentially indifferent to us.

I want to say something more about this notion of an objectively right work to be done in the world. In Subud this is expressed by the word *dharma*. If one looks back to its original meaning in Sanskrit, it is not connected with the law of cause-and-effect, which governs the actions of people and their consequences. That is called karma, or the law of results of the chain of causality. Dharma is something that is objective, common to all, yet in which each one of us has a certain special place. But of course this notion of dharma is by no means something exclusive to Subud, and the notion that there is an objective task to be done is very generally held. But often people forget about it and think instead in terms of some work to be done which is of a quite subjective kind. Let me try to explain what I mean by that. We can see subjectively, from our own feelings, that things are wrong with the world. We can see it is wrong that people should be hungry, and right that we should wish to feed them. We may feel it is wrong that people should be ignorant and feel they should be given the opportunity of learning. We feel it is wrong that people should be neglected and thrown out in

190

their old age, and we feel something should be done to care for the aged and the sick and so on. These beliefs, if we look at them sincerely, come from our own feelings.

We cannot always know objectively. For example, I read the other day, in a quite serious scientific paper written in America, that at one time it was thought that there could be some good in poverty, but today this foolish idea has fortunately disappeared and it is now understood that happiness depends upon material prosperity. This was written as if it were the same sort of scientific fact as the law of gravitation, but it is not only a subjective interpretation of human life, it is not even true, as anyone who has lived among poor people knows, especially in countries where there are what we would call great poverty and low standards of living. I know, from having been among people in all parts of the world, that there is no connection between riches and happiness, yet someone can take it as an axiom that in order to be happy one must be rich! It is not even true that in order to be happy one must have one's belly full. It is just as possible to be very unhappy and ruin one's life through overeating as it is to be very unhappy and ruin one's life through starvation.

I am saying all this because I want you to see something which seems to me, from my lifelong experience, very clear: that there are various subjective notions about what is good for people—what is required. These notions are not necessarily wrong, and they can come from a very sincere love of kind: a wish for other people to have the benefits that we ourselves enjoy. But this is not the same thing as the objective work expressed by this word Dharma. In the objective work there is something much more directly concerned with the total welfare of mankind. Sincere and acute observers who see what would be the outcome of achieving everything commonly regarded as subjective betterment, realize that it can arrive at something like Aldous Huxley's book, *Brave New World*—or other kinds of disastrous utopias. And people who look at it in that way and try to find a subjective solution for the human problem, never can find any solution which, if carried through, would not lead to its own opposite. It seems therefore that the objective work must be something different, based upon different laws from those that simply govern the immediate subjective satisfactions of people. Beyond these quite genuine physical or mental needs there is something else that has to be done, and it is to that "something else" that the word Dharma refers. The objective wisdom that directs the Dharma is of a totally different order from the subjective wisdom that man can ordinarily bring to bear on our human problems. This is why, in Subud—*Susila Budhi Dharma*—the word put in the center is *Budhi*—from the word *bhod* that means the supreme unique wisdom which is the direct contact with reality—without any veil, without anything in between—that same power of immediate perception which Gurdjieff has called "the highest gradation of objective reason." And, again quoting Gurdjieff, it is only those beings who have come to a high gradation of objective reason who can really see what is required in the world and so will not produce subjective and perhaps even disastrous results with the best will in the world—as happens with people who have only the subjective reason of knowledge or emotions.

If that is true, then this objective, real work in the world, is something beyond the understanding of ordinary people. But this does not mean it is totally veiled and inaccessible. If we will really put away our own subjectivity, we can see that the conditions of life that are really best for man can be mirrored in the conditions of life that are best for ourselves. Through really seeing this we can recognize how different they are from our own subjective desires and suppositions. How often we can see in our own lives that what had seemed unmitigated disaster has afterwards turned out to be the very best thing that could have happened to us! How often we see that success in achieving something that we longed for has resulted in our lives taking a turn that was totally unsatisfactory to us, from which we were obliged to turn back with quite a lot of suffering and grief! As we grow older and begin to see such things, we no longer look at the events of our lives in terms of what we liked or disliked—what we hoped for or what we feared—but in terms of the conditions that they create for our spiritual transformation. And it no longer matters to us whether things correspond to our subjective feelings; what matters to us is that they should correspond to our objective requirements. And if it is so with us individually, it is so with the whole of mankind. It may well be that the disasters that have come over mankind in this present century were really great blessings for the world of the future. Who knows if it might not be necessary for still greater disasters to come so that the destiny of mankind can be brought back into its right channel, and who could possibly say that this was for the ill, for the hurt of mankind? If we see what clever people can certainly do, what would be the outcome of the fulfillment of all the subjective desires of people? What kind of Utopia would be created if we could have everything we want? And how terrifying that would be!

As we begin to see and understand things a little bit more in that way, something in us begins to become more sensitive and more aware of the kind of work that is really required in the world. Maybe that helps us to be prepared to find a place for ourselves in it so that we can make our own contribution. It is not an easy thing. But if we do begin to see that there is this great meaning in human life, then it begins to be as important for us that we should serve and take part in this as that we should find our own private perfection, private salvation. Only about this we must never deceive ourselves. There is no use at all having wonderful dreams of how we could do good to mankind. If any of us ever wish to serve mankind, we must know that this means a special kind of commitment. A commitment to disregard, as far as we are capable of doing, our own subjective wishes and hopes and fears. It requires an incessant practice to do that. If we cannot do it in little things, we will not do it in big things. It is certainly much easier to "do good." One can do a lot of "good" and still remain the slave of one's own subjectivity, and not sacrifice anything from one's own inner egoistic standpoint. This does not mean that "doing good" does not produce good results, both for others and for ourselves. If we do good, we shall attract to ourselves corresponding results; this is Karma. But doing good is not the same as Dharma; not the same as the objective work.

I am going to tell you the story of Moses and Khidr. Khidr is the name given in Islam to the hidden prophet, who is always present in the world. He goes about instructing those few who are able to receive his teaching and intervening in events whenever it is necessary. It appears that Moses, during the time of his preparation—he was forty years old—met Khidr one day, and asked if he could travel with him. And Khidr said, "Yes, you may do so providing you never question anything I shall do." So together they boarded a ship, where they were very kindly treated, and arrived at a port. But as they were disembarking, while the sailors were all occupied, Khidr took a piece of iron and stove in the bottom of the ship so that it sank, and went on his way. Next Khidr saw a little boy sitting at the side of the road and, picking up a stone, bashed in his head. Moses of course was getting more and more alarmed by everything he was seeing. They then went past a place where some people were building a wall. It was not firm, and by pushing it hard Khidr made it collapse. This act aroused great complaint, because the wall had belonged to a poor widow with only enough money to have it built and she too appeared ruined by this. Finally Moses could hold his tongue no longer and said to Khidr "Why do you do such things?" He said, "You were not to question anything I do.

Since you do question me, I will answer. But then I must leave you."
Then he explained: "The harbor we entered is governed by a terrible
tyrant, who seizes any ships arriving with merchandise and imprisons
the crew. As this ship sank, he will ignore it and they will be able to
repair it and escape. The child I killed was otherwise destined to
become a monstrous tyrant and kill his own brother and father. I saved
him from the frightful consequences of this destiny. Beneath the wall I
destroyed, the widow's husband had secretly buried all his money for
her. She had been unable to find it, but when they dig up the wall to
repair it, they will find this treasure and she will benefit." Then Khidr
disappeared.

You have probably all heard this story. It is told in Eastern countries
to people who imagine it is always possible to know when one is doing
objective good, or objective harm. But harm even towards oneself one
cannot see without knowledge.

After-Lunch Discussion
Questioner. How can we recognize when we are responding to
dharma and getting free from karma?
JG Bennett. There are two converging lines of understanding that
begin from opposite ends. Only when they meet can we really know
this. One line begins from the whole, the other line begins from ourselves. You cannot start by knowing your place in relation to the whole,
and you cannot know the whole in sufficient detail to understand practically what is going on until these two lines are beginning to meet in
your experience. At first, we can know about the whole only in principle: roughly what I said earlier. But gradually there can grow in us a
certain confidence that there really is such a thing as objective work,
and with that a real wish to understand it and to find one's own place
in it. With that something begins to "come towards us": that is to say,
what is at first very general and necessarily vague, begins to take on a
certain definition. That is one of the two directions.

The other direction is, very simply, immediately from ourselves: it is
the distinction between necessary and unnecessary actions. All our
unnecessary actions produce what is called *vikarma*, or the undesirable results which only make us more involved. They are the causes of
all our human slavery. Necessary actions are called a-karmic, that is,
they do not produce consequences that have to be paid for. When I do
just what is necessary, I am not involving myself in any karmic consequences. For example, my breathing is a necessary function; when I

breathe, it is not producing results that I have afterwards to pay for. Everything that is really necessary for the maintenance of my bodily life is a-karmic. On the other hand, everything I do that is unnecessary in relation to my body will produce consequences, but the consequences will be in relation to my body. Everything that I do with my mind that is necessary for my mind is a-karmic, but everything that I do with my mind that is unnecessary is vi-karmic, and this produces results which I afterwards will have to pay for. Similarly, with my feelings. If my feelings respond only to what is necessary, that is, to give force to my right actions, this is not vi-karmic: it is not producing adverse results. But when my feelings become involved unnecessarily in anything beyond what the situation requires, it produces its own consequences.

As we come to know ourselves and observe what is happening, we can recognize more and more clearly what are necessary and what are unnecessary actions, and also, intermediate between these, more or less harmless actions, which we can allow ourselves without any serious consequences. This develops discrimination, which is quite solid and reliable for oneself; that is, one learns to recognize very well when one is falling into a sequence of unnecessary actions with body, mind or feelings. One knows quite well that this will have to be paid for; and certainly a wise man, who has understood things, wishes as quickly as possible to pay for the consequences of his vi-karmic actions in order to be free.

From that kind of discrimination there comes also the ability to see when an action will have desired consequences, and then one will undertake an action foreseeing the consequences of it, which include making full allowance for the facts which are outside our possible knowledge and control, and accepting whatever they may introduce into the situation. This is a discrimination which is a stage beyond the discrimination simply of necessary from unnecessary. All of this is what I call the line which starts from ourselves and it is based upon our own self-knowledge and self-discipline. The other, the first line, is the one that comes from the whole, from the totality of the entire plan or the purpose of things. This, generally speaking, we require some intermediary help in discerning, and this is where traditions and the seeking out of wise people are important for us. That is why it is always said: "If possible endeavor to live among wise people and not among foolish people."

Q. What can we do if we live among foolish people?

JGB. I did not mean that we should try to avoid all contact with foolish people; it is not true that we should only seek out a favorable and positive environment. I only said it in reply to T.'s specific question about how we can know what is the objectively right thing, or Dharma. This we shall certainly not learn from foolish people! We should be prepared to live in all kinds of difficult conditions. And always remember this: that there is never anyone from whom we cannot learn. There is no person so foolish that in one way he or she is not wiser than I am. Whatever person I look at, I must always know there is something that person understands better than I do. It is always true. Because in every person there is a point of wisdom. That is what we should look out for. And then you will see, sometimes with astonishment, that people who are very foolish in their lives, who live according to very foolish and harmful values for themselves, or who are filled with all kinds of stupid vanities and pretensions and who you know are imitating false things, pretending they are their own—every kind of stupidity that man is capable of—you will always know that any one of these people will always say or do something which can be profitable for you. And it is very good for oneself, always when looking at people, to look for the point of wisdom in them; that is, to look at every person to see not what they cannot understand but what they can understand.

Q. In the story of the three people whom the wise man helped, are we to understand—do apparently evil actions really contain good?

JGB. Khidr only did things that looked like evil actions from the outside, because the difference between Khidr and Moses was that he could see what Moses could not see. This is not a question of good or evil, it is a question of seeing or being blind. Absolute evil is a different question; there cannot be absolute evil because this would mean that there are two absolute powers in the world: God and the absolute evil, and it is not possible to think like that. If you mean that everyone who bangs someone else over the head with a stone is always going to produce a good result, this is not true. Certainly there can be vicious people and vicious actions. And it can be that the vicious actions of people can do real harm to others. Whether or not, beyond it all, the justice of God works itself out behind all this, this we simply cannot know. To try to find plausible explanations so that one can reconcile oneself to whatever one observes happening in the world—and to say "It is all right because of such and such"—this is not right. Really there is here a mystery that we cannot fathom. In the Gospels read in church this morning, there was the account of Jesus weeping over Jerusalem because its people did not know all that he saw in advance, all the disasters that were to come to Jerusalem because they did not know what had visited them. This is an extraordinarily interesting passage to try and understand. Why is it that these consequences came just because they did not see? And also the other side of the story I told this morning of Khidr and Moses. The results of Khidr's actions were good because he could see their results right through to the end, even with the boy whose head he smashed in. I think in one version of the story he tells how many years in hell this boy was saved from, by the fact that he was killed prematurely. In the other cases, the beneficial consequences were either directly or indirectly to be seen. That is probably the reason for the three different parts of the story.

But in the Gospel story of "not having seen the hour of thy visitation," just because of that failure to see, all the subsequent tribulations came upon Jerusalem. One has to see for oneself that there is this extraordinary working. We were talking earlier about Karma. In this case it was very clear how these distinctions T. was asking about worked themselves out. The Dharma, that is, the Providential Purpose—the entry of the new transforming powers of the human life—that was fulfilled; but the Karmic consequences of blindness had also to be fulfilled. They are very interesting, these passages; they strike one deeply when one hears them; because immediately after this part concerning the weeping over Jerusalem and seeing these inevitable consequences of their blindness comes another part about the foolishness of the people buying and selling in the temple. There something could be done directly about the situation, the action was visible, and the people could be saved.

This is the reason why the story of Christ whipping the money-changers out of the temple is so like a story of Khidr. On the face of it He was doing something altogether wrong: desecrating the temple, bullying and ill-treating people who thought what they were doing was very good and so on, but in reality He was making certain things possible. Because He could see what nobody else could see who was round Him at that time. All these things are really to show us what a terrible thing blindness is. How apparently unjust it seems that people should be punished for their blindness! For how, if they cannot see, can they help making mistakes?! The answer is that we have no right to be blind because we have possibilities of seeing.

"We can understand the law of *Harnelmiatznel*—'the higher blends with the lower in order to actualize the middle'—by taking a simple action from everyday life. The material world is passive compared with us people. We can act on it. In that sense we are higher and the material world is lower, or we are more active and the material world is more passive. As an illustration let us think of the material world as a knife and of myself, or my activity, as my hand. The knife alone can do nothing: it cannot cut although its function is to cut. Also my hand cannot cut although it wants to cut. There is a loaf of bread to be cut. This loaf of bread can only be cut if my hand and the knife come together: if the higher blends with the lower. Then something new comes into existence which is neither my hand nor the loaf of bread, nor just these two together. We can call this 'the cutting action.' This is the 'middle.' It is higher than the loaf of bread and lower for 'me'— that is, for my intention."

—from *Talks on Beelzebub's Tales*

27.
BEING PRESENT

16 August 1964

I THINK THE SIMPLEST THING IS for me to return this morning to one of
the themes of the Summer School that is good for everyone to remember; then those of you who have only come for the day can use this as
an exercise to work on today.*

Everyone knows that we tend to have our attention too much in the
mental associations and visual images that are constantly streaming in
front of the "inner mirror" in our minds. This state brings with it an
imbalance of the organism: the body tends to develop tensions because
we are not in our proper center-of-gravity. The result of this is that people pass a great deal of their time in an unnatural state, which produces fatigue without doing anything or showing any results for it. In
this state we are divided between a condition of aimless activity in the
mind—daydreaming, idle thoughts, repetition over and over again of
conversations; or simply brooding over things where our feelings have
somehow been touched, pleasantly or unpleasantly—while on the
other hand our bodies are in a kind of tension which is really a reaction
against this over-absorption of energy into the mental associations.

You must understand that the mental associations themselves cannot be stopped, because they are simply the result of the activity of the
brain. They are simply the result of physiological processes: of the constant discharging of their energy impulses in the brain. It is not a matter of stopping or arresting associations; when that is done it is for a

* This Sunday Talk took place during the activities of the 1964 Summer School. Bennett's usual
practice of answering questions after lunch, which may have been a silent meal, was not followed.

quite different purpose and it produces totally different concentrations of energy. Therefore what I am speaking about now is not of stopping thoughts or emptying the mind, but reducing to normal the amount of sensitivity that goes with it, or (in plain language) learning how not to pay attention to our own thoughts, mental images, dreams and the rest of it. With that the problem also is to achieve a more relaxed condition of the body—which becomes tense, as it were, as an involuntary resistance against this absorption with the processes going on in the head.

The simplest technique for this is the one I describe as "lowering the center," by which I mean lowering the center of gravity of our attention and interest from the head to the region between the two breasts, the navel, and the throat—where most of our feeling concentrations are localized. It is normal for man to be constantly and always aware of himself in this central place. From this place he can maintain a balance between the bodily activity and the mental activity. With that there comes a spontaneous relaxing of tensions in the body and a cessation of this tension in the mind, in the thoughts. This is what I would recommend you to try during the day. Whenever you find that your "interest" (or what we call your "sensitivity") has filled you with this awareness of thoughts, mental images and so on, then bring it down. The way to bring it down is not, as it were, to transport anything, but to awaken the sensitivity which is always latent here in the breast. It takes very little practice and most of you already know how to do it perfectly well by bringing the attention here to awaken a feeling of one's own self: of "I," of "I am here present," of "This is where I am." While I am speaking to you, a comparatively small part of my attention is in what I am thinking and in my body. It is mainly centered as a fairly strong awareness of myself here in my breast, so that I feel in consequence a certain harmony between my bodily state and my thinking state.

This can be strengthened and eventually firmly established in us by practice. We will then even experience discomfort when this sense of being present in oneself goes away and we notice that something is lacking. One sees "I am not here," and then one brings this awareness back again and at once there ceases to be the same degree of absorption in, or noticing of, the mental images and pictures—and a very great diminution of this pestilential inner talking that afflicts practically everyone.

I can recommend this exercise as a regular practice because it is designed to bring us back to what is the normal state for man—or nearer to it—called the "all-centered balanced state": the state where our energies are appropriately distributed between thought, feeling and organic sensation. In this all-centered balanced state it is possible for us to have a certain initiative in our own hands and to be free from the impulses of the body, from the activity of our own thoughts, and also from our own feeling reactions, our likes and dislikes, and the rest of it.

I certainly do not mean to suggest that you can, in one morning or in any short time, arrive at experiencing as a "second nature" (or even a return to the first nature) this all-centered balanced state: but this is what one should look for. We never should be satisfied with having all our sensitivity drawn into one of our functions. In that state there is no possibility of controlling or directing anything because there is no possibility of our consciousness disentangling itself from what is going on.

No one should feel comfortable when their attention is all in random thoughts, bits of conversation, pictures and so on, sounds passing through, music, voices and all the rest of it. All this is a messy way of existing which also produces all sorts of adverse effects on the organism and on the whole of our inner state. We should always be trying to withdraw the sensitivity from this, so that it fades into a more or less vague background in the way that dreams (which are also always present as mental images forming various kinds of dramatic patterns) simply fade away when we are awake, because other stronger impressions block them out.

28.
THIS—HERE—NOW

4 November 1963

I WANT YOU TO indicate with your bodies how you would express what you receive when I say the words "this—here—now." Would you just make some gesture without having to ... ? All right. Thank you very much.

I would say that the most natural way to express this is through some gesture of one's right hand. Had it been "I—here—now" then I might have felt more strongly that I had to indicate my presence in my own breast. But if one says "this" instead of "I" it seems for most people there is an awareness that our right hand is the most natural contact with "this—here—now."

Why is "this—here—now" important for us? Why do we say we should be "present"; and why do we feel if we are not present that something is lacking? Because this present moment is the point of action. It is here that something can be done. We can "repair the past"; we can "prepare the future"; but it is only in this present moment that something can be done, only here that it can be done, and only this can be done. This which can be recognized as able to be done at this moment: *this* is what I can do now.

There are many things that are possible for me, but to make those possibilities real I have to make them actual. That means I have to bring them to "this—here—now." There may be a hundred things I could say: this is what I am saying. At this moment the instrument that I am using is my vocal instrument, my sound-producing instrument. For other things I should use my eyes, my feet, some different

202

parts of my body, but probably the one we can take as typical to symbolize this instrumental element is our right hand. Anyhow, let us take it as that for today.

Through "this—here—now" there is for us a certain anchorage in reality. If we lose touch with it we are hard put to distinguish reality from fantasy. But in "this—here—now" fantasy has no place; and the more fully and completely I can enter into "this—here—now" the more I have that element of concrete complete experience.

It is certainly only one element. Man cannot live just in "this—here—now" because he is more than that. He has past and future. He has the power of understanding what is possible, of seeing the significance of things and how they can be connected. All of that is there for him. But what is the use of all that if it isn't brought into "this—here—now"? When we do different work we are brought into this contact; but very often it is a very imperfect contact: a kind of shortsighted contact where we are only aware of just what is holding our attention and interest at the moment. That is not the true experience of "this—here—now"; the true experience is of something complete: a complete human body with human life in it, serving as an instrument enabling me to act; and also at the same time giving me my own place. If I am not in my "this—here—now" I am just merged into everything else. As I become aware of being anchored in my own "this—here and now" I am both much stronger in myself and much more strongly real—for other people, for other things—for the world. If we have not got this anchorage we dissociate. It is inevitable. Not only do we lose touch with our own bodies, but the different parts of us lose touch with one another. Our thinking loses touch with our feelings and then they begin to disagree and war with one another.

The other side of "this—here—now" is what is sometimes called the "eternal present": the sense of the timeless infinite to which we also belong. It is just as real and just as necessary for us but we mustn't confuse the two—which does happen when people talk of the "eternal present" as if it also gave the "this—here—now"—but it doesn't. One can lose oneself in this contemplation of infinity, so that one's thinking and feeling, one's sense of past and future are all turned towards something remote: with the idea perhaps that if we could cast anchor—get away from this, here, and now—we could get to that other. But that is not how man is formed and not what he is for. Man stands between his immediate present of "this—here—now" and the infinite present that is neither "this" nor "here" nor "now" but everything and everywhere. He has no choice—he cannot say "I will take this and leave that"—because he is made so.

But what I am proposing to you today is not something in these realms of high philosophy but a practical thing. To exercise yourself in keeping a more constant and stable awareness of "this—here—now" with the help of your right hand. You can lay your right hand on your right knee, or anywhere that is convenient so that you can now speak to your right hand. "This living right hand of mine" is what symbolizes for me my power to act. "All the day it will accompany me, all the day it will be working, I wish to remember it and I wish it to remember me; and by this fellowship between myself and my right hand to keep a sense of my own presence." From my right hand my whole body will remember. From my body my inner feelings and thoughts will remember. For that I have to transfer the decision into my hand. It is not enough that I should merely think: "My right hand is my contact with the world." This must be put into the hand itself. "Let it accept this task to do for me today, that in all its actions it will remember it stands for my contact with the world." My right hand must work with all the other parts of my body; it must not claim any sort of precedence (because of this task which it has been given), but it is going to take that responsibility towards me. Many times during the day it will remind me: that is, there will come from my hand an impulse which will remind me that I must be present and by being present I shall be unified—united.

After-Lunch Discussion

Questioner. What is the difference between self-love and that sort of awareness you spoke of this morning?

JG Bennett. There are two kinds of self-love. Right and necessary is the love of self because it is the center of our own being; and we must love this. There is wrong love of self when we substitute for that our own imaginary picture, and project our feelings and interests on to that imaginary picture. This produces a false self-love: a narcissistic love where we only like looking at our own picture, whereas we never look at the real self. But what I spoke of today is really a way from the false one towards the other. When we are in the state of self-awareness, which is founded on our physical presence, we cannot have the same kind of false self-love. That is really the best one can say.

Q. As we have spoken about love could we have some light on what psychologists mean when they say love and hate go together? It is almost implicit that if you have got love you have got hate, and I find that very difficult. I do hate; and lots of people I love.

JGB. This is connected with feeling. Love of feeling always has polarity in it. Gurdjieff for example says, "Love of consciousness evokes the same in response, love of feeling evokes the opposite, and love of body is only type and polarity." Love of feeling is really a boomerang. Because feelings are necessarily divided, like and dislike are inseparable from one another. Love of consciousness is beyond this; so when psychologists speak about it they are only talking about love up to that point where it is no more than the love of our functions—which is the only kind of love that can be studied.

A very sobering thing to realize is this—as it gradually comes to be a truth that one cannot deny—that love of feeling evokes the opposite. Sometimes it is terribly and painfully obvious when pouring out a feeling of love just produces aversion in the object of that love. Sometimes it produces a reaction in us also. But one has to understand that this dualistic or two-edged love doesn't go beyond our functions. It is not the love that comes from our true self; for the love that is from our consciousness hasn't got this. It neither likes nor dislikes, neither approves nor disapproves, neither agrees or disagrees, it just accepts. It unites.

Q. If consciousness is beyond this polarity of like and dislike in our feelings; and we can never remove their action from ourselves, why are they useful for man to have?

JGB. Because out of them he generates the force that he requires for his actions. By overcoming one's attachment to likes and dislikes one gets strength; and each time one does it one has an access of strength. Whenever we give way to likes and dislikes we fall into weakness. If we were deprived of like and dislike—if we had no polar nature at all—we shouldn't have anything from which to draw force. It is like the poles of a magnet. In order to get force from the poles of a magnet you have to hold yourself right in the field of action of its two poles. In the same way, in order to get force out of the dualism of our nature we have to hold ourselves in the field of it—not let ourselves be drawn to one side or the other because this simply neutralizes their polar force.

Q. Mr. Bennett, can you tell me what it is that remembers the hand? This happened for me several times this morning. What is the technique of this? What is it that remembers?

JGB. It is your "will." If we know how to do it we can place our will where we choose; and that point, that place, becomes the center of initiative. When I said this morning: "I decide this, and I ask that my hand will be a source of remembering to me"—and it certainly was, over and over again, during the morning—the impulse to remember my own presence, and so on, came from my hand. It did not come from my head to my hand; it came from my hand to my head. I expect many of you felt the same, wasn't it so? [Yes.] Usually, everything has a little will of its own that just lives its own life; and there is no sense of wholeness in us. But if we choose to, we can bring this about.

Q. Does it mean that we can do this any time if we choose to?

JGB. It is the nature of the will that it is able to divide itself. The One will, which is God's will, divides into everything. A portion is given to you and to me. It is not really our own but it is put at our disposal. We are entrusted with it. But with this that we have been given, we can again do the same. We can distribute this will into our different parts. Usually all this is happening the whole time unintentionally and chaotically, so that we have many different "I"s saying, "I" will this, "I" won't that, "I" wish, "I" think, "I," "I," "I." Each one of these is a little parcel or fragment of will, but this happens by weakness not by strength: our will has divided into pieces into nothing. But there is also the opposite power in us: to put our will where we choose. That power we also have. When you do this kind of exercise that we did this morning, you realize you can endow your hand with something that makes it independent of you; yet it is still part of you. And from that we can learn also about our relationship to a greater will.

Everything in us should be able to say "I" in such a way that it never forgets where it gets its "I" from. When we have asked our hand to work in this way, it does remember that it was given this "I" by us, by this "I" here, and therefore it remains connected with it. We also should remember, whenever we say "I," that we are saying it with a will that has been lent to us by the Supreme Will; and therefore every time we say "I" we should feel this connection with the source of all "I"s. Instead of which we remain separate; and then, from this separateness in the center of us, there comes also a separateness all through-and-through so that every little bit says "I" without recognizing anything else.

Q. Isn't there a danger of one becoming like little Jack Horner? He said "What a good boy am I!" You might say: "Well, how clever of me to do this with my hand!"

JGB. There could be. At first you would say: "Well, thank you very much. I've been shown how to do this." Later on you would say: "Well, now I've learned how to do it," and later on still you would say: "I invented the whole of this." That is how we tend to be. This is one reason why this whole spiritual life of man must be seen as something organic. If you take one particular action and rely exclusively on this, it can produce a certain narrowing of significance; and there is a great danger that one then attaches oneself to it and thinks "I" because of this. Although it is true what you say, that there is a danger, it is the height of stupidity to think that when we do something which we are allowed to do because there is a higher power, we are doing it of ourselves in defiance of the higher power!

If we begin to see in ourselves, for example, how helpless feeling is because it will always evoke or produce its own opposite, this knocks the ground from under a great deal of our self-love and egoism. It is really a good thing to realize for ourselves that what we like in ourselves is only one pole of a magnet and what we dislike is the other pole; for, as you know, a magnet cannot exist with one pole only. When you slowly become aware that you can't have anything good in you without also having something bad—can't like anything without also disliking—a sense of helplessness comes over you. You realize that many things you relied upon and attributed to yourself as strengths are nothing at all, because they are continually being cancelled out by something else. When we begin to enter the regions beyond that, egoism has nothing more to hold on to. But of course, no one can ever dare to say "Here is a safe way and if you follow it there are no pitfalls."

JG Bennett. In order to teach men about reality somebody invented a game called "golf" in which you have to get a little ball into a hole. And they put all kinds of pitfalls and obstacles in the way: hazards as they call them. That game was really invented by somebody to be a kind of reminder to people of what life is like.

Q. Has that any sense in it?

JGB. Yes. It is highly symbolic. Golf was, I believe, invented in Persia at a time when they had great knowledge there.

"The process starts from the moment when the ovum of the oak flower is fertilized. Before that instant there was no single whole in which all the possibilities of the future oak were present. At that moment of fertilization, the future oak tree, with the whole structure of its existence, is in a state of pure potentiality—within the limits of its hereditary determination · everything oak-like is potential but nothing yet is actual. Thereafter, actualization proceeds continuously but in distinct transitions, at each of which a frontier is passed and a new land of promise is entered. The flower dies—the acorn is formed—the acorn ripens and falls to the ground. Here is the moment of crisis, for, each year, millions of acorns mature but few germinate, since in order to do so the acorn must fall among favorable conditions such as pressure and a spot of fertile ground with the requisite dampness. From germination comes the seedling. Once again there is a well-marked transition and, as nourishment begins to be drawn from the soil, the husk of the acorn is discarded. In the next stage— from seedling to sapling—the plant struggles for light and air. If it finds a place in the sun, the sapling becomes a tree of the forest and, unless destroyed by disease, by fire, or by the woodsman's axe, it grows until it reaches maturity. It then begins to decay, and when its strength is finally exhausted, its life-cycle is completed and it dies. This is the structure of its life."

—from *The Dramatic Universe, Vol. I*

29.
SERVING THE WORK

(date unknown)

THERE IS SOMETHING I want you to understand about your coming here. If, as I sometimes do, I were to ask all of you why you come; some would answer that they want to learn more about work or that they see the value, the need, of working with other people; or that they want opportunities for trying out new methods of work in a more concentrated way than is possible in the ordinary conditions of life. I want you to see that there is something lopsided about this way of looking at it. "Lopsided" doesn't mean "all wrong." It simply means that there is not the right balance. I will illustrate what I mean by an example which you all must have noticed. People are given various jobs to do here, and apart from that there is teaching about work such as these talks, or classes of Movements. Some people seem to think that these talks and the Movements are the important thing, and that they ought to drop anything else in order to come to these; even if they have something for which they are responsible, let us say, like looking after children.

I want you to see that that really turns everything upside down. How could we come here and think, "I have a right to hear the talk" "I have a right to do Movements?" It almost amounts to, "I wouldn't bother to come unless I saw that I was going to get something useful for myself out of it." I want you to put yourself in front of that kind of attitude, and really see for yourselves what is missing. What is missing is that there isn't a feeling for the significance of the Work itself. We bring our own personal attitude into it—"What do I get out of it?" "What use is it to me?"—and don't, at the same time, ask ourselves: "What can I give to it?" "What use am I to the Work?" I want you to realize that it is necessary always to feel the need to get something for oneself; but if one is wholly concerned with that and that only, everything will sooner or later get lopsided and quite out of balance. It is not only what you or I can get out of it, or even what use it can be to all of us, to a group of people. There has to be a greater reason for being here than that.

Every one of you, I suppose, has heard the term "Fourth Way." You must have read about it and so must have heard that in what is called Fourth Way work the fundamental motive for doing anything is that there is a task to be accomplished. Work for or with people is for the purpose of preparation for that task. To whatever level of the Work we may refer, the Fourth Way is always the same. If we are unable to be useful to the task that is being undertaken, we have no right to be here. But all of us can be useful if we will set ourselves to understand this. If you scrub a floor, you are useful to the task, but then you must understand that scrubbing the floor—in so far as it is useful to the task—is the most important thing of all; the rest is incidental to it. If you are put to look after children, looking after children is being useful to the task; it is the most important thing of all; everything else is incidental.

Perhaps you have a chance of working at the Movements; relatively few people can have much expectation of serving the Work through Movements. There are a few people who have to become teachers, or who will be able to demonstrate them in front of others. For people for whom there is no prospect of being of some service through doing the Movements, they must be looked upon not as a right but as a privilege. Such people must always remember that, in one sense it is a privilege, but in another sense it may be a help for them perhaps to be able to serve the Work in another direction. It may be that they will never be able to serve through Movements directly, but through Movements they may find something which increases their quality of attention, their ability to perceive, to find a right relationship with their bodies, and through that they may be able to accomplish some other tasks better.

It is the same with the study of the ideas. Someone may be able to take in one or another aspect of the ideas and to help in the working out of the material that has been given to us. It may be that someone else is not able to do that, and he or she will not be able to serve the Work through the ideas. But this doesn't mean that they shouldn't study the ideas, or take opportunities of going to lectures and so on. Only they have to see that it is then a privilege, which can be justified only if it is going to prepare them for serving the Work in some other way.

We have this place here at Coombe Springs. It is not just for the convenience of a number of people living together, to make life a little easier by sharing in the catering or other common tasks. Nor is it just an opportunity for the study of ideas or methods. We have no right to look at it that way, though maybe it is a little less egoistic than the first. This place can only have reason for its existence if it is a manifestation of Work. That means more than the provision of opportunities for people to come down here and do this or that job. It means that we have to understand that everything we do here can be done, if we have understanding, as a service to the Work. Many, many things have to be done which appear to have no lasting results. You scrub the floor today, tomorrow it is dirty, and it has to be scrubbed again. You cook a meal today; it is eaten, and tomorrow it has to be cooked again. You dig the garden this year; next year it has to be dug again. Out of all that, a little bit slowly, slowly—can be distilled. But it remains, and it begins to grow into a concentration of force of work. But you mustn't think that because what you are doing at the moment appears to be quite ephemeral, that nothing is distilled from it. The quality of what you put into your work remains; that isn't lost. The floor becomes dirty again, but the quality of the work that you put into scrubbing the floor doesn't disappear. It becomes part of the concentration of force.

I really wish you to think about this today; perhaps to speak to me seriously about it after lunch. I say this, because, if there is too much misunderstanding about this, it will affect, even spoil, nearly all that we are trying to do. If it is even possible for somebody to have such a thought as I described—that "I must go and do Movements, let somebody else see to the children, let somebody else do the washing up"—it is evidence of such a fundamentally wrong attitude that it must poison everything.

This is something we can study in a practical way. I am speaking now about our relationship and our attitude not so much towards one another as towards everything that we do when we come here. You can study by observing in yourself the sources from which proceed the impulses to be doing what you are doing at the moment. Maybe you can even assess how much really proceeds from a feeling of what work is. It is only in that way—not by thinking about it, not by theorizing about it, but by the way you observe your own impulses—that you will come to understand something about the third line of work.

After-Lunch Discussion

JG Bennett. I asked you all to try to observe where your impulses came from when you were doing anything—from what motive you were doing it.

Questioner. I found that my own motive was really quite selfish. I had finished the job that I had been set to do before ten thirty. I was standing in the hall looking at the notice board, when someone came up to me and asked me to do something else which was not in the book for me to do. Suddenly I took a very strong dislike; and I saw the resentment I felt at being asked to do this new job, which something in me did not really consider necessary. However, I started to do this other job and I saw that I was not doing it in the same way that I had done the first—not as well as I could have done. Then I started to do it better. But I saw this very strong resentment.

JGB. This kind of impulse you cannot help; but you have to see how absurd it is. If you ask yourself how often during the morning you could really say that what you were doing came from the feeling that it is for the sake of a task that you do it, how would you answer? Maybe you thought about that a number of times, but I think you will find you really had that feeling much less than you expected.

Q. What will I find much less?

JGB. I spoke this morning about there being a task that we all have to serve, and that this is the real reason for everything we are doing here. It is not that we are expected to do something if we come—such as working for half an hour, without being asked to do anything else—or that it is an opportunity for observing yourself, or studying—or that it is an opportunity for gaining approval by somebody saying, "Look! how hard he works" or "What a good attitude he has got," or something of that sort. You realize that those are not the things the work here is intended for. It is intended to help us to see how to work for some purpose bigger than ourselves, and not for what we get out of it. I say to you that if you look to see how often that motive really is the force making you do things, you see it is much less than you might suppose. Do you understand what I mean now? You might think you have that attitude, but when you look for it you see you have not got it. That is what I mean.

Q. I can't put my finger on a concrete example, but I did find it's a very big question for me—whether I can give something to the work

212

rather than just receive the work. I have never been able to find that, unallied from anything else, I should be able to give anything. It always comes back to this question. If I make an effort—at digging or anything like that—I always find that there will be a comeback to me from it. Relatively it seems that it is impossible to give the Work anything itself—there is always a comeback, however apparently unpleasant the job.

JGB. This is theorizing. This can never be clear to you by thinking about it. That kind of argument is just something that goes on in your head. I am not concerned with that. It often happens suddenly that you get taken from one thing to another. As you say, you are digging, and then somebody asks you to wheel something in a wheelbarrow and—very, very often at that moment—you have an inner reaction: "Why should I be changed over, I am getting on very well with my digging?" Or perhaps one may think: "I am thankful to have a change." At that moment there is a reaction in oneself; and you can observe: "Do I accept to do what I am asked to do because I am doing a task, or do my own subjective feelings about it enter at this moment—that I don't want to be bothered—that I don't want to be interfered with—that I've found something that interests me?" or even "Thank goodness I'm getting a change!" Is all that coming into it? Or do I really see at this moment that my response is: "Yes, I accept. If I'm asked to do that I will do it"? Do you understand? At that moment there is no room for all this theorizing. But you do realize that, in you, always some reaction comes whenever anything like that happens—does it not?

Q. It always seems an opportunity though.

JGB. It is impossible that you should be working with other people and not feel the action of them—the impulse to consider the other people in yourself—to notice what they are doing—to wonder if they are noticing what you are doing—to find that your work is affected by whoever happens to be looking at you! Who does not? It is not possible for anyone not to come under that action. Do you imagine you do not have that?

Q. Yes, I do imagine that to a certain extent.

JGB. It is only imagination. It is not possible. Nobody can possibly be free from that action. What do you think? Do you just go on doing your job quite unaffected by whether there are people there or not?

Q. No, there is a reaction. For instance: if I take off my shirt, I would have a reaction then; but usually I would try to deaden it down, try to reject the reaction.

JGB. You have to observe. That is all I say. You have to learn how to observe. You have not learned how to observe yet. You only talk about what you think. You do not see anything yet. You have to begin to take advantage of this opportunity to learn how to see yourself. All that you talk about is what you think. This is just a hotchpotch of half-observed things and a lot of imagination and preconceived ideas—and from that you will never get to know how things really are.

Q. I found I was more interested in finishing the job I was doing than in doing the job. If, while I was doing it, somebody came along and disturbed me, I became annoyed about it.

JGB. What is the difference between an objective and a subjective attitude towards what we are doing? Objectively, the situation is this: that we can only have power over a very small proportion of the factors that decide how things go and whether it will succeed or not—whether it will be finished or not finished—whether we shall finish it or not finish it. We can bring something to that, but never all that is required. There are factors we cannot control—or do not suspect—that determine how things will really go. You understand that in principle? [Yes.] But one still does not remember this. If you remember that you have no power to determine the outcome of what you do, that all you have power to do is to bring the best understanding that you have—this is what I call an "objective" attitude. When it is subjective, you forget all about the limitations of your own powers and replace them by all sorts of imagination about what you think you are doing and what might be done and reasons why it does not go this way or that way. With all that you at once begin to take offense when somebody interferes with you, or when some material thing does not happen to come out right and you begin to say "because of this" or "because of that." That is all subjective. One has to be able to observe how far one is in that state of subjectiveness about what one is doing. If one can manage to keep more or less objective, one realizes that there is a big task to be done: but that I do not understand what the task is as a whole and I could not. There are in any case factors that nobody is able to control—they are outside human control. And there are factors that people might be able to control if they understood them, but they do not. And therefore what is going to come from it all is not predictable by us. Yet that does not mean the task is unimportant or that our share in it is not absolutely necessary. What we have to bring is one necessary part of it, but we never can do more than that. If you could manage to remember this to some extent then you would not get affected in the same way when other people change the line of what you are doing, and so on. You must realize that this is all part of the inevitable uncertainty of whatever we do. The trouble is that we increase that uncertainty a great deal, quite unnecessarily, by trying to force things that cannot be forced, and by trying to do what we are not able to do.

Q. I find that sometimes it is not easy to find the immediate motive for what I am doing. For instance, when I undertook the task of doing the seminar notes, I think I did it because I knew it was needed and it was difficult for anyone else to do it. But I also knew that I liked doing them, and that I was pleased to have that justification for getting out of other jobs which I did not like doing—and I found it hard to disentangle all that.

JGB. One thing which is objective without question, is that that job needs to be done; and also that you are the person who has got most possibility of doing it. It does not mean you are the only person but the most natural and hopeful way of getting that job done is that you should undertake it. Once you see all that, it becomes the affirmation in relation to all this, which you need to try to keep in front of yourself. Various things begin to mix with that affirmation such as self-importance and using it for one's own purposes and so on. One also has to observe that. It is so, it is quite true: "Objectively this has to be done and yet I see I am using this in order to get some other benefit for myself." We all do that. You also see how other things pull on you—at moments when you could do something more than this, you allow something else to take you. You see all that. Through that you find where there are moments of struggle. Moments of struggle to keep the affirmation from getting mixed up with all these other things; moments of struggle when you make the denying part of you submit to this. When you are feeling tired or lazy or bored or wishing to do something else, you make yourself submit to the affirmation that you have accepted to do this job. So all the time it remains there for you, but it remains there for you not because it is good for you to do it or because people happen to be wanting to have these seminar notes or anything like that, but because, quite apart from any of us—you or me or the recipients of the notes or anything else—that is a job which is objectively wanted, and you know it is. That stands outside of all of us. And that is really what I want everyone to see—what it means to realize that one is in front of something which is objectively wanted, which therefore introduces into our lives a factor which is not to do with us personally.

Q. The only real motive I can find is that I am working under your influence and I sense that you regard as very important this task, whatever it is; I also sense that you are a person I feel I can trust, and so on. I do not necessarily do it because I want your approval but because I sense that you want it done and that it would be generally a good thing if it was done. But I still do not understand any objective motive of working for work's sake.

JGB. "Working for work's sake" is not the same thing as working for the sake of the Work. Working for work's sake means it is better to make efforts than not to make efforts; it is a good principle. But what we are speaking of today is not that. It is that we all of us need to understand to some extent—maybe I see more clearly than you, but still you can also see—that something is needed; that it would be a pity, to put it at its lowest, if this work were just to disappear—quite apart from what you may get out of it. Do you understand that?

Q. I can see it helps other people.

JGB. But if you say that to yourself, is that all you have to say about it? Helps other people to what? Why should they be helped? Do you consider that this work makes for a comfortable life?

Q. Well, I know certain people have told me that they have been helped.

JGB. Yes, but does it really just amount to that for you? Is the value of work to be measured just by the amount of help it has been to people?

Q. I don't know.

JGB. No, I ask you, how does it seem like to you?

Q. Well it seems to me that it is a very, very big thing.

JGB. Indeed, yes; I am not saying it is not. But then you should ask yourself what you mean by help—what kind of help? Great numbers of people are concerned with helping people, and many people complain and say, "This work of yours—you are not doing much to help people— what are you doing for the poor this-and-thats who have not got something-or-other?" You understand that it is *what kind* of a "something-or-other" that you give, that is the question?

Q. Yes.

JGB. And doesn't it mean something because it is in relation to a bigger whole? If we were simply an organization for running soup kitchens for starving refugees, you would say that was helping. But is that what we are doing? Is it just that kind of thing and not something else? There the help is measurable and tangible. You say somebody is hungry and you give him food. You say here people have been helped. But is it in that way that they have been helped? Here the word "help" must mean help in relation to the whole of life, to understanding something bigger than ourselves. If someone feels themselves better, it is not because they have more food in their stomachs or that they sleep better or got rid of their tummy-ache—is it?

Q. No, I do not think it is.

JGB. Perhaps they say their life has more meaning?

Q. Yes.

JGB. Ah! Now how can life have meaning except in relation to something? Meaning implies context. You can't have a meaning without a context, can you?

Q. No.

JGB. Therefore if we say we help people to find more meaning in their lives, we are speaking about showing them that and making them feel they have some relation to, some position in that. Is it not so?

Q. Yes.

It is in that sense that one speaks about work as something more than people, more than you or more than me, more than anyone who is helped or not helped. We can be helped, and it is something for all of us, because it is bigger than we are. If it were not bigger than we are it would not be doing that for us. You understand what I mean?

Q. Yes, I think I understand a little better.

JGB. If you realize just that one thing, that we are talking about something which is bigger than you are, than I am, more than the whole lot of us put together, then this idea that we are serving something that is bigger than we are has meaning for you. And if it is not bigger than we are how can it help us—except just to sleep better?

30.
THE SECOND DOMAIN

10 October 1965*

THIS MORNING I want to continue what I was saying yesterday about the Sarmoun Parable of the Three Domains in Idries Shah's, *Tales of the Dervishes,* and speak particularly about transition to the "second domain." Because you must understand that in most respects you still remain in the "first domain." That is, in what one might call a state of nature: trying to manage your life with your own native wit, without seeing what transformations are required—what work is necessary.

In order to enter the "second domain" some teaching is necessary. There is a kind of universal teaching that Gurdjieff called "objective morality." Everyone has this influence, whether well-transmitted or badly transmitted. It is still present in the general life of people, and has been for thousands of years. In it distinctions are made between those manifestations of people that either agree with objective morality or offend against objective morality. Of course, as you know very well, there are all kinds of subjective moralities that are invented by people, or are vestiges of good customs which have merely become meaningless habits—just social conventions and the like—or even wrong habits that have been taught as if they were objectively moral, as in Gurdjieff's story of Lentrohamsanin in *Beelzebub's Tales.* But in general we all of us have access to this objective morality. It is possible to refine this, to bring to it a clearer understanding of the two sides of our human nature. This is, for example, very well expressed in the sixteenth chapter of the *Bhagavad Gita* in those very terms, of the distinction in man

* A talk given to the Stoke-on-Trent group.

between that which belongs to the good nature and that which belongs to the bad nature. It is, again, general. It appears in many books—the Gita and the Old and New Testaments for example—and serves to help people to see how to distinguish between and separate in themselves their two different kinds of actions.

When people begin to make this separation in themselves between actions that are beneficial and those that are harmful, they are, to that extent, already engaged in "second domain" activity. There is already beginning to be in them a certain transformation; or as I said to you yesterday, there is a certain preparation of the "salt"; and I asked you all yesterday to think what is the meaning of the other two ingredients—"flour" and "water"—that were prepared in the "second domain'.

It is first of all necessary to understand that apart from this general process of separating in oneself the higher and lower nature—so that there can come between them a man's own "I," his own self, his "salt"—something else is required of us. That is, man is required as an apparatus for the transformation of energies. He is in the midst of life, depending upon life, depending upon materials—earth, air, sunlight, water. These undergo many transformations here in the life of this Earth and reach us in various prepared forms containing the substances that we require, both for our own inner growth and development, and that are also required for higher purposes, which man is constructed to transform—as the green vegetation is constructed to transform certain substances so that all life can be maintained on the Earth with the bases of life-maintenance that are the carbohydrates, proteins and fats. Animals also transform certain things and man does too, of a higher quality. But all transform. And all this is what Gurdjieff calls the "reciprocal-maintenance-of-everything-that-exists'.

In this "reciprocal-maintenance" we are involved in two ways: one is an obligatory way that is built into our nature, built into our construction as it is built into the construction of plants and animals. "Like not like, understand not understand," man has to, and does, transform certain psychic energies in the course of his experience. All his pleasures and pains, all his interests, everything that happens to him of a characteristically human kind, liberates—without his even knowing it—certain energies which are required for higher purposes, which man himself in general does not understand. But it is also possible for man to transform these energies intentionally, and thereby to very greatly increase the productivity of certain kinds of energy. And in doing that he fulfils a higher purpose. When he sets himself to do this, he brings himself into the "second domain" with another part of himself, which has to act intentionally in a process of transformation. Those kinds of actions which, for instance, people are taught they must perform as a duty, such as prayer, worship, are really to bring people towards this transformation—because all prayer is a transformation of energy; a separation of the fine from the coarse. In our own teaching we are told that man must "remember himself" and that the man who is "asleep" is of very little worth. It is quite true that it is in our own interest to remember ourselves, but the real reason why man should remember himself is because when he does, when he is conscious of his connection between the inner and the outer world (because that is what self-remembering is) he multiplies, ten times at least, the efficiency of transformation of energies in him. Instead of a trickle it becomes a steady flow.

So there are many things that are taught to people, not always with the accompanying understanding as to why it is done. Sometimes it is represented to them that the purpose of it is to get some benefit for themselves. This is not lying, not deceiving them, because that is also true; but it is not the objective reason why this kind of work is necessary. It is like saying to a child, "If you take this medicine you will have a sweet." This must be objectively true; the parents must not deceive the child. If it takes the medicine, it must have the sweet. But the purpose of the medicine is to cure, the sweet is by the way. You cannot explain to the child that this unpleasant medicine has to be taken for some reason that it cannot yet understand. So in many cases with us, men are taught things with the idea that they gain some benefit from it for themselves, and they do the things, and in fact the benefit is gained. But what is in fact accomplished is that a higher purpose is being served.

Truly and properly, to enter into the "second domain" one must understand, as well as possible, what this transformation is—so that the right materials can be produced, represented in this case by the "wheat" turned into "flour," ground to the right fineness, to the right condition. Everything that goes by the name of intentional work belongs to this, and is quite different from "morality." Morality is simply a separation of what is already in oneself that has become mixed up—a separation and a distinguishing of that which acts upon us negatively from that which acts upon us positively. Here there is something else. We have to take in, from the natural world, all kinds of impressions and materials, including the air that we breathe. By our own intentional action, by directing our attention, by submitting ourselves to certain operative conditions, methods, techniques, exercises and so on, we bring about the necessary transformation.

But it is also necessary to understand this: that man is everywhere in need of help; he cannot do anything by himself. If you imagine, for example, that we have come into this room together because of our own initiative, you must just pause and reflect: How did you? Whatever could have made such a thing occur to you? It is because something has been transmitted. And not only have the ideas of man's development, of possible transformation and so on been transmitted to you, but something else also that you have not seen, which is the possibility of responding to it.

This is different from objective morality. There man is clearly told something is required of him; and that it is within his own power to obey the commandments—or follow the rules—of objective morality.

But here there is clearly something that is not in our power: to see that something is relevant for us. Help is as important in this whole process as these other two—and really more so—because without help nothing could be done at all anyhow. Help corresponds in the parable to the element of "water." It has not got to be produced or transformed; it is gratuitous, it comes from the ocean and the sky. But at the same time it must be valued. It must be brought to the place where it is needed, and accepted. Help must not be thrown away and help must not be forgotten. If help accumulates in us, then, with that, our own understanding, our own power of work also grows.

What is necessary here, and really important, is to understand the gratuitous character of help. One cannot earn it. One can earn by work certain rewards of work. By morality one can become transformed into the kind of person that a man ought to be. But the completion of man's nature—his integration to reach a different level of being—that is not in his power. Because one cannot lift oneself from one level to another without the help of a higher level. That has to be grasped, and grasped again, and assimilated, and remembered. But just as, in the parable of the three domains, "water"—the universal medium of life on the earth—is always available, so it is true that help is always available.

The help that we receive, each one of us, is limited by one thing only: our capacity to receive it. Here, now, at this very moment, everything that is needed for our transformation is offered to us, but we cannot take it up because our capacity to receive it is so limited. Like water, it can only be taken to the capacity of the vessel placed to receive it. If you have only a thimble, there is nothing to be done: you can only take a thimbleful of water. This enlarging of the capacity to be able to receive is sometimes called the "opening of the heart," because the heart is compared to a vessel. "Heart" here does not mean emotion. If you know, in the language of The System, what is meant by the "higher emotional center," then that is this vessel I am speaking about. For most people the higher emotional center is no larger than a thimble. But it is made of such a flexible material that it is able to grow without limit. The power to see this is rare. It is invisible to the ordinary eye. Once this power was given to me, and I cherished it—not long ago, perhaps twelve or fourteen years ago—and I really saw what is this "heart," this part which is able to receive help, what unlimited possibilities it has and yet how it remains contracted, shut in, in us, rejecting all the time what is most necessary for us. It must be understood also that without this "opening of the heart" the true work of the "second domain" is not possible. That means it really belongs to the transition from the "first domain" to the "second domain": to be able to be helped, to be able to be taught, to be able to be given strength, understanding, love.

If these three things—flour, water, salt—are not understood, there cannot be that intermediary stage called "second domain" which is the preparation for the final stages of transformation. This means that every one of us has got a means of examining our situation. If what I have been saying is clear to you, and convinces your own reason that "It must be so," then each one of us must examine ourselves: "Are we in the presence of these three actions?"

One last thing I want to say: I want to suggest that today we do as we do on Work Sundays at Coombe Springs; that is, that we have lunch in silence. Last night I could see that you had not, for the most part, been aware of the purpose of the silent meal. It is a very important purpose that is at work here. The transformation of energy by eating is a cosmic process in which we participate. It is the transformation, through us, of life. Man should not forget that his existence depends upon life other than his own. He cannot exist here on the earth without the help of other life. This other life must be respected, and in the act of eating we must bring ourselves into a state of respect for the life that has been sacrificed in order that we should be alive at this moment. At times when people were more civilized than we are now, it was regarded as a great sin to eat without a feeling of respect and gratitude for life.

So, for a good practice and also for strengthening in us the awareness of the transformation in which we are constantly engaged, we should, before we begin eating, pause and bring ourselves into a state—in front of the food that we are going to eat—of remembering that this is life, and that in taking this life we also incur a responsibility. If we fulfill that responsibility, we are blameless. In fact we are doing our duty, because we are here on this earth to perform certain tasks. If anyone really wakes up to what life is, and to the dependence of our existence upon the life of the Earth, this becomes a very strong reminding-factor for him of the responsibility of our existence. It delivers us from the kind of wanton disrespect for life which is characteristic of people. Although there goes with it a kind of sentimental feeling (they would not hurt a cat, or something like that) at the same time they will use innumerable lives in hundreds of ways with no respect for what they have done.

"Sacrifice is never easy. Until the decision is taken it seems almost impossible. Not physically impossible but requiring an act of will that we refuse to make. Once a wealthy lady in one of Ouspensky's groups, about 1923, said in the weekly meeting that she wanted at all costs to be free from herself and asked if she could do anything about it. Ouspensky asked her to name some possession to which she was particularly attached. 'Yes,' she said, 'I have a Dresden tea set that belonged to my grandmother and is still intact.' Ouspensky said: 'Break one of the cups and you will know what it is like to be free.' Next week she returned in tears and almost hysterical saying that she had tried a dozen times and could not bring herself to do it. Ouspensky's dry comment was: 'So you see, this desire for freedom is not worth one cup.'"

—from *Transformation*

31.
"I" AND "NOT-I"

5 April 1964

I EXPECT many of you have studied Buddhist Scriptures and know the exercise the Buddha used to teach his disciples: of sitting and looking at one part of themselves after another and saying, when they had really looked at it: "That is 'not-I,' this is no self of mine," starting with their limbs and their organs, and then coming further in, into their thoughts and feelings and various inner experiences and really looking at them to convince themselves by direct perception, that they cannot be called "I." It is a very useful exercise but probably only appropriate for people without life-obligations whose lives are wholly devoted to the search for reality inwardly. He was speaking to wanderers, mendicants, *bhikhus,* who had left everything to follow the Path. Yet this is a necessary realization, without which we are constantly exposed to wrong influences in ourselves.

I have been asking myself what I myself do to keep present in me the awareness that my instruments are not "I." I find it is something I do when I am sitting observing my own thoughts and seeing that they are "not-I" (and I'm usually very thankful they are not, I must say). This is the chief thing that reminds me because of the absurdity of most of the mental processes that go on in my mind and the way those mental processes really lose all contact with reality, almost immediately after I forget they are not "I." As I was thinking about this, I remembered a conversation I had about thirty years ago with Madame Alexandra David-Neel. You may have read her books about her journeys in Tibet and what she learned from the Lamaists of Tibet. She asked me "What do you consider you have really learned from Gurdjieff?" and I said to her, "I have learned that nothing that we call 'I' is 'I'." She looked at me, rather surprised, and said "And how long has it taken you to come to that?" I said, "Oh, about twelve years"; and she said, "Twelve years? I have been trying to do this for thirty years and I am still not sure that I have come to it!" I felt very ashamed of having spoken in this rather glib way and it stuck in my memory. But as I look back over the years since that talk with Madame David-Neel I see that this has become—I can say now—very clear to me and I do not confuse my own thoughts or feelings with "I." I realize that they are just processes going on in me, which sometimes I can direct and sometimes I cannot or do not direct, but at least they are not "I."

So the question is, first of all, is it really important that one should establish this conviction in oneself? I think it is, because I see that whenever this slips away from me and I begin to believe in my own thoughts or feelings, I lose touch, both with my own reality and the reality of other things. Therefore it is something that requires renewal, from which one can easily be distracted by the very activity that our mind cannot help but maintain. Our life requires that there should be an incessant flow of images and thoughts across this screen of the mind. The impressions coming from what we see and hear outside we don't mistake. We don't think the walls we are looking at are "I." But those that arise from our past memories—all the associations that come to us in the form of words—are more difficult. We do tend to fall into the mistake of supposing that we are thinking these thoughts, feeling these feelings; whereas even a little observation shows us they are nothing to do with that—that they are simply images thrown onto the mind with no participation of our own—except that fatal participation of being lost in them, absorbed into them or, as we say, "identified" with them.

So I say that it is really important—for anyone who wishes to find reality and hold on to it—to find ways and means of putting his own mind outside of himself and seeing it as nothing else but a mirror, a screen, a process, but never as "I." And if one finds oneself on that screen to put it away from there, because this is not the place for us. This can be done in relation to one's thinking if one just looks at one's thoughts. Nothing else is required. As soon as you look at your thoughts you can see for yourself that these are not "I." And you can see for yourself that it is not even "myself" thinking. Those thoughts are just "there." It is comparatively easy with our bodies but it is good practice all the same, because by accustoming ourselves to remember that our bodies are only vessels in which we live and instruments which we use, we can more easily see for ourselves that the same is true of our thoughts and feelings.

Also we should accustom ourselves to the shock of realizing that our thoughts very seldom have anything to do with what we wish or need to think. This becomes quite evident, of course, if we have some task to do where it is necessary to think clearly on some topic. Our minds must then be occupied only with that and the screen must be kept clear, so that the images and connections that belong to that topic should not be blurred and distorted by accidental intrusions. Then we see how strong these accidental intrusions are, and we really should not have any doubt that they are "not-I" and do not come from us, but simply from a process connected with the construction of the human organism: this incessant process that works between the thalamus and the cortex, constantly feeding in stimulation, which is constantly producing images. We should no more think of this as "I" than we should think of the working of our liver and kidneys as "I." All these images that appear on the mind are just excretions of the nervous system, just like any other excretions of our body. We must learn to look upon them in that way. That screen of ours, that mind, onto which these images are thrown, has much more important work for it. Sometimes it has got to be put in a position to do that work, and for that it is first of all necessary that we should not make the mistake of accepting the images that are thrown onto the mind as if they were "I," as if they were my own, as if "I am thinking."

So certainly this exercise of the Buddha's of looking at one thing after another, to see that it is not "I"—or something equivalent to it—is necessary for us all. We have to practice this detaching of ourselves from our own bodies, feelings, mental processes and so on. I think one good method of doing this is when we are working with any part of ourselves, whether it is our hands, our feet, our eyes, our thoughts even, our mental instrument, to remember to look upon this and really see what it is—an instrument engaged in a process, not "I." It doesn't matter if we fail to find "I," because "I" is something not so easy to find as that. It is a matter of trust that there is "I" and it will do what it has to do. But it is not able to be handled by its own instrument, that is, it is not able to be thought about by thinking, or looked at by seeing. Therefore never worry about "I," make sure that you practice, as far as you can, detachment from your own instruments.

After-Lunch Discussion

JG Bennett. We haven't got much time before we continue the meeting. Can you speak about anything you want to bring up now?

Questioner. The other day I had to wait for a bus for about twenty minutes on a cold and wet evening and it was all I could do not to allow myself to be pervaded by a feeling of physical misery and annoyance and even a kind of peevish and stupid resentment. I was aware though that this discomfort was only temporary and that there are many people who are permanently or at least for long periods subjected to that kind of thing, and I felt ashamed to see how very fragile and weak my inner detachment is. Can you say something about this?

JGB. Yes. There are two things here. First of all, the human organism and the human psychic functions are enormously adaptable. They are able to adapt themselves to a range of external conditions far wider than any other living thing. As far as heat and cold are concerned, human beings can adapt themselves to live in climates varying from the hottest and driest or wettest parts of the world to the Arctic Circle. I remember the extreme conditions of physical discomfort I and many others had to endure during the trench warfare of the first world war. In a very short time one got accustomed to sleeping on boards, in mud, in freezing temperatures, for long periods on end. The two points to note in this question are: firstly, that the human organism and the human psyche adapt themselves to a very great range of external conditions; and secondly, that what we notice are changes, even comparatively small changes, in the conditions.

It can be very awkward to be conditioned to one very stable set of circumstances because this diminishes our power of response. People who want to keep themselves alive inwardly must be ready to subject themselves to changes of conditioning. The kind of experience you describe can in fact be used for a deconditioning purpose. To remain comfortable in a certain narrow set of conditions is not really conducive to a state of freedom but if one subjects oneself to changes in one's way of living, a certain deconditioning takes place and with that a certain freedom comes. So if one really understands one's own true profit, one will not mind being subjected to discomforts, especially changes of this sort.

There are two things, the range of variation which we can put forth and the extent to which human reactions can be conditioned so that there is no longer any conscious or intentional element at all in this behavior, it is entirely a conditioned behavior. Those are the things that we have to see. If we want to have some freedom of our own we have to be prepared to submit to changes of environment.

Q. Can one prepare oneself for a change one knows is coming? I once had to take an overnight voyage on a boat from Liverpool to Ireland which I knew was going to be extremely unpleasant. Knowing that it was going to be unpleasant seemed to help make it much less a time of feeling miserable like Olga described. What's the right way to prepare for a thing like this?

JGB. Certainly it is quite possible to prepare mentally, providing it is done with a "decision," which is not just thinking to oneself about it. Yes, it's true, you can foresee a journey with discomfort and realize it will be very uncomfortable for your body to go through that condition for that length of time. It is very uncomfortable for me, for instance, to travel across the Atlantic in a tourist class airplane, because I have nowhere to put my feet, and if I know that I have got to be cramped for six hours (at one time it took twelve hours) then I remember how I could foresee that this discomfort was going to come and what it would feel like not to be able to stretch my legs or to have normal postures— and when it came I just slept through it.

In one well-known story three Dervishes were once taken prisoner by some tyrant or other and one of them had practiced intensive fasting and asceticism and the other two had lived very well and were plump and jolly Dervishes. When they had been put in prison and starved for a fortnight the last two were dead and the first was hardly noticing it.

Q. About different "I"s: some of them seem to be very strong "I"s, and these are the wicked ones. I had an experience once. Somebody spoke to me, and I had an awareness that this person was very sincere and spoke from what was a good "I." Yet some "I" in me opposed that very much, and I couldn't control it. Before I knew it, without me saying anything, the other person felt a tremendous force coming up against him from me. Could you say that some "I"s are more wicked than others? Are the wicked ones stronger, in a way, because you can't control them? Could you say anything about this?

JGB. I didn't speak about different "I"s this morning. I simply said that whatever we look at in ourselves, if we look at it carefully we see "This is 'not-I'."

Q. I know.

JGB. It doesn't matter whether it is good or bad, it still isn't "I." The other thing, though, is a different question. If we leave out this reference to "I" and say "Are there certain conditionings in us, certain kinds of reactions that appear to come from oneself?" the question you are really asking is "How is it that there is a certain explosive violence somehow attaching to the destructive ones, and this same sort of force doesn't seem to be attaching to the others?" Really the way I put it, to turn your question around, is half way to showing the answer. These things you call "That kind of "I," that reacts violently to somebody else's action" we all know very well. There is something in us that can't bear to see somebody else remembering themselves, and at once we inwardly accuse them of inward insincerity and piousness, and of "Thinking they are better than we are" or that "They shouldn't be trying it on me." But why is that? It is because that particular reaction in us has been fixed by that kind of energy. That tendency in us to deny and to reject builds itself into a certain conditioning, and it is true it is generally associated with a more explosive and sometimes with actually a stronger than usual force. One of the ways of dealing with this is really to accustom oneself to seeing that "This is not "I." This is simply something that has been formed in me as a result of allowing myself a certain kind of reaction over and over again, until I have been conditioned to that sort of behavior."

Q. I have been thinking of a way of twisting what you said this morning to mean something that you certainly didn't! If I recollect, if my thoughts, my feelings, my behavior-manifestations, are not "I"— then I can complacently reflect: "Thank goodness this is not "I." Then my "I" is quite angelic! There is a trap in it somewhere though, I think.

JGB. Yes, but does your "I" really wish to be yoked to that companion and be unable to be free from it? It is true that the "I" is not whatever it observes. Wherever our consciousness is seated, this is not the part of us that is conditioned. It is able to stand away and able to be quite apart from it all. Though everyone knows that you can be in the kind of state that K. describes—and very probably it actually was like that when he observed it, that he saw that sort of violent and rejecting thing—but how was it that he saw it? It meant that there was also something else in him which saw, at the same time as he was feeling this rejection against the person. When we observe something in ourselves there must be some degree of separation. The perilous time is when we are not observing anything, which means our consciousness has quite collapsed into our minds and there is nothing else but that. We have then no perspective towards ourselves, because we are simply wholly immersed in our own conditioning and our reactions and we believe in them. And because we believe in them, we justify them; because at that moment this appears to be right. As I say, if I see somebody making an effort which I am not making, it seems to me quite right to look upon him as a hypocrite and myself as an honest man. "He is pretending to be good, but I am what I am" or "Why can't he keep it all to himself and not show off?" All that sort of thing seems very good to one—at the time. Why? Because I am just collapsing onto my reactions and there is nothing that stands back and sees. When it does happen that something stands back and sees, then I feel something quite different. I see myself reacting in this way, but I also see that this reaction is nothing else but conditioning. That is the beginning of being free from it. Even this state that you describe here, where you say, "Well, this is 'this, this, and this' but, if this is all true, what Bennett is saying"—which, God forbid, you may say, in brackets—"then my 'I' is all right after all." But the fact that you have been driven into this reasoning, already shows that there is some breach in your defenses.

Q. Is it really not possible for the "I" to observe itself? Because if one goes through all the things that it isn't, you are left with rather a nasty vacuum. There is nothing left!

JGB. If there is nothing left, then it is not nasty. Why should nothing be nasty? No, what is still left at this stage is your habit of taking yourself seriously. You haven't yet got free from that habit and therefore it seems unpleasant to find that there is nothing there to take seriously.

Q. It isn't that, so much as the panic of "Where does one go from here?"

JGB. The panic isn't lasting. There can be a terror of inner emptiness that can be quite authentic. That is another thing, but the word "nasty" is not right for it. If it is really that, then it is something else, because that kind of vacuum really does attract and bring something real. When you come to that experience, it is not for nothing. Something enters, then, of a quite different quality. But because you are not accustomed to it you don't perhaps recognize it, and only have this feeling of nothingness. In this connection the last Act of *Peer Gynt* really ought to make people's hair stand on end! I still remember going to see it and being absolutely terror-struck at the end of that last Act. Everything seemed to me to be aimed at John Bennett, John Bennett. Not Peer Gynt—John Bennett. Everything said by the Button-Moulder and by everyone else in that Act—all seemed to be pointing at me. Then we got up and the people were going out and I looked around and I saw that nobody else cared a bit. They were criticizing the play or the acting—but nobody felt the finger pointing at them. And I felt how strange it was. "Why? How is it that they can't see this?" That onion-skin speech is really and truly devastating! If you can appreciate what he is saying, then it fills you with this feeling of inner emptiness. Otherwise it is just a speech.

Q. Mr. B., in your talk this morning I felt I would like to have had some reassurance that one's instruments, and the things they connect one with, have also something to give one. I'm sure, in fact, that I look to reassurance because my own feeling is that this is the case. There was a certain sense, surely, that in these things are the need that there must be flow and return; that these materials and instruments always have something to show us, and we cannot afford to be superior to anything.

JGB. All that I was concerned to say was that we should look and recognize that the instruments are not ourselves. But the word "instrument" means that it is something through which we can act. If we hadn't got these instruments we should be helpless anyhow, and they are to be respected. But the point is that they shouldn't be mistaken for "I" and this mistaking them for "I" comes from a kind of inward collapse. You see, when we collapse into the instruments and become our thinking, and become our feeling, and become our bodily sensations, and become our desires, then nobody profits—because the instruments have no master, and we have no tools.

32.
CHANGES OF ACTIVITY

1 March 1964

I WANT TO CALL YOUR ATTENTION today to a peculiar characteristic of our connection with our own actions. It is that we do not notice—and hardly ever can notice even if we try—the moments when our activity changes direction. Providing our activity is continuing in a line we can, more or less, detach our attention and see what we are doing; but if there is a change of direction—for example, if we stop one activity and begin another—we don't notice the moment at which the change is made. And, particularly, we can't be aware of ourselves in that moment because our attention is caught. This certainly applies to the major crossroads in our lives. When people make decisions that are going to change their lives they usually fancy that they know the moment at which they make them. But if they look more closely they will see that the commitment was unconsciously and involuntarily made earlier—perhaps at a quite unnoticed moment. This is one reason why it is so very difficult for people to direct their own lives. People often worry about what they should do, and go around asking for advice as to what ought to be done; when in fact they are already committed to an action: the commitment has taken shape in them without their being aware of it. Even when we try to hold ourselves free so as to make a decision (and we may intentionally set ourselves the task of not deciding on a course of action until certain factors have become known to us) we still find that the commitment is unconsciously taken—that we have pre-judged the issue. But that is only in general. This peculiarity can be studied better with relatively trivial things. At moments during the day when we change the direction of our activity—finish doing one thing and start another—we can try to see if we can be aware of what we do.

One example often given for the purpose of this particular study is to try to notice the moment at which you begin to eat a meal. If you make this experiment, and try for a week or two to see if you can notice the first mouthful of food you take, you will see that, nearly every time, you will only remember after the second or third mouthful; when you have already settled down into the activity of eating—or you will notice it a little bit before. To the exact moment when you take the first mouthful, it is almost impossible to bring your attention.

These moments of change of activity are most important for us because they decide what we shall be doing—and very often how we shall be doing it, or the degree to which we need be involved in it—for whatever period of time the importance of the activity justifies. Because of this, from ancient times it has been the custom to invoke Divine help and protection at such moments. We Christians say "In the Name of the Father" for example; or Muslims, at the moment when they start something new, always, if they can remember it (which they do much more conscientiously than we do) say *Bismillah*, "In the Name of God," whether they are eating food or setting out on a journey, or even much smaller things.

The reason why they do this and why this custom, which we have almost lost now, was instituted, is because of the realization that men at that moment of change of activity are defenseless. Because they are not able to remember themselves, they are not able to be present—to be conscious of what it is that they are doing—and therefore children are taught to acquire the habit of invoking the Name of God at the moment of any change of activity. But unfortunately, like every other well-intentioned action of this kind, it simply becomes habitual. Even if they remember to say Bismillah they only do it automatically, without serving the real purpose: which is to bring them to be present at the moment that the new activity is started. But even when it has become something quite automatic with very little participation of one's own consciousness, there still is value in it. These ancient customs are certainly not to be despised.

If you observe many such things you will see how true it is that we are most defenseless at these moments of change of direction. We again-and-again find we have committed ourselves to some action without being aware that we took the commitment. That is the seriousness of this defenseless state at the moment of change. The psychological reason for it is of course quite obvious. When we are already engaged in an action a great deal of it continues automatically, and we have a certain amount of attention to spare and are able to notice more what we are doing. But at the moment of change our attention is all absorbed into the action and there is none left to enable us to be free.

There are various ways in which we can prepare ourselves in advance for these changes of activity, and I am going to speak this morning about just one of these. The one I am going to recommend to you is this. At the moment when you begin to speak to some other person, set yourselves to remember, as the first word is spoken, that this is the initiation of something new. It is a contact—between you and that person—that you are making by speech. Even if it is trivial, it is a pure contact, and the way to prepare oneself for this is to represent, or visualize in advance what it is like to open one's mouth to speak.

I am going to ask you to stop for one minute while we all picture ourselves in front of some person—no one in particular—at the moment of starting to speak. Now, as you come to this moment of speaking, and if it is convenient to do so, you can make a small call for help—like repeating to yourselves the words "Lord, help me" or something of that kind. The Christian invocation "In the Name of the Father and of the Son, and of the Holy Ghost" is too long to say, but you can say something short, or even nothing at all if you like—no words—providing you make an inward act of calling at that moment for some protection, so that what you say will not be quite defenseless. I don't ask you to do this part of it every time you make this experiment, because the opportunity isn't always there, or there may not be time. Nor do I ask that you should do this every time you speak, all through the morning. But at least try it several times; each time you do it you have to renew this representation I asked you to make—visualizing opening your mouth to speak—so that when you next come to it you will again have something prepared. If you don't prepare in this way you will find it almost impossible to remember. You will find that you will begin to speak, and only after you have spoken will remember that you had intended to do it. To be effective, this has to be done a few seconds before the first word is uttered. I hope you will all assiduously try this; then we can speak about it—and what came from it for you—after lunch.

After-Lunch Discussion

Questioner. [An almost inaudible question was asked.]

JG Bennett. Can everyone hear what G. is saying? It is a very interesting observation, I will try to repeat it more loudly now. She asked if we could speak about choice; and said that sometimes, when we are conscious of our own presence at the moment of a decision, it doesn't matter which way the decision goes. You say it is also an uncomfortable feeling: as if you were going to somewhere quite strange—a different country. It is so. That feeling does come when we go beyond the opposites, to a state where we are not affected by like or dislike. We come nearer to a reality otherwise shut off from us. But at the same time we are accustomed to being supported by like and dislike, so when that support is taken away we wonder what is holding us up. Something is, but not what we are used to. This that G. says is very true. It is an important thing to realize that choice, in the true sense of the word, really only comes when we are conscious of "yes and no," aware of the pull upon us of two different impulses—perhaps even just pleasant or unpleasant, or sometimes one affects us and we agree with it with our minds, yet don't like it with our feelings. But this is the condition—that we should be aware of that pull and then, if we are able to go on at that moment, we enter into a world which is much more free, and have that feeling—really I think the best word is "trepidation"—of going into the unknown. When you said that, it showed me that you were talking about something that really has happened to you. As for this other thing of not minding, of realizing that it really doesn't matter to you which way you go. It doesn't mean you don't care any more and have stopped feeling anything. You are just free from it. But what you don't like, you still don't like!

Q. Yes, you still don't like things, but it is not the same.

JGB. This is one thing we all have really to learn: how we can have such experiences as pleasure and pain, or like and dislike, and not be caught by them. So that we have them, but they don't have us—have no power over us.

Q. Could you explain the inner purpose of the self-sacrifice, of the thing that was only carried out, literally?

JGB. Sacrifice is really the separation of energies, and the purpose of sacrifice is to make energy available.

But can't any of you say anything about the task I proposed this morning? Are there no things you have to say connected with today's experiment? Did you all find it so easy—or so difficult—that there is nothing to say?

Q. It makes one realize what a lot of fun there is in nonsense.

JGB. Yes, I can just say something about that. The awkward thing is to realize that we often don't know what we do. Some conversation that has no serious purpose can be very valuable just because of the contact—the sharing—between people. It is not by any means always necessary that our conversation should be utilitarian. The trouble with our talking is, very often, that no one is there talking: because then it is really empty. I mean it is empty of the person who is speaking. It is a sobering thought to realize how often our mouths are speaking, and there is no one there speaking. But still this is only incidental. What I was mainly interested to see was whether this helped you to observe that the moment of starting to speak, like the moment of starting any action which involves some change, is a moment when it is extremely difficult for us to be present.

Q. I have been very strongly aware of what I call the "flow" of one thing after another with no sharp distinction, a problem which I have often thought about. It seems to be impossible to tell the difference.

JGB. Although it is quite true that there is this inertia by which things go on in us, that takes the place of our own will; changes of direction also come when something impinges on this in us which is simply moving on without any direction. The point is that those moments when there is a change of direction are moments of possibility, and they are the moments we miss. It is as if we were put in the awkward position that we can do things when there is nothing to do, and when there is something to do we cannot do it. And this all comes about simply because we are not strong enough to be able to hold on to our own presence in front of the moments of impact. Tiny things can shatter this presence in us. That is what is so revealing when one works in this particular way: to see how fragile our hold over our own inner state is. It will continue providing there is nothing to disturb it, but it can hardly stand any sort of disturbance.

JGB. [To an inaudible contribution.] Well, what M. says is very right to notice. She can hold on to herself more than most of the people in this room because she has worked at it for a very long time. At the same time even somebody who has really worked at this knows how vulnerable we are at those moments, and therefore we begin to see how important it is to be able to prepare ourselves to stand the shock of anything that is going to change the direction of our experiencing. One cannot see the importance of this until one has really experienced it, otherwise we go on with the illusion that we can manage, just because we don't notice the crucial moments when we are most vulnerable.

But M.'s example is interesting again in another way. With this exercise of recollection that you call No. 39, one enters much more deeply into one's self. One might well think that in this state of deep recollection one will not be vulnerable, but it is not really like that. It is necessary to find a state where the inner and the outer are properly balanced. Where you are engaged in more or less incessant commerce with other people (as you were in the job you have been doing today) of course your attention is necessarily drawn out of yourself the whole time, and the problem is the opposite one. The danger is that your attention will be so much out that you will be caught. But one might think: "Well, it should be much easier if one's attention is right in," but experience shows that it is not at all true, and therefore this idea that recollectedness and entering deeply into oneself is somehow a safer and more reliable state proves not to be true. We have to know how to hold on to the middle position between inner and outer in order to have this.

Q. I found this morning that whenever I tried to act as if I was speaking to someone, and to be aware of acting as if I was speaking to someone, I started to smile!

JGB. It had occurred to me before to mention this thing that Karl is saying about smiling. I don't know whether others of you have found it, when there is attention at this moment of change of direction, this power is given to us. It really is part of the protection against the attack if we are able to see it as a humorous thing. You might say: "Why is man given a sense of humor?" This is quite an interesting question if you really think about it. It is really to enable man to deal with a whole lot of situations which otherwise would simply mean impossible tensions. I have found the same thing here, when preparing for this, of sometimes just seeing the incongruities—realizing how embarrassing for people it might be. As if someone said to me this morning: "But isn't this going to be very awkward for everyone here today if they know that everyone is going to have to say "God help me," before they speak." Perhaps the whole universe, if we but knew it, is provided with a sense of humor as a necessary condition of its being able to keep going at all, not only man. There are plenty of indications that humor is a cosmic function. Let's hope so! But what were you going to say? Who started to speak just now?

Q. I hope this is not off-course, but about energy and changing direction I have noticed there are some people who suddenly have a tremendous impulse, are energized and change the whole direction of their lives. And there are other people in whom this energy leads to weakness, who lose it and then revert back into mechanism.

JGB. What is involved here is a combination of "form" and "content." We can think of energy as content, but it has to have some vessel in which it can be contained. If energy of a very fine kind pours into a vessel which is not strong enough to contain it, it will be explosive, and so it produces that kind of experience which may actually destroy it, and you will not recover at all from that, it will be too strong to bear. With others it may last only for a short time and nothing permanent will be left. But others again will be able to contain it, and then the process of transmutation begins, when there is an action between this energy and the vessel, which gradually brings about the integration of their being. According to St. Paul's accounts (as far as we have them) after his first experience on the way to Damascus it took fifteen or sixteen years for him to more-or-less complete his process of transformation, and he was a very exceptional man, who had undoubtedly been leading a life of discipline before having this experience. Therefore there was already the strength there for him to bear it. Aquinas was also another very great man, yet it was a long time before he really had the experience of full illumination.

The important point to understand here is that there are two things, form and content, or energy and containing-vessel. We have both in us. The energy itself can only produce a certain change that may be quite temporary. But if the vessel controls—or at least holds—some of it, the energy will begin to blend with the substance of the vessel, and bring this to life. It then acts like yeast on dough. It brings the dough to life. But the dough has to be mixed. You have to be ready for it, otherwise the yeast cannot make the dough rise. This is clearly why, no doubt, the whole process of transformation of man depends upon the strengthening of the vessel—or instrument, or apparatus—and also on the supply of the necessary vivifying or life-giving energy. Not only have both these two got to be there, but there must be an action between them.

But how did you find the actual experiment? Were you able to form—at the time that we spoke together in the Djami this morning—a representation of the act of speaking? Were you able to catch yourself before you began to speak? If you were to persist in this and try to do it for several weeks, you would begin to find out both how difficult it is and how much you can learn from it. There is no reason why you shouldn't do so if you like. It will have no ill effect and has much to give us. For one thing it begins to give you a taste of what is meant by presence. When we were speaking just now about the words we use, we began to realize how empty of content words can be. It is difficult for us to grasp this, how the greater part of human conversation really is what the Russian Proverb says—pouring from the empty into the void!

JGB. [Responding to another inaudible observation.] Did you find that the overall effect of having this exercise in front of you during the day did make you more aware of the moments of change, in other directions besides the talking?

Q. Yes, and I was aware ...

JGB. I remember, more than forty years ago—in 1923 or 1922—when we were doing this sort of exercise with Ouspensky. It was not quite like what I have given you, but more in the direction of trying to keep a state of separation between our consciousness of self and our awareness of our own activities. People used to come week after week and make reports on it, and after a few weeks it became painfully obvious that everyone was prefixing their observations by saying "When I was on the top of a bus..." What is the use of remembering yourself only when you are on top of a bus? Obviously, when you are being carried comfortably along by a bus, you can have spare attention, and you can do this, and you can do that, and you can remember yourself when getting off the bus and when getting on the bus! The bus here typifies a state when we are just being carried along by inertia. In that state it is not particularly difficult, with a little effort, to separate oneself from the activity that is going on.

What matters is to be able to bring one's own presence to the moment of change! This is why the Sufis use the "Stop!" exercise—regarding it as very important because it catches people—produces totally unexpected moments of change for them. For example, if there were people working here on a day like this, and I were to give the "Stop!" exercise, perhaps a hundred times in the morning—and there were a hundred people here who stopped personally in the morning, and you were to say to them: "How many of you at the moment of stopping were in a state of remembering yourself?" If among all the hundred there is somebody who can say: "I did once," it would be good. The probability, even when you are watching out for it, of being present at an unexpected moment, is so small that it is really astonishing. People will not believe this until they really have it demonstrated to them. Everyone, I think, without exception has believed that they are conscious of themselves to a far greater extent than is actually the case.

33.
TWO LIVES

15 December 1963

WHAT IS THE POINT of having these Work Sundays twice a month all through the year? Most of you who come here to work could find plenty to do in your own homes, or something else that is of interest to you; and many of those who live here and work during the week could very well do with a day of rest. Why work? Why do something which isn't to satisfy some need of one's own, such as putting one's own house in order? There are of course more or less obvious reasons why there is something to be gained from it. You come here in the expectation—which I hope will be fulfilled—that you will learn something useful for yourself. Or also—and I hope that is true for most if not all of you—because you want to contribute some service, or some help, to the life here. And we do need it, because there is far more work to do than we can accomplish ourselves. But these are outward external reasons; and certainly should not be the primary ones. There is a more important benefit which comes from experiencing the work of a group together; of sharing things with people—not because one has chosen those people, but because one happens to find oneself with them. Therefore we have to make the conditions ourselves by accepting the people with whom we work, and accepting the work we shall do. This is certainly a positive thing; very hard to obtain in any other way. Those of you who have experience of this know that it produces an important action for us. But still there is something more; and I will try to explain something about this deeper reason why we should come and work together.

One very simplified way of looking at it is that we have two lives.

One is the unavoidable obligatory life required for the maintenance of our existence, and for fulfillment of obligations to which we have committed ourselves. This first life has to be lived, willy nilly. We have to breathe, eat, sleep and fulfill the external obligations our family, society and mode of life impose on us—also whatever obligations we have taken on by our profession, or to be a husband, a father, a mother, a wife. All those make up an obligatory life which has to be lived as well as it can. This life belongs to the fact that I am here in this body, and it has to live and conduct various actions and operations to hold its place. I clearly owe a debt for its existence, that I repay by taking care of it. That debt is to be paid here-and-now in this life and when this ends it is finished with.

But within that necessary, obligatory life we are free to create a second life of our own. We are entitled to do that insofar as we fulfill the obligations of our necessary life. This second life is independent of this bodily existence. It is not subject to the same conditions of time and place. But there is something else which is not obligatory for me, which I am free to accept. It is not obligatory in the sense of being compulsory and unavoidable, but in a much higher sense, because it is what I am called to—which I am free to accept or reject. This is because my nature is such that I can if I choose confine myself just to the necessary life of this body, but I can add to this another. This other second life is really what interests us; and I am sure that is what brought all of us here together this morning—this sense that we need to fulfill the higher obligation of a second life.

This is a very simplified way of presenting it because both these lives have different gradations of what is compulsory and what is an obligation. A primary simplification is that our first life is, fortunately for us, full of "holes"—or like a land which is only partly occupied; so there is always room in it to take care of the second life. We have to see how to serve the needs of our second life by making good use of these "holes" or unoccupied territory in our obligatory life. One way we can do this is to keep something apart—in whatever we may be doing—for the sake of this second life. This is particularly easy in our situation here together where instead of the first life flowing over everything—as it does for most of our time—it reduces to the simple need to maintain our physical body. So we can remind ourselves that we are here for a different purpose—that all we do today is directed towards the strengthening and enrichment of our second life. Our energies will then flow towards that.

But, as you know, it can happen that even though we have put our-selves under these special conditions, we can still continue to live just as if it was ordinary life. Then sometimes we may wake up with aston-ishment and say "But why am I here in the cold and the wet doing something my body doesn't like that doesn't interest me? What am I doing here?" That moment of asking yourself "Why am I doing this?" should remind you that we are here to get something for this second life, for fulfilling an obligation of a totally different kind to our ordinary obligations. It is a voluntarily accepted obligation to create, within the world of creativity that only exists because it is being created the whole time—the other life.

The practical advice I give you in connection with this is to use whatever activity you may find yourself doing this morning—whether you work in the house or the garden, or wait table, or sit and eat at table—as means for bringing your attention into your other life. Remind yourself that almost nothing whatever you are doing today is really a necessity of your first life. Therefore, every part of it can be devoted to strengthen and enrich your other life. This means that how we do things, how we hold ourselves and distribute our attention, has a purpose and a significance that is not in our ordinary activities.

Now all this doesn't mean that one is only concerned with the sec-ond life every second Sunday! The true man lives the whole time in both lives. Everything really necessary for his first life he does; every-thing else he devotes to his second life—which is present within him always. A man who is really established in his second life is not con-fined by the condition of his physical body. He has an immense free-dom inconceivable for people who only know how to live the first life. So what I am advising you to do is like a rehearsal, training us to strengthen our power to live in such a way that our attention is dis-tributed between what we have to do and what we can create. We never can create rightly if we neglect our obligations. But we will never create at all if we allow ourselves to be swallowed up by this first life to which we are committed.

After-Lunch Discussion

JG Bennett. [In response to a question inaudible on tape.] Yes, quite true, man can remember himself. You can say "A true man is a man who can remember himself." This is remembering oneself, that is just what it means. To have something in us which is able to keep a bridge between the two worlds—this is what it means to have "I." You must understand that people who haven't got "I" can still have this kind of two-world existence; but their second world is all imagination—dreams. One thing we really have to learn is not to mistake imagination for a true inner life. It is not. I mean by imagination a sort of dreamworld. It is not that—it must be real. A dreamworld will go by itself, but this real world will not. One man who produced a wonderful image of this died a few days ago: C.S. Lewis. In his book, *The Great Divorce,* he draws a picture of this, of the ghost-like condition of the people after death who have lived their lives only in dreams and those who have made something strong and real, which can live in this very concrete world where things are really happening, where everything has to be created in order to be at all.

Questioner. I have two questions: In the *Book of Revelation* [20,6] it says (and then St. Francis picked it up again) "Blessed and holy he that hath part in the first resurrection: on such the second death hath no power." Is this to do with this second life? The other is if one is driving a car, one constantly has an empty thirty seconds when the lights are changing. Have you anything to say about those thirty seconds which come, whether they should be left lying fallow or definitely used?

JGB. Yes, the second death is a reality. When the physical body loses the life-principle and disintegrates, all the functions associated with the physical body cease to be available. However, there remain instruments that are not as dependent on the physical body and something remains then, that is an intermediate state of life, when one can say there are still a will and existence linked together. But the true man is the will. If the will is free then it can create its own form of existence—and its own instruments can then be created around that. But if it is not free then it cannot do all that. The second death is the separation between will and existence. The first death is the separation between will, existence and function. One is leaving the functional mechanism aside, and the other leaving the existence aside. Only those whose will is established can pass consciously through the second death. All this I am sure is the truth but no one is able to penetrate from this existence into what is beyond the second death. All that is known about life after death is between the first and the second.

About how to use one's odd moments: it is a wise thing to renew—reintegrate—oneself, when one is engaged in an activity like driving a car. We cannot be wholly in contact with ourselves because a large part of our attention is engaged in the automatism of driving. There are various kinds of short exercises, like just repeating something to oneself.

Or one can bring one's attention in some definite way upon one's body—such as upon one's bones. An interesting and useful exercise consists in becoming aware of one's skeleton—how we shall be when we haven't got flesh and blood any more. Often this brings one very much back into oneself. One way of doing it is to start counting the bones. I used to do this a lot; sometimes I do it quite spontaneously out of habit. I begin to picture what my leg would look like if it were a nicely dried skeleton! But the purpose of all those things is really that one intentionally brings oneself back into contact with oneself. One is being drawn out, and one wants to get in again. One can invent a hundred-and-one ways to do this. It is better to invent one's own ways so long as they have that result of drawing one into oneself; then when the lights change you have to go out again.

JGB. [In answer to a question about imagination—inaudible on the tape.] Take what I was just saying to K.T. for example. To turn your power of imagination on to visualization of your own skeleton is an extremely hard thing to do. Because you are using intentionally a power that people become accustomed to allowing to run idly. We do have a creative power, a real imagination, a power of creating mental images. But it is so very greatly neglected in life, that instead of using this power for a positive purpose, people allow it to go on idly as a form of self-indulgence. To change over from one to the other is not an easy thing. It is not enough simply to direct it into channels and to start having dreams about good things instead of bad ones. Dreams are dreams whichever they are: good or bad! We have this constructive power to make—to mould—the material of thought into shapes; whereas instead of that we allow it just to make all kinds of vague pictures, and stare at them.

Q. Should we ultimately have control of our minds, so that we don't flop around like that?

JGB. No, but we should know when we are doing it. Putting ourselves into a passive state and allowing this to happen must also sometimes be done as a recreation, you know. If you do daydream, which is a perfectly permissible activity, you should know you are doing it in order to rest your machine, not just out of weakness.

Q. What sort of thing could one do when one is working most of the night, doing a hard manual job which forces one to think ahead all the time? Some of your mind is free and therefore does go on daydreaming.

JGB. You can, for example, say to your right hand: "Now, right hand I want you to be my reminder today." You say this to it, so that when you are working like that with your hands, your right hand keeps saying to you, "Remember!"

Q. Remember what, though?

JGB. Remember what you are here for. Remember who you are—what it is all about. Remember this other life that I am speaking of. You treat your right hand as your go-between. My right hand is not going to forget that there is another life. If I really do this, then my hand is able to do it. Or one can put things into one's hand and use them instead. If you are using some utensil you can decide "That saucepan there is going to be my reminder today" and say to it "Now saucepan, whenever I pick you up, remind me." This you really can do, you know. It sounds funny to say, but everything is able to receive force. You know how old things, and things that have been lived with, have something—they can talk to you. Why is it? Because they are able to receive force. This water-jug is only dead because no life has been put into it. If I were to sit in front of it and put life into it, it would begin talking to me. You understand? You know that. Every artist knows it. When he takes his material, it is a friend. It is not simply dead stuff! Do you understand that? Everything can be like that to us.

Q. You said we could let ourselves daydream as recreation, if our body is tired we know we need a rest.

JGB. Do we always know when our body is tired? Bodies can very often just scream their heads off about nothing, you know. And then something interesting turns up and they forget all about this screaming, and this terrible tiredness vanishes! Sometimes also you can do just the opposite. Because you are excited and interested, you can make excessive demands on your body which are not just to it. So you cannot be so trustful about your body knowing when it is tired.

To really know what your body needs is not so straightforward. Everything must be studied. This knowledge doesn't just come by itself; because we are not sufficiently in touch with ourselves to be able to talk with all parts of us. If I really know my body and trust it, and it trusts me, I can say to it "Are you tired or aren't you tired?" and it will say to me "Well, I'm not really tired," or perhaps "No, I'd better not do this"—and I would believe it. The same with my mind: I may think "Well, I could force myself to go on with this mental effort" but I can also say to my mind, "Are you really able to do it, or will it strain you?" If it says "No, I had better not" then I believe it. You must learn to talk to yourself—to talk to your various parts. They are all intelligent, only you must give them the means to talk to you. You must bring them to life.

"The tetrad is the form of all activities that lead to a change of order. For this reason, the four-term system is inherently flexible. We can picture it in the activity of bread making, which calls for four elements: flour, water, yeast and fire. There are two raw materials and two active agents. Yeast ferments from within the flour; fire cooks by an action from without. Good bread requires the exactly right adjustment of the four terms and the adjustment is possible by the very nature of the process. Each element is separately controllable and the place and time of its entry into the process can be selected to give the required sequence of transformations. We can picture the four elements as four Sources from which the activity of bread making is sustained."

—from *The Dramatic Universe, Vol. III*

34.
USING OUR INSTRUMENTS

1 July 1962

WHENEVER WE DO any kind of job we use tools or, for fine work, instruments. To do a proper job we have also to make sure these are in good order, which we can call verifying, or checking them. If we don't do this, we may get quite different results from those we require and expect, because the tool or instrument may be wrongly adjusted and may, for example, veer off to the right when we want it to go straight ahead. We have to learn how to do the same with everything we do. Everything we do today will use tools and instruments. We are powerless to produce any results without them. For example, I am speaking to you now with one instrument and you are listening to me with another. Because we have bodies, we all possess its instruments of our hands, our feet, our eyes and ears, our thinking and so on, but, behind these there are, as it were, a series of "master instruments" or controls that we should know how to check and verify.

In a simplified way we can speak of just two of these: the "instrument of the head" and the "instrument of the heart." The instrument of the head is used to direct our activity, to know what we are doing, and the instrument of the heart is to tell whether we are in the right state when we are doing it. We should learn to be able to verify their condition. Something else in us is able to do that, different from our thinking or feeling. A third instrument is able to see and look at these other two. From time to time, whenever necessary, sometimes often, sometimes only occasionally, it must verify: "Is my head working as it should be working? Is it directing my activity?" (Once this direction is taken, it is the duty of the head to keep that direction; it cannot choose it because it can only know "about" things.) "Is it keeping me in a right relationship with the world around me? Am I really doing what I intend to do? Am I doing it in the way that I intend to do it? Am I adapting myself to changes in the situation?" That verification is necessary if our head work is to be right. The heart I must also verify: "Am I disturbed? Have I some animosity, some anxiety, some fear? How am I at this moment? Am I quiet?" That condition is necessary, because through the quiet state of the heart all the other activities become properly coordinated and harmonized. Otherwise there will be conflict and disturbance between one instrument and another—one part of our activity and another. And we may even find ourselves drawn towards the very thing we do not wish to do. It is always possible for us, with the experience that we have, to bring our feelings to a state of peace and freedom from resentment and anxiety and fear and anger and the rest. We must not be afraid that this is too difficult for us because with practice we can always bring ourselves to a state of inward peace.

Another way of looking at all this is in terms of the "What" the "How" and the "Why" of our activity. "What am I doing?" At this moment I am speaking to you and trying to convey to you something I have learned and tested from my own experience. This must be clear in my mind, and I must keep it clear there. And you in hearing must really listen so that you too can put yourself in the position of seeing— not merely hearing my words, but seeing what I'm speaking of—so that the "What" will be clear. The "How" depends upon our inner state. If I am disturbed, this disturbance will reflect itself in what I am saying. If you are disturbed, you will not be able to listen, because it is harder to listen than to speak—more necessary to be inwardly quiet in order to listen. The "Why" concerns the whole direction of our lives towards whatever goal we are seeking. This also needs to be verified, but verified differently, because this "Why" is perceived in the same inner consciousness which is doing all this controlling and verifying. It is an inward clarity as to what really is important for me. When I am in front of a choice, this "Why" determines what I will choose and what I will deny.

This situation I am describing is also represented by the picture of the chariot, the horses, the driver and the master. The master is the "I." It is the "I" that is able to see why; it is not yet sufficiently awake to see the whole of the "Why," but it is the "I" that can see as much as anything can see in us, and insofar as we have this present in us, this inner self, this inner consciousness, this own will that belongs to "I," then we have also a "why."

Very often we cannot know at all in detail why we should be doing this and not that, and we have to make our choice as to what we will do without having the inner consciousness of why we do it. We then base ourselves on what is expedient, what is taught by morality, what is the custom, the way we live and what we want to achieve. But little-by-little we must begin to see for ourselves why we do everything, why we exist at all, what is the purpose of our lives here on the Earth. Only we must of course understand that this is not the job of these controllers of the head or the heart.

But what I mainly wanted to speak to you about today was the simple verification of the condition of these two controls that we should make whenever it is necessary during the day and while performing any task. Very often we shall find that our head is not really directing our work, that we are just going along with the habits of our bodies. Or we will find our feelings are altogether tied up in some condition or other that has nothing to do with what we are doing at that moment—some resentment, some anxiety, some fear. Whenever we see these, they must be put away. If we wish to have a life worth living, we must cultivate a quiet heart. There is always some means that must be used for this. It is well-known, for example, that quietness of the heart is associated with a relaxed state of the body, and that if our body is in a state of tension, it is very difficult for the heart, or the feelings, to be quiet.

There is a direct technique everyone can acquire little-by-little if they wish to, and that is the technique of simply quieting the feelings whenever one observes a state of disturbance. But before that we must be able to withdraw into our deeper and inward consciousness so that the feelings no longer seem to be "I"—"I feel this!"—where "This!" is simply that some feeling of resentment or anxiety is there. It should not be there. One should never think "I dislike that person, I am worried, I am anxious about something." It should always be: "There is resentment, there is anxiety, there is worry. That should not be." No one should ever accept in themselves that these sorts of states should persist. They are not unavoidable for man—certainly not necessary; everyone knows that. They are really not such that we cannot master them. It is just a bad habit of thought to suppose that we have to remain in a state of resentment or anxiety.

After-Lunch Discussion

Questioner. What do you think about the evolving place of a leader since Gurdjieff's day? I mean the relation of guru to *chela*, of teacher to pupil, that is particularly prevalent in Asiatic countries; and has Bapak's arrival shown up a general world change?

JG Bennett. There was a very great change in Gurdjieff's handling of this relationship between the First and Second World War. The Gurdjieff who is described in *In Search of the Miraculous*—the idea of schools and the rest of it—was partly colored by Ouspensky's own ideas about it, but no doubt that was really there. It certainly remained when he had his Institute in Fontainebleau but it was changing all the time. And when he wrote that first little book of his that was never published, *The Herald of Coming Good,* he said, very emphatically, that people who just acted as he told them were quite useless. And you have no doubt often heard the story of how he sent two devoted followers [the Hartmanns] away from him; and other people as well, because they took whatever he said as gospel truth. He saw that this was useless, because the aim of the Work was to make independent beings and not slaves, and he certainly took steps to stop this kind of thing. On the other hand, he also did say that in order to work one needs a force outside of oneself, that one had to be aware of its presence in order to make one's own affirmation.

When Gurdjieff died, I felt that this force had disappeared, as far as I was concerned, or at least had become very much less noticeable. When Subud came, before Pak Subuh himself came to England, in 1956, I felt in the *latihan* that I was recognizing this force again; but that it was inside instead of outside; that is, that there was something that one had to stand up to, something that was a challenge to one. There is of course the question whether this alone is all that is required. You speak about this relationship of *chela* and guru, of pupil and teacher, being very prevalent in the Asiatic countries, and this is true. It is true that Bapak himself has never been able to change this in his own country, Indonesia, and they will treat him as an infallible oracle and really, in effect, as a *sheikh,* and many people in Western countries have this same attitude. In India, they would consider him as a guru, although he himself says that this can only be a provisional situation and that when people began to be aware of what was happening inside them they would see that they would not have to look for it outside.

The question then comes whether any outside relationship is

required at all, and that, in my opinion, is a question not yet answered; perhaps not able to be answered yet. But on the whole my view is that human beings, at this stage of the development of man, cannot make the transition from dependence to independence just in one leap; that a transition is needed and what really is important is how the help is given in that transition. To be thrown too abruptly out on one's own and be told, "You must rely entirely upon what is within you," is not right perhaps for almost all people. The other extreme, that is, to encourage a constant and continuing state of dependence upon help from outside is equally disastrous, I am sure.

What I feel we really have to look for is a way of dealing with the transition: Something begins to happen inside us and one day we hope that this will come to a point where it is sufficient, that there is nothing required but that. But we all are in need of something to help us to go from one side to the other—a bridge, or a boat, or whatever it may be. The word bridge reminds me: I have once heard Gurdjieff say, "I am only a bridge; when you have got over the stream you can kick me away."

There is another thing you may remember if you have read Ouspensky's book, *In Search of the Miraculous,* he talks there about the distinction between "the way" and "the staircase." It was something he used to talk about a lot in the early days, and it was this: the Way does not begin on the level of life; there has already to be a certain transformation before we can enter the Way. Between the level of life and the Way, a staircase is placed; and you have to go up this step by step. When you are going up the staircase, you require external help, and because you require external help, you have also the obligation to give it, and therefore, if you have gone from one step to another, you have the obligation to help somebody else up to your step. That only applies to the staircase, and only at the end are you able to find your way by yourself. He also said that on the staircase you can be sure of nothing; you cannot be sure of your teacher; he may be leading you wrongly. There are teachers who pretend to be leading you up, but either because of their own ignorance or because they have some wrong purposes they wish to serve, they are leading you down; so that you may think that you are going up the staircase and you are really going down. Therefore as long as you are on the staircase, you have to be on the watch; you must keep your critical faculty. Do not believe what your teacher tells you: test it. There must be no blind faith. You will only know whether your teacher is right when you reach the Way. At the very point where you know your teacher was right, you do not need him any more. There is a lot of interest in that idea, but that was certainly the way Gurdjieff looked at it.

There are three different conditions of life: there is the condition of life of the man who is content with the visible world; there is the condition of life of the man who is searching for the other world; there is the condition of life of the man who has found or entered the other world. These three conditions I call the psychostatic condition, where the psyche is content to remain stationary and not change its level; the psychokinetic condition where the psyche is searching and striving for something different; and the psychotelios condition when the psyche has already found. It does not mean that nothing further happens, but it is not any longer as it was in the psychokinetic state, which properly corresponds to this staircase.

I do not think that these things really change from age to age, because I think that all this is according to cosmic laws, and it is only the forms that change, and with the forms, the emphasis. There have always been teachers who made their pupils dependent upon them; there were always false teachers. There have always been ways offered to people which claimed to give them immediate freedom; like, for example, in the Middle Ages there were the Brethren of the Free Spirits—you know, in the painting, "The Garden of Earthly Delights," of Hieronymus Bosch—and all that was connected with the notion that it is sufficient to receive a certain initiation, to have had a process start in you and afterwards you were free to follow this inner process. The same thing happened in Islam in the tenth century, and from time to time. I think that if it is claimed that this setting free is granted to someone at once, without a transformation, it cannot be right. Therefore, I think that the truth is that there are these different stages at all times. The extraordinary thing in Subud, is that there is an inner action which corresponds to the completion of the process and makes probably the ascent of the staircase a quite different process, but I do not think that it actually can—I do not think anything can—eliminate this process. In one way or another we have to be transformed. And after all, Pak Subuh himself says, "You will not understand Subud until you reach the third or fourth stage," that is to say, so long as the action of the latihan is on the level of the physical body, we cannot understand what is happening; you must simply do what you are told, that is, practice the latihan and not try to understand it. When you are on the second stage, that is, when the action is in the feelings, in the emotional part—or as it is sometimes called, in the astral body—then you still will not understand, although you will already be different. It is only when it reaches the third part, or the mental body as it is called—the understanding—that you will begin to understand. It means that in Subud also, it is taken into account; that there has to be a period, a stage—which may be, and I think always is, quite prolonged—during which one can do nothing except what one is told: to do the latihan and not think. After all, that is doing what one is told.

Q. How do you know which is the right one between two different demands? How do you reach the decision?

JGB. [First repeats the question, which was barely audible.] We may find ourselves sometimes confronted with two tasks, both of which cannot be accomplished, and therefore there has to be a certain sacrifice of the one in favor of the other. Perhaps one of them is obviously important in itself, but far beyond us, and whether we can make an effectual contribution towards it or not, we do not know; whereas the other is perhaps more within our power, and perhaps we also find ourselves drawn towards this, but we do not really know which way the right path lies.

One should put to oneself various questions, like this: First of all, is an obligation to be recognized? There are categorical obligations that are upon us just because we are human beings in a given situation; we have the categorical obligation to take care of our own bodies; we have a categorical obligation towards our own family; we have a categorical obligation to anyone towards whom we have entered into a relationship of obligations; where we have accepted a certain dependence of someone else upon us, which has been consciously accepted and exchanged, as it were

Further, there are those kinds of obligations that every man and every woman has to fulfill. If I am in front of an obligation of this sort I have to think to myself: "Is in one of these various duties that I am confronted with the character of an obligation?" That must come first. If I find that that does not help me out of it, and it seems to me that there is no categorical obligation anywhere, then it becomes a matter of my own choice and decision. I am not obliged to do either this or that; both of them can be useful but I am not committed by that sort of bond, which I cannot break without betraying my human responsibilities.

Then I may say: "Of these situations, which do I understand best?" When I see my way through this one or that one, can I see the nature of my contribution to it? If I do this, can I see how I should be acting in front of the different situations that would arise? Or am I likely to be confused in one case and wonder whether I am doing the right thing or not, whereas in the other one I can see fairly well what I ought to be doing? If I can see between two situations, one that I understand and the other where I do not understand, and where in neither case is there an obvious issue of obligation, then I should clearly choose the one where I understand. Whether it is large or small, or interesting or uninteresting: because if I understand, I will be effective. If I do not understand, I might do more harm than good. In either case, I should not be influenced by my likes and dislikes. I will naturally be drawn towards a situation which interests me more, which seems to offer a better use of my powers or something of that sort, or which may be flattering me, I may feel myself more important in this than in that. Or the people I shall have to deal with in this situation I like, in that situation I do not like.

Clearly, I ought to try and put those feelings away if I really want to come to an objective decision. Similarly, I should not be thinking: "What will people think of me; if I do this, will they think well of me; if I do that, will they think ill of me?" I should not be influenced by that if I can help it, and if I can observe in myself fear of criticism by some if I choose course A and fear of others if I choose course B, I must not be influenced by that sort of thing. It seems to me that by reasoning in that way and not acting from feeling, we will understand which one to choose. We have to try to bring understanding to bear on these sorts of situations, not feeling, not habit. You may well find that you do one thing just by momentum because you have been in the habit of doing it: You do not realize how much it is from habit. It may be that it is from feeling, and you do not see for yourself how much you are doing this just from feeling. If one aims at perfection, one must look to see what is right, and not anything else.

Q. I find since Subud appeared I want to do certain things which are right, even if they are difficult. I do them with joy!

JGB. That does not conflict with what I have just been saying. I did not suggest that it is a question of morality or the reverse; asking oneself, "Am I influenced or am I not by what people think of me, am I influenced by comfort or discomfort?" is an essential question, but it certainly always happens that to do what is right is also to do what is joyful. It must be so. A thing that is right can never be an unpleasant or painful experience. Unpleasant and painful experiences all come from not doing what is right, or from not doing what is true for oneself.

And sometimes, it is quite true, it is possible to tell what is true and right by being able to see in oneself what will give one real satisfaction.

Q. Might it happen that we disregard obligations of one kind in favor of another, when both are strong?

JGB. I do not believe, truly, that there is such a thing as conflict of obligations. Obligations are an objective reality, and it is a mistake to think that there would be a conflict between them. There are, of course, some situations where it is not very easy. Where I feel "I have committed myself to doing something and I do not want to let so-and-so down"; it is a personal commitment, but my responsibility of taking care of my own body, my own parents and wife and children, and those who depend upon me—that is not something I have chosen. All this has been given to me and I have got to look after it.

35.
FOUR KINDS OF ACTIVITY

21 July 1963

ONE OF THE PURPOSES of our coming together like this from time to time is that it takes us out of the routine of our ordinary lives and gives us an opportunity of entering into an activity which we ourselves choose; that is outside our necessary obligations in life. I want to say something this morning about distinctions we can draw between different kinds of activity.

There are four kinds that we can learn to recognize. First of all there is the *automatic* activity which is not directed to any purpose at all. It is simply the passive response of our organism to whatever happens to be stimulating it at the moment. Partly it is the effect of the habits, the momentum of our own past lives, and partly the effect of just what attracts our attention or our interest. In this there is no intention or purpose. Secondly, there is the activity that is *necessary*. There is a great deal of necessary activity for man, most of which is looked after by the construction of our own organism, with its nervous system. There is everything that we do to keep our bodies alive and, outside of this, there is the very limited amount of activity that cannot be avoided just by the fact that we are here in these bodies on the earth. This is different, because there is a reason for it all; that reason is the necessity which requires it, that is how it differs from the first. The third kind of activity is all that is directed to the fulfillment of our *obligations and purposes* in life. It is all that we do because we are in a given situation in life and have to respond to what that situation demands of us. Then, fourthly, there is another kind, quite distinct from the third one, which is the *creative* activity. That is where we exercise our own freedom and our own powers in order to bring something about that could not come otherwise.

The first activity one could call mechanical, because it is not even connected with the purposes of life. It is just the way this mechanism of reaction works in us constantly. The second can be called vegetative, because it is just the same as what a vegetable does in order to keep itself alive, to nourish itself, to find the sun and the air, and so on. The third is more like an animal activity because every animal has a certain situation in the world which it has to fulfill; and it does many things, either because it is a solitary or it is a social animal, all of which serve to fill that particular place in the scheme of things. We also have to fill our place according to what we are and our own powers and so on. But over and above this there is something that we are able to do, chiefly because we are human beings with the power of understanding in relation to past and future; and that is, to create something that comes from ourselves and from our own decision. This power that we have is of course a dangerous power because it also leaves us free to create the wrong kind of thing. But the way we wish to look at it is that we should learn how to use this power for its true purpose; that is, to bring into existence something which is required from each one of us.

To understand this and to develop and exercise this power, we have to begin with small things which are within the compass of our understanding, because if we try to create outside of our understanding, we shall only produce a mixture of different activities, not a true creation. And we must never be disappointed or offended if we discover that our creative power is limited to doing extremely simple things in a way that would not happen of itself. Some of you have been working at this already in various groups, so you know about it in relation to doing things particularly well on a limited task that one sets oneself to do, to the limit of one's power, well. But it is possible, by keeping oneself alert, to discover situations many times during the day when a genuine creative act is possible, and then to do that. Sometimes it can be in our relationship with other people, sometimes in our relationship with material objects or living things, sometimes in relation to ourselves; that is, I can discover that in my inner state there is just a confusion or various impulses that have no purpose in them. I can bring myself into such a state that I am at least, for the moment, what I should be. When I do that, I really create myself for a moment. If I am not able to make a lasting, enduring, creation, this is because I have not yet power over the whole of myself. But I can at least do it sometimes with sufficient clarity and definiteness to recognize the change that comes over me when I do that, when I see that something can come which would not have been there if I had not made that decision and carried it out. It does not necessarily involve any striving or prolonged effort; it requires understanding and seeing what can be done, and it requires a decision to do it.

For the rest, it is important and useful to everyone to distinguish between the different activities; to see when we are doing things which are necessary and unavoidable for our lives—such as sleeping and eating and breathing and so on—and to see when something that is unnecessary enters and we inevitably fall back into the first kind: mechanical activity. For example, we may require a certain amount of sleep, let us say of seven and a half hours, and we then wake up; but instead of taking the decision to pass into the active life, we allow the moment to pass, and remain in a state half between waking and sleeping. Then we are no longer doing what is necessary, but something that is unnecessary for us, and this brings our state down into the mechanical condition, and no benefit for our organism comes from it.

That is to say, we remain another period of time—half an hour or an hour—somewhere between waking and sleeping, and we are not at all refreshed or benefited by that. Similarly, if it is necessary for our bodies to eat a certain amount of food—which the body itself knows—and we are not attentive to the moment when it is enough, or in taking our food we do not measure the needs of our own body when we look at the food, we find ourselves eating more than is necessary, and again this becomes an automatic activity which is of no benefit to our organism, but on the contrary, leaves it with unnecessary work to do in digesting the extra food.

Or again, with our thinking. If we have a certain problem in front of us, we should be able to measure the amount of attention we should give to that problem in order to see as much of it as we are at present capable of seeing. This may be a matter of minutes. If, instead of giving it the minutes of fruitful time, we spend half an hour or more turning it round-and-round in our mind, all that time is useless for solving the problem.

On the contrary, turning back into this automatic activity confuses and befuddles our mind. That is quite harmless as a kind of background, or substratum, of the purposeful activity. It is like loosening pulleys on machines being driven by a belt and pulley arrangement.

You have to loosen them, from time to time, when you don't want to use the machine. But if you spend a great deal of time with the driving engines running and the pulleys loose, this is not only wasteful, but in fact everything tends to go out of order because of it.

So we really have to learn how to allow the right amount of time for this unconnected activity, where nothing is being accomplished. It is harmless for some purposes, but harmful for others. There is, for example, a necessity for our mind to have freedom from pressure. It is very bad to keep the mind under constant pressure of attention; and it is very good to release it and to let it run idle for a time. But then one must know how to measure the amount of this idling of the mind which is going to be sufficient to relieve it and enable it again to return to an active state—if this is required. All this has to be studied; it is not a difficult thing, because it depends only upon our having the wish to do it, and watching ourselves.

36.
INTENTION AND ACTION

5 July 1964

TODAY WE HAVE the special task of getting the grounds of Coombe Springs prepared for the Reception we are holding next week for our neighbors and the Civic Authorities. I therefore ask you all to work as well and as hard as you can at this job. I am also going to give a short talk.

What I have to say is about something which, if we can understand it, is of real importance to us. This is the marriage of our intention and action. When these two are divorced it is always bad. Intention without action, or action without intention, are both of very little use to us. If we act and have no intention in our acting, our action may be taken over by any kind of impulse. If we intend without acting, then this is poison for our will. It is a good practice to bring one's intention right into contact with one's actions: that is, really to marry the two together—not just to let them look at one another from a distance, but really be married. One way of doing this is to pause at certain moments and ask oneself: "What am I at this moment intending?" Maybe I'll find nothing at all, yet I'm still doing something—worrying. Or maybe my action is just going on by momentum; which often doesn't very much matter, because many actions can go on very well automatically. But is there an intention which is united to this action? Even though I'm not conscious of it at the moment of questioning, it can still be a genuine marriage.

So I recommend to you today that you should practice this immediate connection—immediate uniting—of intention and action. One help to achieving that is by this self-questioning: "Am I acting at this moment with intention?" "What do I intend, and for what reason?" "Am

I doing it to serve some purpose?" "Am I doing it to please myself or because it is an unavoidable necessity?" With such questions, we can bring our intention into focus and then carry it into the action.

After-Lunch Discussion

Questioner. How can we distinguish between working with intention and being self-willed?

JG Bennett. Self-will is one kind of intention. To be able to see that one's intention is simply to have one's own way; even that is one kind of intention.

Q. Could you enlarge on the other kinds?

JGB. For example, if I intend to do something that I have been asked to do, in the way I have been asked to do it, then my intention is to conform to that; in which case it is not self-willed. Or if my intention is just to do the job as well as I can, then that is the direction of my intention. I may be able to see what my situation is at the moment if I ask myself: "What is my intention at this moment?" I may very well be able to see that I am really trying to justify myself, to impose myself, to have my own way. If I see that, I see it! I may have thought that I am doing something for some quite high reason, then if I look more closely I see that my real intention is nothing else except to do it as I like.

Q. Where do you draw a line between intention and impulse? I have often married impulse with action without results.

JGB. There should come between impulse and action this question: "Why?" Only in that way is an impulse turned into an intention. It is because we don't ask ourselves this question: "What is my intention in doing this?" that we act impulsively; and then the result may be quite contrary to our intention, simply because this test hasn't been applied.

Q. You get an impulse first as a rule don't you, and then …?

JGB. An impulse is usually to change what one is doing. But we may find at a given moment that we are doing something, and when we ask ourselves "What is my intention in this?" we see that we are just going on doing it by habit: neither impulse nor intention, just habit. But what the test does is to see "Am I there as I am doing it, or not?" What is sometimes quite easy to notice is that our intention is going along one line and our action going along another. They are just quite merrily following their own bent, and neither has anything to do with the other.

Q. Well the first obstacle was that our clock was a quarter of an hour wrong! That was a thing that couldn't have been the fault of anyone. And then I was going to fetch something from the kitchen and walked along with intention and action going along together; and suddenly I walked in quite a different direction, up to the herb garden, and seemed to have forgotten about it! That sort of thing has been happening all morning.

JGB. It sounds (from many groans of sympathetic agreement) as if you aren't the only one!

Q. How does one gain a sense of spiritual companionship which makes you feel that there is almost a sense of integration between ourselves, and we find real oneness in our spiritual consciousness? It has been suggested that there are techniques of reaching this—meditation and inspiration. What would your recipe for this be?

JGB. Before I reply to what you ask me, I ought to explain that you have not been on one of these Work Sundays before. You weren't here when I gave a talk earlier this morning. (I'm saying this for others who also weren't there) in which I recommended everybody to look at one simple thing: the marriage of intention and action (or the divorce between them) and to try to observe how much we lose through the incessant divorcing of our intentions from our actions.

We have to bring the two together at the same time. It is no use intending something now and doing it in an hour's time, because by that time my intention will have changed. I have to bring it back at the moment of action. I asked people to experiment with this by finding, at a moment that they are doing something, whether or not there is an intention accompanying their action. Is action and intention really married in us? For example I at this moment have as my intention to try to make clear to the people here what I myself have seen and experienced about this. Therefore what I find to say to illustrate it must always accord with the intention of communicating it clearly.

But you were asking about something different: about the techniques that are necessary. It is one of the greatest mistakes to suppose that we could dispense with techniques in the deep and difficult things of life, when we know we need them for the simple ones. We know that speech is a technique of communication; we know that there are techniques for cooking, for clothing, for providing ourselves with the necessities of life, for learning various sorts of skills. Yet somehow we suppose that the inner life will go rightly without any technique. It isn't true. We don't suppose for a moment that we can say to a child: "Now read!" We realize that we have got to teach it how to read. We think we can perfectly well say to somebody, "Act in such-and-such a way!"

263

without telling them how to act in that way. This is a most strange illusion: that the easy things have to be learned and the difficult things don't have to be learned. One must at least understand that something has to be prepared and fashioned to make it possible. You see, you spoke about union with God, and awareness of the presence of God. Something in us has to be fashioned, to be able to have that kind of experience. It may happen accidentally to people, and then they have no doubt about its possibility. Then they want to find it again and can't; and they wonder why they can't. The truth is that this doesn't come by itself when one asks for it. It comes by itself sometimes unasked, but really to put oneself into such a disposition that this is possible, is a technical matter. You spoke about meditation. Yes, there are techniques of meditation, and techniques for adjusting the consequences of meditation. By this, I mean it is possible to learn a certain way of meditating that will produce results, but also produces all kinds of other things that may be quite undesirable. A great deal of "science" is needed if one is really going to get something which is what one wants, and not get undesirable reactions from it, and that applies to meditation.

Q. Is there a technique for... [inaudible].

JGB. No, there is not a technique by which one can feel that. There is a technique by which one can dispose oneself to receive this, but that is a different matter.

Q. Would we pre-condition our minds, for instance?

JGB. "De-condition" or "condition?"

Q. "Pre-condition" our minds to that extent. For example, trying to compose some music by playing over, let us say, inspiring music, classical music. It helps to condition our mind so we are rightly adjusted to compose music. Is there a parallel technique whereby we can become conscious of God in our brain, or in our minds?

JGB. They are not the same thing and it is not quite right to say that. If you speak about composition in the sense of constructing music, this is one thing. If you speak about composition in the sense of a spontaneous creative act it is quite a different thing. If you speak about the first kind of composition, you have to learn the theory of composition and you can certainly put yourself under the kind of influences which suggest various musical forms to you, but all that can happen without the slightest creative content. If you are looking for the creative content of musical composition there is something else involved. You understand the difference?

Q. I only offered that as a sort of ...

JGB. It is the same with the other thing. There is a technical side to it where you put yourself under certain conditions that are favorable to being in a state of prayer, and you may have states of prayer arising out of it. All that is one sort of technique, but the actual content of it is subject to the same sort of difference as there is in creative music—there is something which is not under our control in both cases.

Q. I noticed when I was working this morning that when I started I had intentions of doing the job in a certain way and this formed a pattern in which I could work. But I found I was getting lost in the pattern an awful lot, and my intention disappeared completely from the action. Whereas the intention gave me a little freedom it did tie me to a certain way of working, but the pattern gave me a tremendous amount of freedom and I could use this. Was this working properly: to form a pattern beforehand to work to? Or should one just try and form the intention and work with that? Does one have to plan ahead and form a pattern of work? Or should the intention be sufficient impulse to afford one to work almost spontaneously?

Q. Before Mr. B answers, could we understand what a "pattern" would be for you?

Q. I was doing some clearing and I said: "This is the way I wish to do it: I shall take this, and clear that, and clear this." I held this pattern; and started working to it; and quite often while I was doing that I asked myself: "Am I doing this with the intention?" I was just conforming to the pattern, but when I was working it was almost as if my intention just disappeared!

JGB. But why did you come here today? For what did you come?

Q. Because I wanted to! To say why would be difficult, but I wanted to come, that's all! The reasons I wanted to come would be because I found—last time I came—I learned things. I discovered things I didn't know before, and this helped me.

JGB. So this "wanting" you speak about turns out to be "having understood something"—or as you yourself put it—"there is something you can learn." Situations, which you find it worthwhile being in, come about this way, and would not if you were arbitrarily doing something else on your own. And it's from this that the wanting comes, isn't it? But at the same time you can realize that you may also forget all of this: You could come-to with a start, and realize that for perhaps half an hour you have been working away without getting any of the things out of it that you really came for. That is what I mean by "losing the

intention." We all—not only you, but everyone—find that we put ourselves into situations which we choose, and which, as you say, "we
want to be in." And behind this wanting there is some purpose, some
wish, some need, some understanding. And then, when we are in the
situation, it all begins to go automatically and the purpose of it all disappears. And it is only by accident—by some lucky chance—that
something happens that reminds us. And then we begin to get something out of it again. Isn't it like that for everyone? But it needn't be so
haphazard as that. We have power to bring more often our intention
into contact with what we are doing; and whenever we do so there is a
profit in it which there isn't otherwise. It also has a special kind of effect
on us. It shows us one or two other things like those other people have
reported—particularly what A. was saying—that when you begin to
apply this test, "Am I doing what I intend to do?" you find with astonishment how often you are not doing what you intended to be doing,
but have gone off at a tangent.

Q. Could we talk about intentions? I was through Gloucester lately
and met a Subud member who was a painter. She had been about two
years in England, and had got bogged down in building a house, so
she couldn't manage to paint at all. But she couldn't see any sense in
that, so we agreed that until we met in Paris (when Bapak comes)
whatever happened, for two hours we were going to do our house-
painting job. She had painting to do and I had something else. We were
doing this for a week. Now firstly, I found I often do have the intention
to do something for two hours, but I found it easier with her, because
another with the same intention seems to help. That is one thing I
wanted to ask you about.

The other thing is that, some years ago, I heard that it was a very
big mistake ever to set one's mind to do something and not to do it. So I
tried to discipline myself never to imagine that I was going to do anything that I didn't carry out. And so I try to cut down my imagination
before I get up in the morning. I don't allow myself to think too much of
what I'll do, because everything I do think of, I have got to do. I still
don't think I get out of myself, as it were, anything like what I could, if I
could get this a little bit further. But I think I need to link it with other
people. I can't do it on my own.

JGB. First of all, there are two or three important things here, in
what you have said. I will come to the one about working with other
people afterwards and include this painter. First of all it really is true
that false decisions, decisions which are not taken with genuine com-

mitment, but where one says "I will do such and such" without having really committed oneself—so that it still leaves one in doubt as to whether one will do it; and as likely as not one won't—this is really a bad thing. It truly is a thief of one's own power—to let that enter. Therefore I am sure what you say about setting oneself to reduce to a minimum the sort of plans for the future which are not carried out, is very desirable. Much more so then merely not wasting time. It is a much more positive thing to set yourself directly to take an obligation, so that whenever you say "I will do such and such" you do it. This is enormously valuable in a very deep way. And, also interesting, it is something that connects us with others; because the absence of decision, and living with that intense imagination, isolates us from other people. Whereas when we begin to do what we decide, we begin to come into a world of reality where we can really meet people; and this encounter with other people is not a dream-encounter, it is a substantial encounter. This is certainly so when two people take together a decision that they will do something; so that the obligation is not only towards their own essential truth but also towards the other person's. This is well-known and there is no question about it. It more than doubles the strength of the decision.

By this means a link is made, I think, whenever people have shared in a decision of this sort, and that link is a sacred matter. This is literally what the word sacred means in this case. Because it is to a reality greater than themselves that they take this commitment, a bond is made between them which is never broken. And every time this bond of shared decision is made between people, it leads to more and more connection between more and more people. Therefore, because of that very quality of being imperishable, it is not under the same law of time as our other things. If you come to understand better about decisions, you see the decision is really a timeless act. Because you decide as an act of your own and that act, if it is really appreciated for what it means, is something eternal and imperishable. It cannot be destroyed. Once one begins to feel towards one's acts in that way, then one is getting a real footing upon reality. And another thing about it is that it never isolates us, it never separates us from others. It makes it much easier for us to come into contact with other people who are feeling for the same realities. Whereas as soon as we begin to allow ourselves to go in the other direction—of letting dreams predominate and planning ten things and accomplishing one—this may be very pleasant, and the one may really be accomplished, and you may say "Well what does it matter if I dream of nine castles in Spain and only build one castle in England?" But it does matter! Because those unreal things tie us to an unreal world. Of course, this doesn't at all mean we mustn't have imagination and visions have no importance. They have. What we must not have is visions which take the place of reality, that's all.

Q. This morning, I put a question to myself, perhaps half-heartedly, "Am I doing this with intention?" and replied, "Of course it is my intention, every word that comes out of my mouth is really what I intended to say," and I noticed that I had missed something. But another time the reply was "This is all just happening, this is all just happening anyway!" and once there was a sort of vacuum, and another time some lack of intention came up.

JGB. Do you understand why I used such a strange word as "marriage?" And why I said the union of intention and action is really like marriage? How there is a certain oneness that comes about, which cannot be spoken of, that one can only know if one has had it? The second time you spoke of—when you had the feeling of a void and awareness of a state of separation—the divorce between the two—and the unreality of intention. Then an intention could really come and, what is more, it could come as it ought to come: in full union with action. Our intentions haven't always got to be at the very moment of action. Intentions can be directed to the future, when we call them commitments or decisions. But they must still be united with the action.

This is why I said there must be a sense of sacredness about the union—the connection—between intention and action. If I intend to do something and I really take that intention into myself and accept it, it will not be possible for me not to do it. As long as the conditions allow, it will not be possible for me not to. One must know that taste of what a commitment is. Even if I forget all about it—or if I don't want to at all and quite change my mind about it—if I have committed myself I will not be able not to do it. This we must learn to have, and when we do we begin to take it terribly seriously, because we see that to take a real decision is no joke! "At this moment I think I want it!"—"Do I really?"

This is what I was saying about impulse and intention. I must be very sure that this is really my intention and not just an impulse, because if I have only done something on impulse—when it wasn't really my intention—I may afterwards very much regret it and wish to undo it!

"You know the picture of St. George and the dragon.* It tells us how we can master this dragon in ourselves. Eternal vigilance is required, represented by St. George on his horse, watching it, with his spear just touching the dragon's neck. That is all that is required. As long as the dragon knows he is being watched, he is quiet and peaceful. Then the soul—represented by the lady—can lead him on the silken thread. This represents the state we have to learn to establish in ourselves. So long as the dragon was in the cave, he was a threat. He could not be seen. What he would do next was unpredictable. Only when he was brought out of the cave, making all of him visible, did the situation arise enabling St. George to see and control him.

"The ordinary state of man is one in which he is identified with his dragon. His dragon is 'I.' The desires of his dragon are his desires. That is the state when the dragon is in the cave. There is no possibility even of fighting with him. The dragon is inside us and we are the dragon. … How to see this? How to come to the point where one sees that one's dragon is not oneself? How to arrive at having one's own St. George?

"St. George does not come on the scene, you understand, a novice in the matter of dealing with dragons. He has probably been to a dragon-taming school, so the dragon soon becomes weak when confronted with him. But now a dreadful thing can occur, for it can happen that St. George himself turns into a dragon! A terrible risk is run here. For if he ever thinks he is the real beneficiary in the taming of the dragon—that the dragon will become his own domestic animal—he is in great danger. …

"This is why the lady is there, representing the highest soul-principle in man. Why is it represented as feminine? Because it is obedient, it is loving, it is receptive. It is not seeking for power. She only holds the dragon with a silken thread. The real meaning of this is that one must have power as if not having it."

—edited, from *Intimations*

* Uccello's painting, in London's National Gallery. See page P8, photo insert.

37.
BEING REALISTIC

21 June 1964

WHAT DOES IT MEAN to be realistic? I am going to talk about three kinds of realism. It may help us if we distinguish them and know how to come to terms with each of these. First of all, there is being realistic about the facts: not to disguise from ourselves what are the facts with which we are confronted and also to see how we stand in front of the actual situation whenever we have to make a decision or perform an action. It is necessary not only to look the facts in the face, but to look for the facts. That is, to realize that there is almost certain to be something in the situation that is there to be seen and known, if only we will look more unprejudicedly and intently—in a more free way. Every one of us has a great tendency to see the facts according to our own habit of thought and just notice the things that we are accustomed to look for. Therefore a training is also required in being realistic about facts.

The second kind of realism is to be realistic about what we really want and hope for. We can easily pretend to ourselves that we want something which we don't really want; or intend to do something that we are not going to commit ourselves to doing. In this realism about intentions it is also necessary for us to make sure that our intentions do correspond to possibilities. This second way of being realistic is just as important as facing the facts. It is also a question of facing what we intend to do about it: what we can do about it.

The third kind of realism is the realism of decisive action. The opposite of that realism is drifting: just letting things happen to us. Even though we may know enough about the facts—and even though we

270

may have an intention—yet we still don't bring to it the third kind of realism: the realism of the act. You can see that these three kinds of realism hang together. If any one of the three is omitted there is no realism; or one can say "One kind of realism is not realism at all, two is only half realism." One is realistic only when one is firmly grounded on fact, one knows one's own mind, and one acts. The enemy in each case is that kind of imagination in us that allows us to pretend to ourselves.

I am going to say something specially about the second kind of realism, that is, the realism connected with our own intentions—with our alignment in front of the possibilities of the situation. The first thing is really to satisfy ourselves that there is something to be done, that there is an opening.

You know very well that one can be planning, working out schemes for doing things, and really if we are quite honest with ourselves we know there is no intention of doing anything: no intention of finding an opening. This often happens because we go beyond what is really possible; and we do that because we go beyond what we are able to understand. Therefore we should bring this second kind of realism back to a certain starting point. And this starting point is the recognition of openings, of "holes," as they are also called. If everything is fixed and has got to happen as it will happen, then intentions are no good, they waste. Sometimes the situation is for all practical purposes like that. If you jump off the top of the Empire State Building and change your mind half way down and say, "But I didn't intend to hit the ground!" it won't help. This is an exaggerated example; nevertheless it still corresponds to things that happen to us in our lives. We do get ourselves involved in situations where the outcome is almost as inevitable as jumping off the Empire State Building, and then afterwards, when things have already begun to go with an irresistible momentum, we begin to want to change them.

Learning to look for openings is really nothing else but a way of facing the facts. That is the point I want you to see more clearly. An opening is really a place where a fact is missing. If there were a fact there, it would have to produce its results and there would be nothing to be done—the outcome would be inevitable. But the world of fact is such that it is not full, but has plenty of holes or empty places where facts are missing and we have the possibility of putting in what we intend. If the world were packed tight with facts like sardines in a box, we should have no more chance of moving about than sardines have. You must understand that this other world, the world where we can have intentions, where we can take commitments, where we can make decisions, is different. Facts are only half of the whole reality, this is the other half.

In *The Dramatic Universe,* I called these two the worlds of Fact and of Value and said the first of all values is the awareness of an opening. This I called "contingency" or "uncertainty," but both words really mean there is an opening—something to be done. Learning to recognize this possibility of doing something is the beginning of the second kind of realism. It is not enough to be honest with oneself and say "I really want such and such" if we are not able to see a hole for such and such to enter. This is why, even with good intention, one can still only achieve something if there is a hole, a place for it; and putting something into it has to be done by an intentional decision of our own; it will not come by itself.

All day long holes appear in the world of fact around us. We recognize these holes whenever we notice that something can be done—when, as we say, it occurs to us to do something. If you have the wish not to be completely stultified in the world of facts—if you wish to come into a richer world where you have freedom to do what you want—then you have to make use of the moments when there is the possibility of inserting or adding something. And those moments have to be recognized and valued. As you gain experience in this you come to see it as the beginning of value, so that this "thing that might be" really matters much more than all the things that are already there. This is being realistic—we may have good fine and beautiful intentions about what we will do with our lives and how we will behave towards people and the sort of things that we will accomplish, but in the end it all comes back to the moment when it is possible to do something and the recognition of that moment. Until you have understood this, you haven't understood at all what the second kind of realism is. When you do begin to recognize this, then you can begin to care. When you begin to care then this world opens out to you, because your caring comes from yourself.

But then it still brings us back to the third kind of realism: "What do we do about it?" That means it brings us back to the world of fact: of doing. This is a way in which we combine the two: the world of what-is and the world of what-might-be—the world of fact and the world of value—these come together and become reality only through action. If you think about it, it couldn't be otherwise than that. This is why we are given the will—this is why we are given the possibility of understanding—so that we should be able to achieve this third element of reality: of doing what we choose to do, doing what we wish to do, doing what is possible to be done, not neglecting the opportunities. It may seem very small compared with the kind of intentions and dreams and hopes that we have of what we will do with our lives, but all these things will come if we begin here—at this point of learning to use the moments when there is the possibility of doing something. When I said the world of fact was full of holes I meant more like a sponge than an empty place. The trouble is that for the most part we don't see the holes. If we look at something like a sponge that has got holes in it, we tend only to see the material, tangible aspect of it—what is there. We don't see what might be there, and all that is concerned with "might-be." We lose touch with the possibilities of things because we don't get close enough, so that our world, and the lives of most people, consist in just living with the facts which they only half face, and living with dreams which they hardly ever realize.

So I suggest you reflect a little on these three kinds of realism and during the day that we are here and working together (because it has to be done in the middle of action) practice looking for the moments when it is possible to do something intentional. Observe for yourself just how much and how often in the course of the next two hours you actually are able to do something that you are intending to do—and how many times in those two hours—and for how long.

After-Lunch Discussion

JG Bennett. First of all, were there any of you who were not at the talk at half-past ten this morning? Did you all find out about what was said at the talk? Did anyone who wasn't at the talk fail to get told what was said at it? When we come together for these Work Sundays we undertake something together. We do various jobs together outwardly, but also direct our inward attention on a theme and that theme should also be shared by everyone. So if you are prevented from coming to the talk at half past ten you should always ask someone to tell you what the theme is. Now I would like somebody to tell me briefly what they understood the theme to be, and what they understand that I asked you to do this morning?

Questioner. I understood that we were trying to look for three different worlds: of facts which we could encourage; of values or possibilities which could exist—potentialities which could happen; and of intentions that came from ourselves.

JGB. Wait a minute, it is very important that we should test for ourselves whether we have heard what is being said. ... Did you do any-thing M. R., during the morning, to verify that you had understood rightly? Did you speak to anyone about it?

Q. I didn't, in fact, verify that I had understood rightly. I took it that I had.

JGB. But you hadn't! Well, go on then M. What specific thing did I ask you to try and do during the morning?

Q. I took the specific thing to be that we should look at facts and attempt to see if anything could be done, something intentional. Looking for what I think you called "holes." During the morning I tried to do this, to see if there was anything among the things I could see with a potential of changing, of having something done which I could do. This is what I did.

JGB. All right. In a minute I will ask you what came of it. I would like someone else who came for the first time to say what they thought about it, and also whether they did take the opportunity of speaking to someone to verify that they had understood? What would you say? At the end here, I would like both of you to tell me.

Q. I'm not going to worry about whether I understood properly, what I did was to relate my capabilities—to be aware of the relation of my capabilities and my intention with ...

JGB. All right, what do you say?

Q. The interpretation I got was that I should try to be aware of the world around me, of myself, and of my own ideals. I brought my ideas into action to better the world around me.

JGB. [Asking a third person.] Could you tell?

Q. I saw today to be a means of concentration on realism in the form of looking for opportunities. Opportunities for the individual to play a part in his environment.

JGB. [Sitting up on the side of his chair.] I will make myself a little bit taller so that I can see.

Q. To see the opportunity, see the hole, but also to have a concrete intellect and general attention, taking all the facts into consideration.

JGB. That is the general theme of the talk. What did you gather was my suggestion for the actual practical experiment to be made during the morning?

Q. Looking for opportunities in what we are doing with regard to doing something with intention rather than allowing the external things to just happen.

JGB. [To another person.] Can you say? Don't bother to stand up.

Q. What I understood was that there were three points. One was to find out the facts as far as we know them. Secondly, to realize one's capabilities, or the limits of one's capabilities to find cracks or holes I think you said, in the edifice—find some new opportunities. And then, what was really important was not only to find these opportunities but—when you had found something—to act and to do it. Action, not just thought, not just knowing what to do, but getting down to it and doing it.

JGB. And what did you regard as the particular experiment that I asked you to make, that we could make?

Q. To find an opportunity and then to grasp this opportunity and do it.

JGB. All right. Who else now can tell something? You see, everyone that has spoken so far has merely reinterpreted for themselves what I said. Not one single person has referred to the crucial point which I asked you to note. ... Yes?

Q. It was to see if within two hours we could have two opportunities when we were actually doing what we intended. But for some people....

JGB. At least it brings back one of the tasks I set. It is much nearer to what I was saying.

Q. Would you say that the moment of decision of this whole situation in bringing oneself into relationship was letting yourself go into it?

JGB. But what did I actually ask you to do? R. G. has referred to ...

Q. I understood you to say that we should try to find out if our actions corresponded to our intentions; and you gave us two hours to do this. Bob has already pointed out that two hours is a very short time. I have found that my actions most often don't correspond to my intentions; but this is something which takes years to see sometimes, and in those two hours I couldn't really do it. I knew that there was a job of work to be done. I was working on the chimney; but at the same time I wasn't at the head of that working party. I couldn't determine exactly what had to be done, because I wouldn't have had an influence over it in any way. I could tell, for example, that I was going to mix some mortar. so I decided I would mix some mortar. As it happened it did fall to me to do it, so that in that respect my actions did correspond.

JGB. Anyone else?

Q. I am not sure whether R. G. has already covered the point I had in mind or not; but you asked us to take note of how many times during the whole two hours we became awake enough to do something about this or to.... I am not sure about this.

JGB. That is right. That is what I said; but you are the first person to tell me so!

Q. I thought that R.G. was trying to say the same thing.

JGB. The specific thing I asked you to do was, during those two hours between eleven and one o'clock, to observe how many times you could be aware of an opportunity—actually see that there was a possibility of doing something. I purposely put it that way round instead of putting it in a language that might be familiar to you, like "How many times do you remember yourself?" or "How many times do you wake up?" because it would have just suggested all that simply by association—so I said the same thing in slightly different language. But the thing I really did emphasize was that I asked you to take note how many times—and, I also said, for how long—can you find yourself in a state of being able to do something. Because in order to be able to do something you have to be aware of your being there. And I said the first beginning of it is to be aware of there being a hole. But this very fact that you remember is itself a hole.

Now, I want to know how many of you—having heard B. describe it—recognize that as what I asked you to do? Could you...? All right, that is very good …. Now how many of you did it? Yes.

You will recognize that the particular account I gave you—with its background of the three elements of realism—was all to help you see where the possibility of a real moment comes. I put it in that way: "Try to observe and actually count up on your fingers." I remember thinking to myself, "Not many people will have to go beyond their two hands in this." I said "Try to take note of these moments when you see that there is a possibility of doing something and see how often they come, and how long they last, how long you are able to be in a position of being aware that there is something that you can do." You rightly said that I did stress this side of it, that is the awareness of being in front of a possibility. I didn't emphasize that there is a third side, that is, of actually doing something about it, because I especially wanted you to notice these moments of "coming to," and remembering yourself as we sometimes call it, without describing it in just those words, by using an equivalent description which would not just produce associations in your mind. About thirty of you have said that you did recognize that as what was asked. Now I want to know how many—you also said a good number of you—actually tried this experiment. How many of you really could in the course of doing that recognize these moments of coming to something quite unmistakable? Could you put up your hands? Yes, very good. And now how many can say that they did it ten times? Or nine? Eight? Good. Paul hits the jackpot. All right, I won't torture you by going all the way through.

Q. My own experience is that it is rather like being in, and standing at night in, a thunderstorm. Between that and the lightning you don't see anything....

JGB. Yes, it is like that. What is very extraordinary is to realize that upon these moments everything depends. They are the only moments when we have really the possibility of doing something with our lives. Therefore, in a way, to feel realistic about this is the key to coming to reality. What I find strange is to see how these moments can come to me and I can just wait for them. Although I know from years—and decades—of experience, that they are those moments when I can do something to change my situation; it still can happen that they come to me and I only think about it and don't actually translate it into the third step of an act. This is really what I am talking about today: the key to the understanding of human life. The ordinary way of looking at life is that we can do what we choose to do, that we are responsible all the time for our actions, and that we can make demands on others— as if they too could choose what they want to, and as if they too were responsible for their actions. Whereas the truth—the real truth—about man is that he has very little possibility of being responsible; because responsibility means reality. A byproduct of this—which I must say I foresaw beforehand, before we started—should be to show you how difficult it is to listen: how difficult it is to repeat back—just after two and a half or three hours—something which I said and repeated and said, "This is what I want you to do." The question had to go round about ten people and then come to somebody who has had many years experience and, if I may put it that way, had his nose rubbed in it—somebody who can really say what it was that I had said. Well now, [to K.] did you want to say something?

Q. I was going to say that I listened very carefully to what you said this morning. It was very interesting, and I just became aware, sitting here, that I couldn't remember a thing of what you said. On the other hand, I was quite certain that I absorbed it. This often happens to me. I actually did the exercise, but I couldn't tell you about it at all in the way that B. was able to.

JGB. Yes. Would any others of you say the same as K. did? That is to say: you felt that you got the gist but couldn't possibly have repeated it correctly in words? [A certain number felt the same.] That is also quite possible. At the same time it is not sufficient. One should be able to bring things into some kind of focus—bring the image into focus. Are there any other things that anyone wants to say or talk about?

Q. There were five times when, perhaps against your request, I carried this to the point of action.

JGB. Oh, I did not mean that you were not to! I was only concerned with you counting up the number of times that you recognized the nature of a hole. Go on.

Q. In one case a hole appeared which I needn't do anything about, but if I had, the job would probably be much smoother and better managed. When I brought myself to take the decision to act, and acted, it seemed to produce a tremendous feeling of harmony, purposefulness and steadiness. But I only noticed that in the very last half hour of the job, which was bricklaying. It's probably about ten years since I've done any, so none of it was easy and therefore the harmony went. But it became real work because to get anything done I had to continually try to see what I was trying to do with my hands … .

JGB. What you are saying now illustrates something else I said this morning—realism of one kind isn't realism at all. Realism of only two kinds is still only half-realism. What you are describing now is that half-realism when we are in front of a challenge and we do something about it. This can happen while we are asleep. The second kind of realism isn't there, yet it is half-realism and something happens. A great deal of life is lived in this half-real way; and people who have only that at least have something. But there is an unmistakable difference between that and the three-term realism; because you know you are real only when the three are there. Another interesting thing emerges about that, which is how our own reality and the reality of the world are one and the same thing. There cannot be a real world and we not be real, or we cannot ourselves be real and not be in a real world. This, you remember, is the title of Gurdjieff's Third Series of writings, *Life is Real Only Then When "I Am."*

"I will give only one example of a 'personal' symbol. Once in the latihan I put out my hands and felt that a globe had been placed in them. Its surface was as smooth as glass, and I turned it over and over to make sure it was perfectly spherical. Although my eyes were closed I could see that it was perfectly transparent, like a crystal. It was heavy and yet it had no weight. As I was wondering what it meant, I opened my mouth and the great globe—as large as a pumpkin—entered my mouth and I swallowed it. I could feel it inside myself gradually being absorbed. All this had no meaning for me whatsoever, but the same evening, after the latihan, I was able to describe it to Pak Subuh. He said that this was to show that my understanding had been purified and that in future I would be able to see the true meaning of ideas presented to me from outside or from within."

—*Concerning Subud.*

38.
UNDERSTANDING VERSUS KNOWING

(date unknown)

IF SOMEBODY ASKS YOU whether there is a difference between knowing and understanding, you will probably say "yes." But if you are asked to explain this difference, I think you would not find it so easy. I myself have been trying to make clear to myself how I understand the difference. I just used the word "understand"—as you would probably also—that is to say, you would not say, "Do I *know* the difference between knowing and understanding?" but "Do I *understand* how they are different?" That is because understanding is more intimately connected with ourselves than knowing. We feel at once that when we have understood something, it really has become part of us, whereas we can know something and it can remain altogether outside of us.

Certainly we can use the same words in different ways. We can see that there is obviously a difference between knowing about things and knowing things. I can know "about" a person without knowing the person. When I know a person there is something different in our contact. It is better, I think, to keep the distinction between knowing and understanding as clear as we can for ourselves by using the two words with a clear idea of what the moment of knowing is and what the moment of understanding is. Evidently we know something when we are told about it, and we connect it with what we already know. That connection has to be made, for we cannot know things in a complete void without any context or environment; that context or environment is always there somewhere. We are told something about—let us say—Persia, and we already have some picture of Persian history and Persian art and, maybe, Persian people; and what we are told fits somehow into this framework that we already have; so that as soon as we hear of Persia, this new information goes in and finds its place alongside our previous knowledge. We would not say we have understood it, even if it has found the right place and even if we have seen how it fits into what we have heard and known about life in Persia, its history and so on.

Why would we not say that we have understood? Because understanding is something that comes from inside ourselves, not from outside. Because understanding cannot arise at all without our own experience; something has changed in us when we have understood something. This is why we say, for example: "Do you know?" not "Have you understood?" We would not say "Have you known?" When I say "I have understood this," it means that something has happened to me which has brought this into contact with me. It can be said that it has "entered" into me and I have "entered" into it: we have blended together and something has happened between us.

Just as we have to bring something to knowing—a certain framework or background or context so that we can know that we know—so also do we have to bring something to understanding in order to understand that we have understood. This is different, because what we bring to understanding is not a framework of facts and pictures and images and memories and habits of thought and so on, but a certain quality that is developing in us which makes it possible for us to understand. And we can very well see that as that quality is developing in us it becomes less and less dependent upon knowing this or that piece of knowledge or this or that fact. It is a certain possibility for us of experiencing in such a way that we have some understanding.

We can also see that knowledge is something quite specialized. You cannot pick up some quite new item of knowledge about some subject—such as Persian art or Oriental languages or Mathematics—unless you have a good strong background in that particular subject. If you hear some piece of knowledge and have not got the context, you cannot see its significance at all. That shows how knowledge depends upon something which is outside of us, on something we have acquired from outside. But understanding is not like this. It is sometimes quite possible to understand something where we have practically no background—no context at all of the ordinary kind. It is just that we are able to enter into this something, sometimes quite unexpectedly, and we realize we have "understood" a thing which we hardly knew about at all. And also the other way round: we can often be sure that we know a lot about a subject and yet do not understand it at all.

As our own experience expands, it brings with it the possibility of an expansion of our understanding. This can be an expansion in the upward direction—so that our experience begins to acquire a more spiritual quality and therefore we have more understanding of spiritual realities—but this alone is not enough; there must also be a more penetrating quality which will enable us to understand also the nature of things that are below the level of our ordinary human life and working. It also spreads out to right and left: we understand better others like ourselves where before we perhaps had only glimpses of how they would behave—what we could expect from them in certain situations.

When understanding begins to grow, it is not a question of knowing what people are like and how they will behave; but some sort of merging—or blending—of one person with another. As I picture it, this helps us to see how understanding is like a kind of sphere that slowly grows in size and embraces more and more. It embraces partly towards the spiritual and partly penetrates into these realms of existence which we call material, and partly also it spreads out sideways to help us to merge with and blend with others like ourselves.

When you get this picture in yourself of that quality of understanding as something which expands, you see much more strongly the difference between understanding and knowing: how knowing is much more like having more and more material spread out on a table—perhaps better and better arranged so that you may place one thing in relation to another—but it has not got that quality of embracing, holding within itself, that you get when you really understand this growing nature of the quality of understanding. It is important for us to see this clearly for ourselves, because then we can recognize where something can and has to grow in us through our spiritual development, and how we cannot look for a growth through it of something which is of the same kind as knowledge.

One may develop spiritually, but still one requires to get knowledge in the same way as knowledge is always got: through contact with the outside world. Whether that contact is directly through seeing and hearing, or through different kinds of powers such as clairvoyance, visions or telepathy or participation of some kind or other (I think one can say it is quite certain that man can have certain powers by which he can know without having to receive solely through the senses) none of that is any different, nothing of that adds anything to our understanding. I may sit here and have a vision exact and correct of what is going on two thousand miles away instead of what is going on in this room; or of what happened two or ten thousand years ago; or maybe even of what is going to happen in the future—but none of those things will by itself add anything to my understanding. The reason is that all such experiences still belong to the domain of knowing; they are simply different ways of knowing, just as we know of distant things in the past through records and calculations and so on. It is simply the better and better ordering of all this as it were on a great big table. Understanding is altogether different from this, because one clear way of recognizing understanding is that it is not something that is exclusive: if we understand one thing we understand another. It is not such that I can understand myself but I cannot understand you, or I can understand spiritual things but I cannot understand material things.

The power of understanding is really a transformation of the soul of man; an enlargement, a greater embrace that comes through something which is happening to us, not something that we do. Glimpses of understanding can happen to us, a kind of expansion where one really sees the meaning of things that previously one only knew; and this shows us why understanding has so little connection with the ordinary powers of man. We can see quite unlearned people, with very limited perceptions in the ordinary sense, who have real understanding "all the way round" as I put it. Others will have great sharpness of mind, a wonderful memory and many other things, but not have that power of embrace of the understanding.

In order that our understanding should grow, we have to allow it to be "stretched" so that this kind of change in its capacity can be brought about. This means we must not hold back understanding by thinking that at any moment we have reached a final understanding on any subject whatever, by supposing that there is any moment when we can say: "This I have understood and my relationship with it is now complete." As soon as we say that, this possibility of inward growth is stopped; but when we let go, we say: "I have seen (and what a great thing it is to have seen) but I can see so little." If there is always a readiness to accept that our understanding has to go through constant transformation, and that we must never at any time trust that the understanding we have reached is our final understanding, then we allow the growth of the inner vessel, or growth of the soul, which will be able to increase its embrace and understand more and more.

Certainly, in order to allow knowledge to grow, we must always accept that we are ignorant of many things; but it is doubly necessary for the growth of understanding that we should always accept, not merely that there are many things we do not understand, but nothing that we are able to understand fully; because only an infinite consciousness—an infinite spiritual power—is able to understand anything at all fully. So, although we can know separate things quite well enough for practical purposes, we cannot understand anything enough—neither the smallest thing nor the greatest—because understanding is a totality which has to grow; the growth of which may even stop and even risk being strained and spoiled if we hold on to the idea: "Now I have understood and my understanding will remain as it is now."

That cannot be: what is understanding today will be misunderstanding tomorrow. Nothing in the domain of understanding remains stationary: it must grow or it will die. If you grasp this all-important truth, you will see that we must be constantly opening ourselves to understanding. Great understanding can be built on very little knowledge; but no amount of knowledge will give understanding automatically. We must have experience and we must live it.

After-Lunch Discussion

Questioner. What in man is really capable of freedom and how is this related to individuals? What is the nature of the actual division involved in free choice? What is the *source* of freedom?

JG Bennett. Properly speaking the word "I" should represent that part of a person which is able to be free. You could put it that way round: "What is 'I'?" and then I should say: "That in man which is able to be free." The "I" in man is not something which is always the same for all people or even the same at all times for a given person. The man who, at all times and in all places can truly say "I am" is not an ordinary man. He is the perfected man that we aspire to become. Such an "I" is the goal, not the starting point. Therefore, to say "The 'I' is that which is able to be free" is probably the best way of describing it. It is possible also to say that there is a certain place in man, a certain position within him, where freedom is possible. I will start by explaining that, because this is a complex thing which has to come from several directions, and therefore I cannot give a logical exposition to answer it.

What does it mean that the "I" in ordinary man is relative and therefore that freedom is relative? There can be a temporary local freedom in front of a temporary local situation. For example, supposing there is a packet of cigarettes here; at the moment I am aware of these cigarettes and of the desire to smoke and at the same time of a previously taken decision that I will not smoke, there is a possibility of choosing, in that temporary local situation, whether I will smoke or not smoke. The condition required is first of all that I should be aware of the two possibilities: to smoke or not to smoke. I am aware of them as present in me now; that is to say, there is something in me which is related to the actual situation of taking a cigarette or not taking it. It is altogether localized and temporary. Just so long as I remember about the cigarettes and so long as something relates me to the cigarettes in terms of smoking, or not smoking. As soon as this passes away, the situation ceases to exist and so does that possibility of choice and freedom.

This same choice can be applied to the question you asked me. When you were asking it, I paused and put myself in front of it in the same sort of way I would have done in front of the cigarette. I was aware that I could speak about principles of freedom and choice and individuality, or I could speak by taking a specific limited example. I was free to choose which way I would speak about it and I chose at that moment to approach it by a specific example. But I could not be free at that moment in relation to what I am saying now, because I could not foresee how the conversation would develop; what would be the result of speaking about it in terms of specific examples, and therefore I cannot say that when I heard you asking your question my freedom extended to this moment now. I could only commit myself to start speaking in one way or another about it.

If we take examples of that sort, we can see that in front of a limited situation there is a limited power of embrace of our "I," a limited duration of awareness of our "I," a limited situation within which we can effectively choose or not choose. As long as we keep it down within the practical limits of the actual experience, of choosing and deciding, it is not difficult to understand about freedom. It is when we try to go from this to something much bigger; or try, for example, to answer your third question before we answer the first; then it becomes difficult.

Now, let us come back to what I said just a minute ago: I cannot be said to be free or to have any choice in relation to a situation that may present itself to me in an hour's time or tomorrow, unless I am actually able to be present and related to that future situation. It so happens that I know my "I" is of such a nature that as it is now, it is able to take decisions which will be valid and that my choice will be able to carry beyond the present moment to something an hour or two hours or maybe even two or three days hence. At one time I could not do that; I could not be sure how I would react to a certain situation that had not yet arisen. In other words, I can see from my experience and my life that my "I" today is something more that it was twenty, thirty or forty years ago, and therefore I know that the "I" in man is something which can change. And also, not only that it changes in its power of embrace and its duration, but also in the seriousness of the decisions it is able to take and the choices it is able to make. Therefore I know, from my own experience, that freedom is something which is progressive; that everyone has a small degree of freedom, and that it is possible for this freedom to grow. The growing of freedom is also a growing of the "I," and therefore "I" and freedom are the same thing. One of the ways one can recognize the condition of one's "I" is when one can really understand—and not just imagine to oneself—what it means to be able to take a decision which will be valid for a situation that has not yet arisen, or for a situation which is perhaps complex, where one sees in advance that one is going to be involved in emotional reactions and one will change from one emotional state to another, and yet one may see clearly that in spite of all these changes in one's feelings and the various influences that will act upon one, one's manifestations will still remain the same as when the decision was taken.

Now, there is something else connected with "I" and connected with freedom that is very important. That is, that it is really possible to distinguish two kinds of freedom. There is the freedom of the "I" to relate and direct the reactions of different parts of oneself, as shown by the examples I have just given. Another sort of freedom is the freedom to relate oneself to what is higher; where it is not a question of acting upon any part but of relating oneself, or of accepting a relationship of submission; and this in itself is more complex and there is much to be understood about it because it is not always the same. But the main thing about the two is that the "I" can either occupy a position of self-affirmation in relation to our outward activity, or it can occupy a position of self-denial, or self-surrender in relation to a power which is greater; which means, in the final analysis, to the Power of God. Both are acts of freedom. It turns out that when one's experience grows in this, one comes to realize the existence of these two kinds of freedom which, up to a certain point, are so different as to be almost opposite to each other. One is the freedom to do, to assert oneself, to act and so on; the other is the freedom to not do, to deny oneself: to submit. At a certain point they cease to be in opposition to one another—and then one realizes the presence of a further stage: and that is, that the "I" becomes transformed by a kind of inner change within the "I" itself;

where it is not "submitted to" nor "affirming that"—it is just free. Then the "I" is really not different from God, and that is why it is said that within the "I" is the real place where God enters. This is the true "I am" that I spoke about at the beginning of my answer to your question.

There is very much more to be said about this, but if you follow these suggestions, you will see that conditions can exist in man where the "I" is something transient which allows you to have the power of choice and freedom just in relation to a situation which is immediately in front of you—either Yes or No. It can develop to a point where it begins to be to some extent exempt from the successiveness of time and "I" can then take a commitment with full consciousness that "I" shall be exactly the same at some future moment as I am now. The strangest thing about it is that one can even be free in relation to the past. This experience—when people begin to notice that they are free to change the past—makes them realize that this power also exists in man. It is connected with the transformation of the "I": the "I" in this transformation becomes differently related to time and space.

Gradually, from this transient, changeable "I" we become aware that something or someone has entered us that is strong and free and that this "someone" is growing freer and stronger. And then we begin to be aware in ourselves: "There is now something in me which is never touched by anything that is happening, but remains free whether there is activity or non-activity, whether I am turning in this direction or that direction, I am always the same." We begin to realize that this new "I" is quite different from the other way of experiencing "I" we had before. And that again can go through various transformations until a time comes when we realize that there is really no difference between any of these relationships—between responsibility for the lower and submission to the higher—because it is all God and it is all "I." Everything depends on the transformation of the "I" and as I said all the way through, from beginning to end it is inseparable from Freedom.

This brings me to the last part of your question. "What is the source of freedom, how is it that there can be such a thing as freedom?" The answer is, there can be freedom because there is God; because God is free and we all have a part in His freedom. If we only have a very small part, then our freedom is only like this "to smoke or not to smoke" or "to think or not to think." The more part we have—that is, the more it is possible for God to enter into us—the more we find that this freedom which in reality belongs only to God has entered into us. It is always from that Source, but how much we can have of it and how much we can exercise it depends entirely upon how strong, how mature the "I" is.

Q. Is it a state that comes from awareness?

JGB. It is something more than a state of awareness. If you try to describe the "I" in terms of something else, then you are describing the greater in terms of the less—the real in terms of the only partially real. The "I" is what is real and reality is not the same as awareness—even awareness of the spiritual nature.

Q. Is not the "I" formed with the awakening of the soul?

JGB. It seems to me that we can say that the "I" enters the soul and awakens it—like the prince of the fairytale who awakens the sleeping beauty. The soul is the true home of the "I." But this does not mean that we can understand yet what is meant by "soul." It is different with "I" for this can enter different parts of our nature. We can say "I walk," "I feel," "I think" and so on, and each time the "I" is in a different place. But when "I am in the soul," in the very center of my being, it is different. "I" am always related by my awareness to some experience, and with that relationship "I" can be free to act or not to act. Without that awareness you cannot have an "I" at all: there cannot be an "I" except in relation to the difference between one thing and another; then my "I" can relate itself to either of these two different things. The more I become aware of how everything is and how things are different from one another and what their nature is, the more I can have a complete experience of "I".

Q. Could you say something more about the power of the "I" to change the past?

JGB. The past is the way in which we are connected with it. This means that there is no past except the trace it has left. There is no other kind of past. Even if we have forgotten about it, we are connected with it in a certain way; but this connectedness with the past is not something fixed. A simple kind of example which is not too inaccurate and does not give too false a picture is this: Suppose there is some incident in my own past which I refuse to accept; which I do not wish to look upon as my past, by realizing "I did this" or "This happened to me." That past event is in a state of tension with me and, although it is past, I am certainly connected with it. If anything tends to remind me of it I shall be tense and upset and I will avoid it. Or, if I do remember it, I will suffer or brood over it, and so on. So there is no doubt whatever that I am effectively connected with that incident; as effectively connected with it as with this chair I am sitting on, or as I am here with you sitting opposite me. The fact that it is past does not mean that I am not connected with it; and so my connection with the past is the reality of the past. My connection with you is the reality of you for me. My connection with those trees out there is the reality of those trees for me. Without those connections they have no reality. My connection with tomorrow is the reality of tomorrow for me. And that is why I say that if I make a decision for tomorrow I am connected with it and also that I really am free with relation to something which has not yet happened; because I am connected with it.

If you once can grasp the fact that the reality of anything is your connection with it; then you can see that if you change this connection then you change its reality. One is so much in the habit of thinking that the past is something which has happened and cannot be changed, that it sounds as if I was talking of some sort of psychological trick: "If I think differently about it I shall feel differently about it." It is much more real and concrete than that. It is not at all easy to grasp that the reality of everything is my connection with it; and if it is nothing else, then changing my connection with it really affects its reality.

Q. If I feel remorse about something in the past, it seems that my connectedness with it is changed. But I cannot see that the event itself is changed.

JGB. Remorse is what enables you to be aware of the nature of your connection. Before you felt remorse about it, you may have been falsifying the connection. Let us take the stages that can occur in a situation: In the ordinary way, there are certain events in our past that do not fit the picture we want to have of ourselves and do not correspond to the "I" that—one may say—is longing to form itself within us; and we reject them. This means that we live in a false state, repudiating ourselves, and the result is the tension we experience in the present. Then there comes a time when perhaps we come to see: "I cannot repudiate that; I must admit that I myself was in that situation. That is how I acted in that situation," and then we feel remorse. But still the remorse itself is not sufficient because you can have remorse without really being prepared to change what you are. I can wish that I had not behaved in that way; I can suffer because I have behaved like that; but I still want to keep the picture I have of myself and therefore I have not really changed the connection.

On the other hand, if I am ready to take into the present this condition of the past and say not merely "I was that person" but "I *am* that person," then I feel repentance, which is a different thing from remorse; because remorse is concerned with what we have done; but repentance is concerned with what we are. When we experience repentance, that itself changes the connection with the past because repentance is really freedom. Everyone knows this bitter feeling of remorse over something one has done, and yet knows also that one is no more free than one was before. What is more, one sees from experience that remorse does not stop one from doing the same sort of thing again. But repentance is different; it is freely to accept that my "I" is connected with and bound to that event, and this free acceptance now liberates me from the past event.

There is therefore a condition of man where he refuses to admit the connection with the past; there is a condition where he accepts it, but keeps it in the past; there is a condition where he accepts it and brings it into the present by connecting it with what he is at the moment, and this is a condition of freedom: this is change.

Q. You said something in your book, *Witness,* about this question of non-identity that interested me particularly, when you said that "fear is negative identity."

JGB. This is something one can only really verify psychologically; but it is interesting to see that it is connected with what I said about the state of the "I." In the ordinary state of people their sense of existing at all depends on whether something is supporting them. You are supported by likes and dislikes, by feelings about things, by your thoughts and everything. And if any of this is taken away, you experience fear.

Q. I once had a very strange experience which I have never forgotten. I was in a state of great annoyance and indignation about what somebody had said or done, and a friend of mine said "It is not necessary to feel like that." I was suddenly overcome with the revelation: "But if I did not feel like this, then I would just not exist!" I could not go on for long facing what seemed to be an unbearable void.

JGB. Yes, quite true. Such a moment of clear vision can change our entire life. This is just what I mean by "understanding'.

Q. I suppose it means waiting for the "I" to be strong—to be non-fearful when not identified with our feelings.

JGB. All of us are entitled to have this trust that we do have in us the place and the seed of the "I." We do not need to bolster ourselves up with pretense "I"s, only it is a very strong habit. It is just incredible to notice that many people have no trust in themselves that they exist at all unless somebody else shows signs of believing that they exist. One way we can cope with this to some extent is with the feeling: "I do not need that somebody else should acknowledge my existence—I AM."

39.
WHOLE-HEARTEDNESS AND COURAGE.

(date unknown) c. 1961-2

WHATEVER WE DO, whether inwardly or outwardly, we are making use of our various instruments of body, mind and will. All are involved in our every act, and so the way in which we perform every act should be a total thing. Yet this is very difficult, and it leads me to what I wish to speak about this morning, and that is whole-heartedness in what we do in our search for God. I would like first to remind you of what the Shivapuri Baba said about the possibility of seeing God—which I have already quoted on various occasions. He says: "Every man who wishes can come to see God; but for this there must be a complete and uncompromising surrender and abandonment of everything that stands between us and God."

This attitude of whole-heartedness—of finding God at all costs—is easy to recognize in such people, as he, whose lives are clearly dedicated. In him you see a very aged man whose whole life has been devoted to this one thing only, and having found it, he has lived according to what he found. But it does not mean that this is possible only for those who renounce everything in the world, become *sanyasins* and retire into the forest for twenty years or more, as he did. Bapak says it is possible also for us; but how is it possible for us if we remain half-hearted? Is not the reason why these people who go into the forest really do find God, not that they go into the forest, but that they are whole-hearted in their search? Their going into the forest comes from the fact that they have the courage to go out of the world in order to surrender and abandon all that separates them from God. It is not that the forest has anything special that makes their path easy.

In one of the talks with the Shivapuri Baba, somebody asked him a question about the difficulties of modern life, and I said: "Is it not easier in a village, where there is not so much pressure?" His answer was: "Pressure is everywhere, there is no difference." So I added: "Then in the forest?," and he answered: "It is the same in the forest, because it is all in the mind, there is no difference, the pressure is not really from the outside conditions." And what is it that can change this? It is only our own whole-heartedness in turning towards that which is beyond the mind instead of towards what is outside the mind; that is, the external world. So I think it is probably true to say that those who go into the forest and do find God, succeed because they are whole-hearted, not just because they go into the forest. And those who do not go into the forest and do not succeed, fail, not because they have failed to isolate themselves from life, but because they are not whole-hearted.

Yesterday at a meeting we were talking about these questions and someone spoke of the extraordinary sense of awe one experiences when one finds oneself in front of something too big, when this deeper consciousness begins to stir in us, and how one lets it go just from lack of courage. It is quite true, we are afraid of that greater world and this fear makes us cling to this small world, because it seems safer. Reflecting on this, I remembered how in the *Bhagavad Gita,* in the chapter on the higher and lower natures of man, the first quality ascribed to the higher nature is fearlessness. Fear certainly is a strange phenomenon in this spiritual life of ours. We want to come to Reality, but every step towards Reality makes us afraid, and so we often turn back and have to start again.

You could ask: "But what about those who get into trouble because they plunge too rashly into action, looking to get something?" It is really important to make the distinction between true courage and the kind of foolish haste that disregards the dangers. Certainly courage is not that which ignores danger: it is that which sees the risk and why it must be taken. Of course, it is a risk to go forward in the spiritual life, because all progress in the spiritual life must come from dying in order to be born again. Every step is a death, and everything that one finds is a new birth. Death is always such that, until one has died, one is afraid of dying. But there are also plenty of people who just rush into death by folly, not seeing what they are doing, and then they die the wrong kind of death, which is what we call "crisis" or "psychosis." This is then very awkward for them, because perhaps what comes out of it is not ready to be born and it may be necessary to retrace one's steps.

I really do not think that for anyone who reflects on it, there is much difficulty in distinguishing between what is courage—freedom from fear when facing a new way of living—and what is foolish disregard of the reality of the process of transformation. We sometimes trust ourselves to this in a foolhardy way, expecting to get something particular that we want, and get it very quickly. We throw ourselves into it with a complete lack of reflection and honesty. Our own vanity is always mixed up in this, as is our self-love, our belief that we are different from other people and that we can accomplish things that other people cannot accomplish and so on. None of this is courage, none of this is that fearlessness which belongs to the true human self of man. Even when we know that there are many foolish imitations of courage and put all those aside, it remains true that true courage is necessary if we are to be whole-hearted.

The real steps are not easy to take. It is not easy to let go of attachment to this or that thing. Then the moment comes when we are faced with the choice between the world and God—and it comes over and over again, every day. I know for myself how often it is just an act of cowardice to allow oneself the easy way of letting one's attention be completely occupied with some worldly thing which is not at all necessary. I think everyone knows how easy it is to get into the habit of disregarding opportunities that arise all day long for living on a level different from the ordinary. When they come and we begin to take them, then courage is needed. Courage is not needed so long as one takes no opportunities; then one just drifts along as one likes. When we begin to take our opportunities, then something in us starts to get nervous and says: "Can I really bear to live like this? Can I stand this kind of life, where the spiritual reality is going to mean more than the power of any outward things on me—more even than my own vanity and self-esteem?"

And then we have to make the decision: "I *can* bear it, I *must* go this way!" And it has to be made over and over again. We can always get a little way without much risk; we can come to the point where our life really is made easier and more comfortable both inwardly and outwardly. By this I do not mean just material comfort and ease of life but to feel oneself psychologically better—to feel more confidence, a little freer in relation to external things, a little more sure in our relationships with people. One can be satisfied with that; these are fruits that come relatively easily. But when it is the question of going further than this, then it is certainly true that courage is needed.

It can be immensely valuable for us to be confronted by someone who has wholly taken such a decision. That is what a number of us have found who have visited this old man in the Himalayas. It is an inspiration to speak to someone who, when he says "You must want only God," really means it, with all its implications, with everything taken into account that has to be paid in order to have that. We mostly live our lives otherwise than this—too easily, forgetting that if we really set ourselves on that way, the end of it must mean that everything will have to be given up in order to come to God.

I remember vividly how at one moment, ten years ago or so, I discovered—after having gone through some very difficult and hard experiences—that I had the power within myself, if I decided to, to act in one way and not in another way. And I remember how I had always wanted to have this power, and when I saw that it had come to me, instead of being delighted and thankful that I had it, all I felt was a sense of terror: "If I can do this, I must do it. Am I really going to live my life in this way that has now been made possible for me?" All I wanted at that moment was to run away. Then it was that I really began to see for myself how great a part courage plays in this spiritual life of ours. When opportunities are offered to us, it is often out of fear that we do not take them. This may not be fear of suffering, of harm coming to us, or even fear of losing something; but simply fear at the thought that "I am facing the possibility of living a different kind of life which will put an end for ever to the way I have lived my life until now." This may be the very kind of life that it had been my aim to live for long years, and yet now the door is open for me I am afraid to go through. That life, into which I can enter, is too strong. The temptation is to go back to the weaker life, the shadowy life, and not the new substantial life that is offered. This I think many people know in one form or another. Spiritual progress is from the illusory to the real, from the shadow to the substance, and every time there is a chance that substance, reality, will be given to us, there is the fear: "Will I be able to bear that much more?." The only answer to this, I think, is that one must go little by little; one must go step by step, realizing that it is always possible for us to bear to be a little more real than we are. If we go forward, then our reality will grow.

After-Lunch Discussion

Questioner. You quoted the Shivapuri Baba as having said that it is possible to see God, but somewhere it is said: "No one shall see God and live!"

JG Bennett. It is also said: "Blessed are the pure in heart for they shall see God." When the Shivapuri Baba says: "It is difficult, but not impossible," he means that the mind must be empty of everything else. By "mind" he does not mean just "thinking," he means the axis of our inner life around which our feelings and desires are built. So long as there are small things in this mind, if it comes in front of anything very great, it will be destroyed. Therefore a veil is put down for man—really out of mercy—to save him from this, so that he should not see what he is not yet able to see, which he is not ready for seeing.

It is said in religion that we cannot see God until we are dead—that this vision belongs to the life after death. But this life after death can come without dying, if man "dies before he dies"—that is, if his mind can really be emptied of everything, including his own self-will. How is it possible to be empty and yet to have something with which one can see? When the Shivapuri Baba was asked: "What is it that can see God?" he replied: "I—it is only I." If this "I" is not attached to anything, or in other words, if it is free from everything, then it can see God. But in order to be free from everything one has to die to everything. If one were to see without that freedom, then all attachments would be destroyed; it would be impossible for anyone to see God and care for anything else but God; all else would be destroyed. It is therefore true, as is said in the Old Testament, that "No man shall see God and live."

Q. What properties of God can we see?

JGB. The properties of God can never be described. Every attempt to do so really only amounts to describing properties that we approve of in men. If we approve of those properties and think of them brought to perfection, then we say these are the properties of God. We have no right to make that sort of deduction. There is a possibility of an assurance of the Presence of God—of being aware that "I am now, at this moment, in a state where the Reality of God's Presence is a truth for me," but no more. Nothing can be said about it except just that assurance. This does not mean that God has no properties, nor even that His properties can never be experienced; but simply that the attempt to describe them is bound to fail. My own personal conviction about this is that there is an infinite variety in the nature of God—an infinite richness. Perhaps each being can appreciate this richness of God's nature in only one way. Therefore it may be that everyone who sees God sees something different.

I think it is probably like that, but one thing I really am sure about is that the higher we ascend the scale of Existence, the more uniqueness we find. The lowest things are the only ones that are all alike. As soon as you begin to go up the scale, no two things are exactly the same. It seems very probable, for example, that two electrons are just like one another—one can disappear and another can take its place and there would be no possibility of knowing that this has happened. Various other simple things have this property of being so much alike that they have no identity of their own. A little higher up the scale, things begin to be recognizable as themselves; even dead things—material objects—have a certain identity and uniqueness. Even things that are made by man off a machine have something or other which makes them distinguishable, though not very much. Living beings are much more so; human beings are unquestionably all different from one another; there is probably some significant difference in the actual raw material of every single human soul, but not so much as all that.

Men of a higher order—that is, those men who have reached the degree where their higher nature is already formed in them—are different from other men: they are differently unique. Each one has become more wholly himself. Man is probably only a little way up the scale, and I think there can be no reason for doubting at all that every step up this scale leads towards uniqueness and at the same time towards an enrichment of nature. We see this among human beings, that the more perfect beings are both unique and also very rich in their nature—their qualities. We can surely say with confidence that God is the most unique and God is the most rich, and that is why we can never hope to describe Him or His nature.

Question: A week or so ago I read an article on the situation in Notting Hill [racial incidents] and I was horrified by it, in a normal way. But about five minutes later I was suddenly sobbing with a terrible feeling of compassion for all these people. I do not know quite how this fits in. It did not last long, but it just shook me.

JG Bennett: This is compassion, because it means you accepted to have this within yourself instead of it being outside you. When we look on suffering and see it from outside, we may have pity, we may have kindness and so on, but it is not compassion. When that suffering enters into our inner house—because it can be like this—then we suffer, even if perhaps we do not know where it comes from. In your case, your inner place is able to be open to that.

This is why, when one gets delivered from one kind of suffering, one then enters into another kind of suffering. That second kind of suffering which you have experienced is inevitable. It is not something that comes from your own nature. It is not suffering because you are weak or because you are bad or have made some mistake, or because you treasure something too much and cannot bear to lose it. That kind of suffering is simply the suffering of our egoism. If that suffering can go away, then we are open to a different kind of suffering, which is the suffering of the world. That cannot go away. We do not even wish that it should go away, because we realize that we cannot isolate ourselves from that.

—from *Towards the True Self*

40.
HASNAMUSS

(date unknown) c. 1950

THIS WEEK I will try to explain to you about the meaning of the term *"Hasnamuss,"* which appears very frequently in *Beelzebub's Tales to His Grandson* and which, perhaps, is not one of the terms specially invented, like most of the new words you find in *Beelzebub,* which were invented by Mr. Gurdjieff himself. It is a word that has a very clear meaning if you understand its etymology and origin, and also a very clear meaning appears in *Beelzebub.* It is a conception that it is necessary for us to understand.

Firstly, in a simple way, a Hasnamuss is a person without a conscience, or a person who has cut himself off from his conscience. A Hasnamuss is also a person who sets himself aims that, however he may describe them, are in fact founded on his own egoism. But there is a special twist in this idea of Hasnamuss that it is important to try to catch. The word *"has"* means "special" and *"namuss"* means "honor." *"Has"* also means "privy," in all the different meanings in which the word privy is used. When we say "privy purse"—or the private treasury of the King—this is called *"has,"* and when we talk about a privy (an outdoor toilet), *"has"* is used for this too. It has a double meaning in Persian and in other languages where it is used—both a meaning of something that is specially important and something that is specially learned. In that double meaning of the word much is conveyed, so that a *"has"* is a person whose honor is very special, special in this dubious sense. Throughout *Beelzebub Tales,* the idea of Hasnamusses as beings who, because they set themselves aims that are clearly defined for themselves and are able to direct the course of events, is a very important one.

You remember that I read to you some weeks ago, in the last series of lectures, the story of Ashiata Shiemash and the establishment of an organization for the welfare of mankind. One or two people asked me after that lecture how, if such a good organization was established, did it break down and what hope is there for anything that may be achieved on the earth. I promised at that time that I would read the description, which is also given in *Beelzebub's Tales,* of the way in which this organization established by Ashiata Shiemash was ultimately destroyed, and destroyed by the work precisely of an arch Hasnamuss.

This illustrates the general idea that the troubles of the world are not solely due to the inertia and mechanicalness and blindness of things which are in themselves sufficient to cause the disintegration of any structure which may be set up—unless there is a conscious force struggling to maintain it—but that there are also conscious forces working against this higher purpose—or better purpose—and that this "conscious evil" is exercised through Hasnamuss. Not conscious in general with their understanding of the nature and the extent of the harm that they do, but conscious in the sense that they allow themselves, for their own purposes, to follow a line in which they see that they are able to succeed.

A Hasnamuss can be of different grades; and this depends—just as in the same way with positively developed beings—upon the singleness of their purpose, on the efforts that they make to attain it, and the degree of consciousness they bring into these efforts. In *Beelzebub's Tales* it is even conceived that they can be beings who, seeing what they are doing and understanding what they are doing, nevertheless strive for egoistic means and bring quite considerable forces to bear on this striving.

But more generally, a Hasnamuss is a being in whom there is gradually lost the capacity for hearing the voice of his own conscience, and who therefore thinks himself in the right, who feels that his whole activity is justified, and who may even be certain that he is doing good when in fact he is serving a destructive aim—destructive, that is, of any higher possibilities.

There is also a general conception that we have to think about here. Many times people have said to me that there is something painful in the idea that "many are called but few are chosen"—painful that one should have to accept that attainment of higher levels of being is only for a few, and that the possibilities of the greater number are very limited. But those who have big possibilities have them in part without deserving them, owing to accidental combinations of circumstances. Not only circumstances that are in some way connected with their own essential being—such as their heredity and the conditions of their birth—but also accidental conditions of environment, accidental contacts, and other properties connected with their physical body.

This means a repugnance that some should have great possibilities and others only very limited possibilities. We have been taught for a long time the doctrine that people are born equal, and that everyone has equal rights and must be given equal opportunities—even though this doctrine is contrary to all our everyday observations of how life is on every level and in every form that we know. We see, moreover, that every attempt to create equality only worsens the general lot even of those for whose apparent good these efforts are undertaken. If we have to abandon this idea as being contrary to anything which can be realized in fact, what are we to do about this feeling of ours that somehow in any doctrine of inequality there is an injustice?

First of all, it is quite true that the possibility for work on oneself does not arise equally for all people, and that for some people it arises in a much greater degree than for the majority. Those whose material conditions of life are, for example, favorable—whose bodily existence is not reduced to a low energy level by insufficient food or by harassing and difficult external conditions—do have opportunities: they not only have opportunities of learning but also possibilities of making efforts over and above the needs of their life. They have the possibility of impartial thinking in a way that is not possible for a person in a state of hunger or in a state of extreme danger or strain. However, for such people of opportunity the corresponding responsibility is increased, at least in the same proportion.

In the chapter on war, "Beelzebub's Opinion of War," this particular point is emphasized: those who have the possibilities of impartial objective thinking have a correspondingly heavy obligation; and the same, of course, is true of those who have possibilities of making being efforts, of making efforts to increase their own inner strength. Because this is an objective fact—that those who have the power of making efforts have the obligation not only to make efforts for themselves but to make efforts on behalf of those who cannot—then, if they fail to fulfill this obligation, then the consequences for themselves are correspondingly terrible.

All this is not seen in relation to the conditions of our world, and so it appears that the people who have favorable conditions of external existence and yet do not use them, or use them for selfish or wasteful ends, simply do not count and disappear out of the picture without any serious consequences, but this is not right.

The world is so constructed and so arranged—and all worlds are the same—that opportunities are not equal. Comparatively few people on any planet are able to attain the highest things possible to attain, but in order to attain them they have to make a correspondingly great payment. This payment is a very big one: they have to sacrifice many of the things that are, quite legitimately, to be enjoyed by those who have not these same opportunities. Objectively, there is no injustice in this, especially if you understand the situation of the Hasnamuss Individual.

Generally speaking, the Hasnamuss Individual is one for whom favorable conditions of existence and work arise so that he has the power and the opportunity of efforts and of being able to think. But if he fails to use this power to make efforts and to think for the good of others and makes them, on the contrary, for his own selfish aims, he creates by this process something in himself from which he cannot afterwards liberate himself without very great suffering. He must liberate himself from it, because anything which is built upon egoism has a definite limit beyond which it cannot go. There is a certain threshold beyond which egoism cannot pass; and if something is created that is permanent and therefore able to survive the death of the body, and if this something can neither go forward nor by its nature can go backwards, then it has only one thing remaining—and that is that it should be destroyed. There is no other way out for it.

I am not attempting this evening to go into a detailed explanation of this, but if anyone thinks about it, and if you have understood what I have spoken about the last few weeks in connection with the chapter on purgatory, "The Holy Planet Purgatory," then you will have seen clearly that if this process of crystallization of higher matters goes forward, it must always produce something which is not destroyed by the forces which work on the surface of the planet, whether or not it is produced on the right basis or on a wrong basis. The greater the opportunities and the greater the corresponding efforts, the more completely formed is this "something" which is able to survive, and it may be formed to the point at which it becomes conscious of its own situation. Then it either has to be able, by some means or other, to purify itself of its own egoism—so that it can pass through this threshold of which I have spoken—or else it has to be destroyed. Or, possibly, even a third thing: it may be returned to a lower level of existence in which the destruction of this egoism can be made possible. This is necessary and follows inevitably from this conception of the higher chemistry of man, as does everything that we have said about the formation of the higher bodies.

So the situation of those who have possibilities is a correspondingly serious and dangerous one. Those whose possibilities are very limited have less danger of arriving in this terrible situation. Those whose possibilities are great have to make very great payment before they can square their account, before they can liberate themselves from the debt of their own existence and, particularly, for their favorable existence. In periods of the world's history when these sorts of things are lost sight of, it can happen that men and women with very favorable conditions for work on themselves—and therefore favorable conditions to be able to help other people—are so educated that they are entirely unaware of this, so that they are entirely without fault of their own in this case. Owing to the faults of their parents and those who educated them, they think they are entitled to pursue quite egoistic and self-centered aims—and they use their capacity for effort accordingly.

In that way, they become Hasnamuss. And in these generally unreal conditions of life, such as we have at present, a Hasnamuss may be the most respected and the most honored person in the community, because people judge him in terms of his external manifestations and his own declarations about his aims and intentions. So, at first sight, certain people may appear to be working for quite good purposes, yet when we see them and are able to assess them with an objective eye, how they really work and what they do, we see that it is from very profound egoism, and an egoism, what is more, which is combined with the conviction of their own rightness and their justification in pursuing this sort of aim. They pursue it because they think that through this they will be able to do other good things. This can apply to people whose whole life is devoted exclusively to the ostensible good of others, not for material gain, but to gain ascendancy over others or to win their praise and esteem.

After-Lunch Discussion

Questioner. Is there such a thing as justice, or is it only a concept of ours?

JG Bennett. There is justice, but objective justice is not at all as most people conceive justice. For example, the principle "that as a man soweth so shall he also reap" is the principle of objective justice. But then people will say, supposing he has nothing to sow, what about it? Then they begin to bring in subjective factors that arise only in their imagination. Obviously if a man has nothing to sow, he will have nothing to reap. It may not be his own fault that he has nothing to sow, but the fact that he does not reap anything still is bound to remain.

Remember the parable of the sower and the seed. This, from the point of view of the seed, is quite contrary to our conception of justice. Why should it be that some seeds fall on stony ground and others on thorns? It may be that one seed is as good as another, but one thing happens to one and another thing happens to another.

Q. Can it be said that those with very few possibilities have another kind of evolutionary hope?

JGB. I am speaking not about those who have very few possibilities but about the serious situation of those who have possibilities. I said this to illustrate what I said about Hasnamuss. In reply to your question: yes, certainly these people have some reward.

Q. How can one be sure that one is not acting from egoistic aims? Is there any acid test you can apply? How can anyone be told who does not come into contact with a school?

JGB. I said there are certain bad periods in the world's history when people can be so brought up that without any fault of their own they are filled with quite inverted and destructive aims, and think them good aims.

Q. If they think them good aims, they may be acting not from an egoistic point of view?

JGB. Various factors come in, connected also with means as well as ends. It is one quite characteristic feature of Hasnamuss that he will pursue a legitimate aim by illegitimate means. By that I mean that there is a certain compromise that offers itself very frequently, by which people can attain or appear to be attaining a worthy aim by allowing a certain thing which their own conscience tells them to be unmistakably wrong, to happen at a given moment. They may also justify this. This is very characteristic of a Hasnamuss: that he quite unhesitatingly justifies this sort of compromise. The truth is that no good aim can be achieved through bad means, and the end can never justify the means. Very often it is more by observing means than by observing ends that we can tell, by judging each action as it arises.

Q. Referring to the previous question on justice, would you agree that true justice is our own effort in the long-term working of the law of karma?

JGB. Long-term things can be very deceptive.

Q. Were some of the spectacular people in history Hasnamusses? Peter the Great, or Caesar?

JGB. Yes. Very often. There is one property that Hasnamuss can have—a certain illegitimate kind of knowledge—I mean he can have a certain illegitimate knowledge of the future which can give him an indescribable confidence about the course that events are going to take. This is why the idea of Hasnamuss has been connected in people's minds with the idea of selling one's soul to the devil. This peculiar property of knowing for certain what course events are going to take is connected with the existence of something of a higher order on a lower level than it should be.

You know this conception of different levels of time: on the lowest level everything follows a determined sequence. Ordinary people who live on this level are blind to the future and therefore the future is just as uncertain to them as it is on the higher levels where it has to be created—but a Hasnamuss Individual can live on that level and in a certain way know.

Q. Is it because he only knows up to a point that it usually goes wrong for him?

JGB. Yes. Very often. At a certain point a transition takes place in him, when he goes mad, in effect, and thinks that he is creating the future instead of merely knowing it. Then he ceases to listen to this knowledge that exists inside him—and he proceeds to do things without this.

41.
THE WORK

3 January 1965

I AM GOING TO TALK THIS MORNING about a subject which is appropriate for the New Year and that is Work. We use this word and, I suppose, slowly the greatness of it begins to dawn on us. We use it in various ways. We use it as a verb to say: "I work" or "I wish to work" or "I don't know how to work" and we use it also as a noun when we talk about "the Work." And when we use it as a noun we sometimes just refer to this general activity that we expect—or hope—will bring us to the goal we are all seeking. Sometimes we also use it, and rightly so, as a something to which we belong: in which we have a place. So ever since this word Work came into our vocabulary we have spoken about being "in the Work," or "belonging to the Work." But we have also noticed over the years that it is unfortunately possible also to take this word in these ways: of assuming that people who do things such as coming to these meetings, or doing various exercises, are superior to others because of that; and then make a distinction between people who are "in the Work" and people who are "not in the Work"—and even talk about people who have "left the Work" with sadness!

But what does it really mean? In one sense Work means life, certainly when you have a choice. That is in *Deuteronomy:* "Behold I have set before thee this day life and death, blessing and cursing, choose therefore life, that thou and thy seed may live!" and the life spoken of there means the same as we mean by the word "Work." For this work is certainly set before us as a choice. There is life that we can choose and when we choose it we belong to it. It becomes part of us. We live it.

All of that is true about the Work. It is also called a New Life—or Rebirth—or Regeneration. It is also true that Work is above all connected with choosing between a way of existing that leads to our eventual extinction—our disappearance from the scene—and a way of existing in which we shall grow without limit until we not only become part of what is without limit, but even one with it. All of this is implied in "Work, Rebirth and Regeneration." But there is still something in this which is not close enough; and I know that for me this has changed over the years, so that to me now Work is not something which is an idea, or an action, something to be done, a duty, or even a state in which one wants to be. It is not only Life but it is Living, it is not only the Way, but it is the Life itself.

I remember one saying of Madame Ouspensky's that "You must come to love the Work as the woman loves her lover": which means to give yourself altogether to it. To understand this love towards the Work; this wish to give oneself entirely, holding nothing back from it, that certainly comes with a deepening of one's experience. Another thing about it is that Work is very different from a human lover who can betray, forget, fail us. But the Work never betrays, never forgets, always repays. I am sure every one of you knows from your experience what this generosity of the Work really is. How when you give to it, always so much more is returned, that one is humbled, abashed by what one receives in return for so little that one gives. How often we find that one sacrifice that is really small, yet genuine, which we make in the name of the Work, changes so very much more than we ever expected or hoped for. But certainly, of course, the Work also hides itself. It isn't always producing and offering us tangible returns for what we give to it; and it shouldn't be. Because we have to be drawn to go deeper, so that it is drawing us on always to something more than we have at this moment. Always to more understanding, to a deepening of our union with it. And for this it hides itself. This is what is called the "play" of the Work. You see this described in the *Proverbs of Solomon*, where Work is called "Sophia" or the Wisdom of God. It goes by many names. There it is said how, before the world was created, the Work was already there, how it plays with the children of men and draws them to her. If you know that chapter—one of the most beautiful chapters in the Bible— you can see how Work has that quality also. When we take the Work solemnly, as if it were something to be heavy about, we are really unfaithful to it. We used to use such phrases as "Work faces"—or "Work behavior," or "Work personality"—to try to convey to people the absurdity of imagining that if one is solemn and heavy one is somehow in a better state than if one is light-hearted—or more likely because of this heavy solemnity to remember oneself, or to do what is right. The essence of the Work is joy. The closer you come to the Work, the more you find joy in it—and the more you understand, of course, that joy and suffering are not to be separated; and that one doesn't shirk or avoid what is hard. But certainly Work is as much what is joyful, as what is suffering.

In saying all this I seem to be, as they say, "hypostatising": making the Work into a person. That is how it is for me. Work isn't just an abstract idea, or a process, or an activity, or something like that. Work is my home, my reality. Everything that is of real value I find in it: wife, children, friends, interests, studies, everything. All are "in the Work" so that the Work is both like a person to be loved, and also like a home to be lived in. It is the security of our old age; it is the guarantee of our finding, after we die, the Way. Certainly I don't picture the state after death as one of repose, quiescence, disappearance of activity—very much the contrary! You know, in the description of the parable of the talents—of the one who has worked and produced the talents, it is said: "You have been faithful over small things, I will make thee ruler over many things, or over great things"—and this means bigger responsibility, bigger possibilities. The Work is like that. Strangely enough, if you look in the New Testament at the things that Jesus says about life after death, you will see how often it is connected with judge- ment and ruling, for the people who work. He says: "You will be seated on twelve thrones judging the tribes of Israel"—to the apostles—"And I will make you ruler over many things. You will judge." This is because people who work are needed. They have a role to play. They are not passive. They become one with this Wisdom, with this Love of God. But one must truly understand this about Work, that it is not an idea. Don't let it be just an idea for you! It is the most intimate reality. It is the reality of our innermost self. When we find ourselves, we find that.

After-Lunch Discussion
JG Bennett. This is the opportunity for asking about anything you like, and if I can I will try to answer.
Q. Mr. B. "Positive thinking" was a very popular phrase, some years ago. Is there such a thing really as positive thinking and does it have a place in our work?
JGB. I suppose "positive thinking" really starts with Mary Baker

Eddy, and is the basis of Christian Science. All the New Thought movements in America are based on positive thinking. It has a place, but only a small place. When anything of this sort is made into a unique principle, it always fails. With Christian Science the only thing you have to do, in effect, is to think positively; and the same with all the New Thought movements that stemmed from that. Nevertheless it is quite true that thoughts attract situations: negative thoughts attract negative situations. But this can all very quickly spill over into nonsense; either into a kind of sentimentality or into some form of self-suggestion. Certainly you can get courses in America on "How to get a Cadillac in six months by positive thinking." The germ of truth in all this is that negative thoughts are not necessary; that we can, without any harmful reaction, put negative thoughts away from us.

But to eliminate some things can produce bad results. For example, we may struggle with some habit that we dislike, and overcome it, only to leave behind some other habit which is even worse, because we like it. Somebody may have some kind of weakness like unpunctuality, or untidiness, and set themselves with great determination to overcome this; and when they succeed they become extremely intolerant and find fault with everyone else, and are satisfied that they have achieved something; so their second state is worse than the first. At least their untidiness was something they were not proud of. It is not like that with not having negative thoughts.

Q. Mr. Bennett, it seems to me that in the world there are very few people who give reasonably clear explanations about the Work, and explanations in a different form from those I am used to. Are there in fact few people and if so, why so few?

JGB. There never have been many. It was said in the time of Christ: "The harvest is plentiful and the reapers are few" and it is like that now. It is particularly difficult at times of transition when new ways of thinking—great ideas—are entering into human understanding. This because people are accustomed to thinking and speaking and expressing themselves in only one way, so a time when things have to be said differently is bound to be a time when people understand each other less than usual. This is one such time. You ask: "Why are there so few people who can speak about Work?" The answer is that Work can only be spoken about from experience. You must have within you the experience of the reality of Work; otherwise you will only speak round about it. It can certainly sometimes happen that many people have the experience of Work, but feel no obligation to speak about it. It is for them something personal and they have no need for any communication about it. Perhaps they are not right in that; perhaps, sometimes, they are. There is a possibility of taking the Work into oneself and treating it as a private affair, not to be communicated; but this is not really right.

You see, one of the difficulties is that the Work is not really something that can be brought within the compass of our thinking and feeling. Some people can express themselves about it emotionally, but what they express is only their own emotional reaction to it, and this doesn't convey the true character of the Work. Somebody else will know the theory of it all, and they can express and speak about this, because they have learned it; but this too cannot convey what Work is. Again true is that it is so easily looked at from one facet, and then one takes that facet to be the whole; as when we were speaking about "positive thinking" just now. When one taste of Work enters into a person, something extraordinary can happen to them, as it did with Mrs. Eddy. She saw one real thing; and on that she built a whole movement which has continued to this day. And yet all that she wrote about it in Christian Science was only a small part, but she never saw that it is. Such people that only see the part don't really serve the Work, because they are serving instead their own imagination of what Work is.

Q. If she had seen the whole, then there would be nothing to say. Yet Christian Science has moved …. Isn't it that blinkers were put on her, as it were, in order that she could get this grounding?

JGB. With her it came certainly from an actual experience of something that did really happen to her. That is genuine and cannot be taken away from her; and some part of her genuine experience she did contrive to communicate to others. What becomes misleading is the tremendous thing that is built around it—not only Christian Science but all that I call the "Science of Mind." It is extraordinary what it has done in North America and is much stronger there than in other parts of the world. It has entered into the very fabric of thinking there, where people perhaps don't even realize that they are affected by it. When you see that happening, you are seeing something which has been overstrained and has then spread because there was a force in the initial moment. An explosion occurs and enables it to expand; and then you see how very different it becomes.

In relation to what T. asked: "Why do so few people speak about Work? Why are so few people really able to?" Because those who are on the verge of being able to, become more and more cautious about it, and maybe quite rightly they refrain from speaking, although what they say could be helpful to many people, but they also see at the same time how easily it can be changed into something else.

Q. Suppose somebody asks you—or it comes up in a discussion— you have had actual experience of the subject and yet you know the person you are speaking to doesn't think the same way, is there any possibility of knowing whether you should or shouldn't speak?

JGB. It is very difficult to give a general answer to a question like that. One has to face that one will make mistakes and maybe do harm. Always to avoid speaking because of the fear of doing harm, this is not right. The fear of doing harm must be very strongly present in us. This is really very close to the "Fear of the Lord that is the beginning of Wisdom" and the certainty—not merely the possibility, but the certainty—that what one says will be misunderstood, must always be taken into account. Even if you speak from a quite authentic experience; and even remember and are living the experience as you are speaking, so that your contact with it is intimate—even so you will be misunderstood, and maybe you will do harm. And yet at the same time it must be understood that to always refuse to share one's experience for fear of being misunderstood is not right either. One must really be prepared in this to learn, the hard way, how to be able to share things with people. Never, trusting in oneself; never expecting to be understood; yet knowing one is obliged, if one has received something, to share it.

Q. Mr. Bennett. This point about not trusting oneself—it does seem to me that a certain kind of trust is important somewhere in this. If one is endeavoring to understand somebody who has had authentic experience, one accepts willingly that harm may be done to one—that the risk is on both sides. There is a certain trust that "Well, this is the way it is," and therefore there is a risk on all sides. Otherwise we as mere men might seem to be claiming infallibility.

JGB. Yes, but what is the point about what you are saying? We have to feel that it is worthwhile taking the risk of sharing and trying to arrive at a common understanding that is given us, but all the time we must remember that it is a risk! As for the other thing you say about claiming infallibility: of course, even if I have had an experience that is for me valid and I really am seeing that it is like that, nevertheless, when new experience comes it will all have to be changed. Providing I work, something will have changed in me and I will not see things next year, or in five years time, as I do today. I know this, because it has happened to me all my life and I know that it will go on happening as long as I work, that my understanding will change. If it didn't, it wouldn't be that I have reached the limit of understanding, but that I had stopped working.

Q. There seems to be a point that one does really feel sometimes that, within limits, one is seeing the problems before oneself almost as if one is watching oneself doing it, and knowing the relative truth; and yet when in my place I think about my own problems, they seem quite impenetrable and any conclusions that I arrive at seem completely inadequate ....

JGB. There is a certain threshold that we cannot recognize by ourselves, which has to be passed before anything can be communicated. You haven't passed that threshold in any way; and therefore you can neither say anything to other people nor anything useful to yourself. You see, you simply have not come to the point where you can understand anything. This you must accept. It will come, but not yet. You have to take it that you simply don't understand—neither your own problems nor other people's problems—and when you think that you can say something useful to other people, it is not true.

Q. And is this ever recognizable by the person concerned?

JGB. No. Maybe the person who tells him this doesn't really understand him or may even be wrong. Everyone may be wrong. But suppose I look at myself in this way, over my own lifetime. I first heard about these ideas and began seriously—sometimes under very favorable conditions of intensive work—to study them in the early 1920s. But I had no idea of what I was like, nor of who I was—and I did not even realize this. Yet I could give people wonderful advice and explanations, and talk to them about work and everything. Then one day in about 1932 I saw myself., and I saw that everything was nonsense and it was all secondhand rubbish that I had talked. It took me twelve years to come to see that.

Q. Mr. Bennett, if a person is hoping to find someone who can speak —I take it there is no general test—he must be able to depend on his own judgement—must not he—in deciding who is really speaking the truth ... in judging between teachings?

JGB. There are two general rules, with which I always used to answer this question. One is that a teaching that puts people to sleep and only helps them to sleep comfortably—to live with their own egoism without being troubled by it—whatever else it may give, is not a true teaching. The other is this: that any teaching that has a tendency to label some people as chosen and others as rejected, is also not to be trusted. If a teaching has *not* got those two tendencies in it—one to make you comfortable and go to sleep; the other to make you think you are one of the chosen people—then, at least, you can put a certain amount of confidence in it. This, I think, everyone can agree to. I think you could say: "Yes! This is how it must be," and therefore you could look at teachings and say, "What is that teaching doing to people? What is it assuring them of, this or that?"

I remember how this principle first became clear to me. I was still a boy at school. At the time it seemed the worst kind of bigotry; but since then, I'm bound to say, I'm grateful that it should have happened to me. We had two divinity teachers at school, both nominally Church of England. One was what in those days was called "High Church," and used to talk about Mary as the Mother of God and always call himself a Catholic. But the other spoke of the Church of Rome as the "Scarlet Woman" and gave us all to understand that the Virgin Mary was practically the source of all the troubles in the world. We went from one to the other in successive years. Fifty years or more have passed since that time, and I still remember how shocked I was by this: that two men, both clergymen, both presumably knowing about God, could tell us things so completely contradictory; and so I thought, "I never can belong to anything which talks to me in that sort of way."

"When the smallest fragment of truth enters a man
he can do nothing but obey."

available from Bennett Books Catalog
PO Box 1553, Santa Fe, NM 87504 • 505 986-1428 phone/fax
office@bennettbooks.org   www.bennettbooks.org

For a
CATALOG OF BOOKS, TAPES & MUSIC

in the tradition of
JG BENNETT, GI GURDJIEFF, AND THE FOURTH WAY

please contact
Bennett Books Catalog
office@bennettbooks.org
www.bennettbooks.org

•

To be informed of
EDUCATIONAL PROGRAMS & GROUP WORK

in the tradition of
JG BENNETT & GI GURDJIEFF

please contact
Bennett Books Educational Seminars
registrar@bennettbooks.org

•

BENNETT BOOKS IS AN INSTRUMENT for publishing ideas on the Transformation of Man. Since 1988 it has concentrated largely on making available the writings and talks of JG Bennett, one of the major developers of the ideas of GI Gurdjieff, and from whom Bennett Books takes its name. The founder and current associates of Bennett Books studied with JG Bennett and Elizabeth Bennett in the 1970s.